# CIRCLING
# SAN FRANCISCO
# BAY

Steep Ravine Trail, Mt. Tamalpais, by Paul Feder

In beauty I walk
With beauty before me I walk
With beauty behind me I walk
With beauty above me I walk
With beauty around me I walk
It has become beauty again
It has become beauty again
It has become beauty again
     p. 44 "Navajo Prayer" in The Navajo,
by Lana T. Griffin and Tommy J. Nockideneh
     Austin: Raintree Steck-Vaughn, 2001.

# CIRCLING SAN FRANCISCO BAY

## A Pilgrimage to Wild and Sacred Places

Ginny Anderson

iUniverse, Inc.
New York  Lincoln  Shanghai

Circling San Francisco Bay
A Pilgrimage to Wild and Sacred Places

Copyright © 2006 by Virginia Anderson

iUniverse books may be ordered through booksellers or by contacting:

iUniverse
2021 Pine Lake Road, Suite 100
Lincoln, NE 68512
www.iuniverse.com
1-800-Authors (1-800-288-4677)


ISBN-13: 978-0-595-39191-2 (pbk)
ISBN-13: 978-0-595-83581-2 (ebk)
ISBN-10: 0-595-39191-5 (pbk)
ISBN-10: 0-595-83581-3 (ebk)


Printed in the United States of America

To my parents, who taught me how to live the journey,

To my children and to Paul, who walk the journey with me.

# CONTENTS

# ACKNOWLEDGMENTS

I give thanks to these helpers in my journey of writing this book:

- The Stone Dancers Circle, who participated in visiting with me the first round of sites upon which the book is based, adventuring, telling stories, singing, being willing to share the truths of their lives. Our ongoing celebrations and explorations will continue to season my life.

- Patria Brown, for her sustaining presence and creative assistance.

- Sandy Miranda, for photographs and for encouraging me to share *Circling San Francisco Bay* more widely.

- A wonderful community of companions ready to explore consciousness and spirit, adventure and heart—Meg Beeler, Dellalou Swan, Jenny Creelman, Carolyn Clebsch, Carol Fitzgerald, Debbie Colbert, and Geoff Brown.

- Macha Nightmare and Rose May Dance, who helped to place me on the path of women's spirituality.

- Shelley Thomson, Ruth-Inge Heinze, Alberto Villoldo, and Americo Yabar, who served as doorways into the practices of shamanism.

- The Quechua Indians in the Andes who shared their native wisdom.

- My parents, whose unconditional acceptance blessed my life ten times over.

- My husband, Paul Feder, who sustains me through laughter, patience, and great cooking.

- My children, whose support has taken so many forms—Marci's encouragement, questions, and supportive editing; Brian's creativity and web know-how helping a vision emerge; Stephen's and Eric's musical contributions to ceremonies.

- Lauren deBoer, Lorraine Anderson, and Ann Davidson, who have been such valuable allies in commenting, editing, and providing knowledge and personal support in a process that continues to be a revelation to me.

- Those who have circled the bay with me, sharing their lives and stories so profoundly.

- The Unseen, whose presence is felt and takes away doubt.

- The ancestors and guardians of the sacred places.
- Indra's Net, spread from mountain to mountain over the paradise of the San Francisco Bay Area.
- The indiayogi team, at www.indiayogi.com, who gave permission to use the story of Vishnu.
- Lynn Marsh, whose artistic contributions to the book are among the many contributions she's made to Circling San Francisco Bay.
- David Sanger, www.davidsanger.com, whose photograph, "Hiker on Ridge", appears on the cover.

# LIST OF EXERCISES AND CEREMONIES

## KIRBY COVE

Discover sage's power through its fragrance
Take a tiny step in evolving consciousness
Explore your own issues of protection on a site that remembers protection
Follow the model of the eucalyptus tree's capacity to shed
Share your story with a tree and listen to the tree's story
Invent a group story with the characters and story line inspired by stones

## RING MOUNTAIN

Link past and present through children
Eat the shadow
Speak your true concerns and opinions with the support of Ring Mountain schist
Create a group mesa, a collection of power objects
Journey to the heart of the boulder
Healing journey for the lineage of the mothers

## MOUNT TAMALPAIS

At the portal to the woods, shift to mindful presence
Turn fretting and distractions over to Mother Earth
Purify yourself with running water
Create an offering to honor your connection with nature
Travel along serpentine's umbilical cord to the earth's belly
Dream with the California bay laurel plant spirit
Find compatible camping companions
Honor a life that has passed
The path of distant ancestors
Make prayer ties for a fire ceremony
Honor a beautiful place by engaging it

## MOUNT DIABLO

Follow a vulture's carrion quest
Fill yourself with the beauty of a flower
Help to heal damaged earth
Prepare a projection offering for a fire ceremony
Deepen connections to the power of fire

## MOUNT HAMILTON

Take a heron walk, an experiment in elegant concentration
Let the melted-ice-cream topography support a transformation or honor a shift
Write about the hangouts in your community
Let go of someone else's blueprint for your life
Write your own obituary
Journey to the stars in search of peace
Deal with a worthy adversary
Journey with a boar ally
Celebrate the summer solstice, longest day of the year
Get some perspective at a star party
Meet a tarantula and be present with something you fear
Exchange issues of humiliation and survival with a gray pine

## MOUNT UMUNHUM

Journey back and forth across time lines
Let an earthquake fault become your teacher
Practice reciprocity—cleansing the water
Create a written meditation on longing
Invite a visit from a hummingbird

## SAN BRUNO MOUNTAIN

Let lichen show you how to be tenacious
Do a moving meditation to bring balance to your life
Let the butterfly's life cycle guide you through a transformation
Do a writing practice to give the mountain a voice
Feel the presence of the past
Following a buckeye teacher, gather your power
Let your hand guide you through a burned knot doorway
Send fresh air from the ocean to the bay
Through an offering, spin a web to encircle the bay

# INTRODUCTION

We live in paradise, and all the world knows it. Exuberance, adventure, creative thinking, and beauty give an unsurpassed pulse to daily life in the San Francisco Bay Area. For hundreds of years, diverse world cultures have brought vivacity and values that add flavor to the evolving communities. For thousands of years before that, Native Americans lived in nomadic communities near the bay, following the seasonal food supply along dozens of trails and trade routes.[1] Their homes were built of willow branches, redwood bark, and tule reeds; they fished from small boats made of bundled tules. Fish, shellfish, birds, rabbit, deer, elk, and other game were plentiful.

In 1542, Spanish, Portuguese, and other European explorers began roaming the Pacific waters, hunting the elusive entrance to what is now known as San Francisco Bay.[2] Not until 1775 was the bay actually entered and mapped by Juan Bautista de Ayala. In 1849, hordes of would-be gold miners came to California. Now, immigrants from all over the world still come with the expectation that along with freedom, the streets are essentially paved with gold. But we are teetering on the brink of totally destroying this Eden, and we may find our treasure instead in a shift in consciousness that comes not a moment too soon.

What is the source of the area's sparkling energy—the deepest spiritual essence that allows the area to rebound and thrive when humanity sometimes weighs upon it so heavily? What mysterious characteristics make this portion of the world unique? For me, the magic that forms the container of our lives is sustained in the mountainous terrain that surrounds the bay. The bay itself flows through the heart of that container, mingling cellular information carried through the fresh water of creeks and rivers from inland sources with the information in the salt water that has roamed the distant reaches of the globe. We are gifted with the powers of the land and the sea, which together provide the chalice and the mead for our changing consciousness.

The mountains are the foundations, the pillars of our paradise. Their presence creates a visible, tangible circle around the communities of the Bay Area. They hold us, lovingly cupped in the hands of Mother Nature. They shape our weather, create a geographic enclosure with permeable boundaries, and hold secrets about life-sustaining processes that continue to function whether or not we pay attention.

Because of the greenbelt surrounding us, we in the Bay Area communities have an opportunity for a profound relationship with the natural world, a chance to retrieve the threads of knowledge held in the weaving that sustains us among the life forms on the planet. This circle of protected open space held in public trust creates opportunities for hundreds of thousands of inhabitants to access nature. The most valued treasure held out to us here, the gold most precious, is the opportunity to return to an intimate relationship with the earth. With few human guides—fewer still in a direct and unbroken lineage of relationship to the places of power that exist here—we are able to turn directly to nature to teach us.

This book invites you to walk through seven very special places in the San Francisco Bay Area, discovering ways to be present that will expand your intuition and your sensory awareness, and enhance your connection to the natural world. Six mountains are included in the journey—Mount Tamalpais, Ring Mountain, Mount Diablo, Mount Hamilton, Mount Umunhum, and San Bruno Mountain. The seventh site, on the Marin Headlands at the foot of the Golden Gate Bridge, is Kirby Cove. Here our journey begins. Kirby Cove designates the physical gateway of the bay's existence, symbolically marking the point of exchange between San Francisco Bay and the Pacific Ocean. Along the shores of the bay and within the circular presence created by the mountainous pillars of paradise, our lives unfold. This pilgrimage allows us to experience the unique contributions that each site offers to the vitality of our lives.

## Why I Wrote This Book

During a series of trips I made to the Andes some years ago, shamans in the high mountains shared with me and my companions approaches to the natural world they believe open us to deeper relationships with nature.[3] The shamans took us to sacred sites, which they consider gateways to elemental knowledge and to the wisdom of the spirit of nature. As important as the individual sites were, even more valuable was the gift of ways to be present in nature that deepen our power to connect with them. When I returned to my Bay Area home, I was eager to explore the places of power surrounding our own communities, and to share with friends the perspective of the people of the Andes.

A group of friends began to consider the project, talking first about our intentions for the exploration and the ways our goals differed from ordinary hiking. We wanted to

- experience the sacredness of the space in which we live, and the places in nature that create and support the atmosphere of life in the Bay Area,

- discover how to communicate with nature,

- learn how to sense the wisdom we know to be there, but whose language we don't always know,

- move into a consciousness of another simultaneously co-existing reality, and incorporate that understanding into our day-to-day lives, footsteps following footsteps, and

- encircle the bay, container of sacred waters and pivotal center to which all Bay Area communities relate, in our walking.

In the greenbelt surrounding our communities, we recognized the opportunity to rebuild a direct relationship with nature. *Circling San Francisco Bay* records our journeys, just as it records the opening of my own heart to my home in paradise. Writing it affirms my connection not only to the earth itself, but also to all forms of life, each with its own language and unique presence. The book is an expression of gratitude to that circle of life for the privilege and pleasure of being here, in this very body, in this very place.

## The Power of Visiting Sacred Sites

The seven sites that this book describes are places of power. Although I chose them with friends, primarily through extensive exploration, some of them turn out not surprisingly to be among those considered sacred to Native Americans in the Bay Area. What exactly is a place of power, and what can we expect to happen when we visit there?

The earth abounds with many varieties of energies. Among them, as Paul Devereux points out, are gravity, geomagnetism, natural radiations, infrared emissions, and natural microwaves, as well as many artificially generated emissions of the modern world.[4] When people sense an amplified energy, and when they intentionally engage that energy through meditation, dreams, ceremony, or shamanic journeys, they often consider the sites of these occurrences as sacred. Devereux attributes this amplification of energy to the earth's magnetic fields.[5] He offers examples of the role of stones with enhanced magnetic properties in the political affairs of Japan (where the emperor incubated dreams while sleeping on a bed made from polished stone) and of England (where the Stone of Scone is placed in the Coronation Chair at Westminster Abbey).

Involvement over centuries of use seems to lay down a residue of emotions, thought forms, and intent that contributes to the "power of place." Many sacred places of power are widely known throughout the world. The Ganges, for example, is revered as the soul of India. Machu Picchu in Peru draws pilgrims from all over the world. Numerous Christian cathedrals (such as Glastonbury in England and Chartres in France) were built over sites already in sacred use for centuries by pre-Christian peoples.

Places of power can be found wherever we live or travel. They attract us; when we are paying attention, we might have experiences there that are hard to put into words. Places of power might create a sense of belonging, of peace or healing,[6] or of a presence deeper than we are able to perceive through our five senses. They sometimes initiate a process of transformation unique to individual lives or circumstances. People sometimes come purposely to a place known to be connected to a transformative process (the Inca Trail leading into Machu Picchu, for example, or the circumambulation of Mount Kailash in the Himalayas). The unusual sense of presence can also occur unexpectedly, often connected with a person's openness to the present moment.

A striking rock formation, a place where water emerges from the earth, or some other natural phenomenon might mark a site as a sacred place and be the vehicle through which a particular bit of knowledge is transmitted.[7] These sacred places are gateways, where the subtle energy that flows through all of nature is somehow amplified, more available to be experienced. Many of the sites have been used ceremonially in past generations. Some people in our own era discover them independently, walking or sitting attentively, and respond to them according to their own needs, perceptions, and modes of expression.

Every place on earth that has come to be considered sacred, or a place of power, holds unique and specific wisdom concerning the web of life. Our learning is supported by the power of these places. We take away from our visits not only a sense of place and of pleasure in their beauty, but also a transformation in ourselves that can accompany us wherever we go. Recognizing our kinship with other life-forms, we can shape a way of moving through troubled times as well as times of leisure and delight through celebrations of all life and meditations about the animals, the plants, and the land itself.

Fortunate are those who are part of a lineage in which rites of passage introduce people at appropriate times in their lives to communication with the presence of Spirit, usually at sites held sacred within the culture for generations. Sadly, in the United States, the style of conquest and the scorn for the spiritual practices of the Native Americans have broken the continuity of human relationship with many sacred sites. To this day, places regarded as sacred to many people are often wantonly destroyed, spray painted, or gouged. Identifying these sites increases their vulnerability. Still, human life will only continue if we learn to be in appropriate balance with the rest of the natural world. Visiting these sites, where subtle perceptions are more amplified, provides our best opportunity to understand how that equilibrium might be achieved.

# Transforming Our Approach to Nature

The decimation of entire tribes in the San Francisco Bay Area (or at very least, failure to acknowledge their existence), coupled with the contemporary mindset of industrialization, has created a rent in the fabric of human connection with the natural world. But while our culture might have broken a link in the continuity of widespread reverence for the land, the earth itself still calls out to be heard. In the Bay Area, several factors create a fertile brew for the revitalization of our connection to nature.

First among them is the land itself. Not only are we surrounded by the greenbelt, but also the quality of the land is unique. Here in California, the ground itself is shifting. This is a land of earthquakes, upheavals, changes in our very foundations. The state stone is serpentine; a current theory of its origin is that periodite underlying the oceanic crustal rocks has been metamorphosed (transformed) into serpentine near subduction zones (where one plate of the earth's surface slides under another) that have existed in various periods of California's history. It rose to the surface along major regional thrust faults (where subduction results in the material from one plate being thrust upward by contact with the other plate).[8] So the land itself models and encourages change and transformation.

Second, within the protective circle of the mountains, the culture is dynamic and fluid. An exceptional opportunity is created by the spiritual, social, and intellectual ferment of the people who have come from all over the world to live here. Silicon Valley is known worldwide for innovations in communication technologies, but it is a culture that rests more essentially on a profound underlying strata of connections that permeate the lives of every living being and await our rediscovery.

The third factor is the bay itself. Contained for a while within this circle of mountains and ridges, the waters of San Francisco Bay pause long enough to be admired, to nourish us in a variety of ways, and then silently slip out of the Golden Gate to shores beyond our knowing. Fed by rivers from all directions, and by whatever we contribute to the bay through our actions on its shores, these waters carry with them some part of the identity of each person who lives in relationship to them. The exchange of water between bay and ocean makes information about life throughout the world available to us on a cellular, nonverbal level.

Nature is full of circles—beautiful variations in flowers, redwoods growing around a burl mother, a fairy ring of mushrooms surging hungrily outward from decaying plant matter. Time follows the circular cycle of spring, summer, fall, and winter. Some people circumambulate sacred mountains—Mount

Kailash in the Himalayas, Ausangate in the Andes—as a prayer ritual. The native people of North America ritually acknowledged the context of every formal activity as contained within a circle of the four cardinal directions, combined with heaven and earth.[9]

The circle of mountains around San Francisco Bay calls attention to the sacredness of the unique space in which we live as we create our present and our future. Within this sacred space, we can discover how to take our place in the web of life. Here, the paths are truly paved with gold—the "gold" of a relationship sustained through reciprocity. Beauty and wonder heal and recreate us, give us perspective and vision. Beneficiaries of these gifts, we can find the insight, motivation, strength, and actions that can sustain human life on the earth.

So how do we move from the paths we walk in an ordinary way, placing one foot in front of the other, to an awareness of the subtle energy, the pulsing presence, emanating from the web of life in which we ourselves are embedded? How do we open ourselves more fully to the wisdom, the gifts, and the needs of our paradise, our natural home? By what transformations of attitude, action, attention, do we incorporate into our consciousness the weaving of energies that sustains our lives?

The transformation has as much to do with ways that we present ourselves as it does with the individual sites that we visit. There are multiple levels possible on our visits. Adventure, discovery, the pleasure of physical activity are available to all. If we add other ingredients—experimenting with new ways of moving, of breathing, of holding intent, of observation, of experiencing the senses—we can reach another level, in which we open to spiritual presence.

Being in silence, moving with intent, we can allow every aspect of the natural world to communicate with us. It is a communication beyond language, one to be learned by being fully present, listening with our hearts, and reciprocating through our actions. The chapters that follow offer very specific suggestions for deepening personal presence in nature.

## Using This Book

I have combined the events of a number of journeys shared with many different friends and companions for the sake of the narration in each of the chapters that follow. The book describes only a sample of the gifts that each site presents. Many other gifts await your personal discovery.

*Circling San Francisco Bay* is a spiritual guidebook, suggesting practices through which you can expand your senses, extend the power of your imagination, and discover new ways of paying attention, deepening connections to the natural world everywhere. These practices include writing, meditation, ritual, ceremony, and storytelling. They exemplify freedom of movement, of thought, of varied art forms to provide channels for nature's multiple forms of expression. Above all is the encouragement to be quiet, to be fully present, and to discover how to use intent to further the exploration of your relationship to nature.

*Circling San Francisco Bay* identifies places of power in the San Francisco Bay Area and some of the vehicles (rock formations, trails, plants, birds, animals) that speak powerfully at those sites. The book calls you to sacred mountains; the places themselves might call you to specific locations or experiences other than those that are suggested here. Follow your heart, for the connections of the heart are the supplies of the Weaver.

I have written the book for the solitary adventurer as well as to be used to plan group expeditions. I encourage you to read through each chapter first at home in order to whet your interest to visit one of the sites. Then visit the site alone or with a single companion initially, even if you plan to lead others there later. Responding to subtle communication is easier when you are free to follow your intuition, undivided by attention to or responsibility for others. Anyone intending to lead groups to the circle of mountains should spend as much time as possible alone or with one partner in nonleadership capacities on each mountain. Facilitating the experience of the mountain for others comes out of your own intimate personal connection with the mountain over time.

As you visit each site, you will discover the aspects of the site to which you're most attracted, and how you might use or adapt the practices presented in the book. Sharing the site with others expands it for yourself and helps to clarify your own experience. Everyone comes with a different background, set of experiences, and way of perceiving. You might be drawn to places on the mountains other than those mentioned in *Circling San Francisco Bay.* Some presence on the mountain might ask to speak to you or through you. Trust your intuition and be aware of how the mountain calls to you.

Incremental steps toward new ways of perceiving can be facilitated for a group when you start with a familiar point of connection. With people from groups that already exist (such as members of environmental organizations, home schooling parents, a whole classroom of students, members of foreign student organizations at a college), certain information or approaches may be more appropriate or useful than others and may also provide jumping-off places for helping people expand ways of perceiving the larger picture. A group experience allows you to expand your individual perception of a moment in time or a place in the circle of life.

Each of the sites hosts a number of endangered species. By and large, we are unaware of the constant threats to these species. In these sacred places, however, we have an opportunity to discover ways to be in relationship with nature that reopen the doors of communication. Extinction of life-forms through the actions of human beings is commonplace; as we become more aware of the power of some of these threatened lives, we might discover how to move differently through the world we share with them.

## Finding Our Fellow Star Beings

For a number of years, I traveled periodically in Peru with shamans of the Andes, among them Americo Yabar. Once at dusk, as we came with friends out of the mountains toward the town of Cuzco, we approached the main square of the town. "Let's have an adventure," he said. "Pretend that you are a Star Being, fallen from your home in the stars. During this long plunge from the sky, you've forgotten exactly where you've come from, and who your companions were in this journey. You sense they're around you, but you've forgotten your common language, and you don't know what they look like, or what your own true self looks like. You are Star Beings, and you've lost your way home. Go into the square and begin to look for those who fell with you. Find your companions. Being alone on an unknown planet is hard. Do whatever you need to do to reunite with them."

We separated. The soft lights in the public square grew stronger against the background of the evening, creating dancing shadows as people moved about selling candy and small packets of gum, weavings, artifacts, and clothing. Others sold their services in shoe polishing or guiding. An army of people surged forward, each person bent on making enough money for a meal or to feed a family. This press of desperation slammed against my purpose. I needed to hold my intention very strongly, or it would be washed away by the survival quest of those around me.

Each person was a possible candidate, however—and how was I to discover my companions if I armored myself? How was I to look for other Star Beings, and not become overwhelmed by their pressing concerns? I began to walk, my heavy hiking boots making a staccato sound that made me aware of my own presence. I sent deep breaths down the length of my body and into the ground to feel the connection between myself and the square, between myself and the earth.

Toward one corner of the square, a young man extended a tray of postcards and invited me to look at them, to choose five for a bargain price. A child's book I had read to my children years ago came to mind—P. D. Eastman's *Are*

*You My Mother?* In it, a young chick hatched while his mother was away from the nest. He searched the countryside and posed that question to road equipment and a wide variety of animals. In the same vein, I searched for a connection with the postcard seller. "Are you a Star Being I've traveled with?" I wondered.

Noticing many cards were photographs taken outside of Cuzco, I asked which places he had visited himself and which had been his favorite. In moments, a group of his friends had gathered around, all pointing out the places they had seen, reminiscing about past adventures at a pace and in a vocabulary much beyond me, which clearly animated the men with cheerful memories. Pressure to buy dissipated, and they slowed down to include me in their conversation. In the end, I bought ten cards, favorite places of many in the little gathering, and I knew that any one of these friendly people might have tumbled with me from the stars.

I crossed the plaza and at the far edge stepped onto the sidewalk, lined with women whose blankets were spread before them displaying jewelry, sweaters, and figurines. Next to the door of a restaurant, a tranquil woman sat weaving on a small loom. Another woman chatted with her, and as I approached, they looked up and smiled, inviting me to inspect the array of woven goods. I knelt beside them and asked about the patterns being incorporated into the tapestry. The weaver showed me symbols traditional in her community—animals and their powers, lightning, rain, and fire. She began to describe her village, and soon small children were listening to her, nudging one another for a spot closer to the storytelling. I offered the children some chocolate and discovered that none had eaten since the day before.

Shocked, and regretting my limited cache, I asked their mother if I could take them with me around the corner to the grocery store. She was as pleased as they were, and the giggling children multiplied to half a dozen before we rounded the corner. We left the store with yogurt and cheese, bread and fruit, and returned to the weaver. As we said our goodbyes, the children's laughter and a creative woman companion seemed welcome additions on the journey from the stars.

Rejoining my friends in the center of the plaza, I realized every part of the square buzzed with possible companions. All those around me had been revealed as children of the stars, valued companions on the journey. It had been challenging to remember our shared identity connected in our starry past. It was equally challenging to hold the remembrance of this discovery as I prepared to return to California.

The mountains that shape our weather, the streams and rivers feeding San Francisco Bay, the life-forms whose existence is the silent pulse of paradise—

these are all part of the web to which we owe our very lives and vibrant lifestyle. All these life-forms are Star Beings, matter from the universe. We are shaped by their presence, as fundamentally as our lives depend on our hearts and other organs. Come meet your companions on the journey.

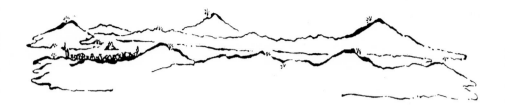

## Chapter One

# KIRBY COVE:
# Gateway to the Bay

Four hundred feet below the cliffs of the Marin Headlands, Kirby Cove lies curled within a protective arm of the Franciscan Complex. The battered visages of three rock formations rising from the water offshore toward the west end of the beach reflect centuries of clashes between land and sea. Late afternoons, they shelter the beach from the setting sun and pull an early blanket of dusk across the sand. Standing with me near the trailhead, geomancer Richard Feather Anderson once pointed out how these massive sentinels, surrounded now by water swirling around their bases, mark the cliffs' ancient territory.[1]

The only route to Kirby Cove begins at the far edge of Battery Spencer, about half a mile from the entrance to the Marin Headlands. The trail is a narrow dirt fire road that winds down toward the cove from Conzelman Road, which runs along the rim of the headlands. Most days the dirt road is barricaded by a white metal bar, essentially making a wide footpath of it. On a weekday, stepping around the barrier, we're granted near-privacy. I've come with a small group of friends to begin a series of expeditions around the bay. Although some have lived all their lives in the area, it's a new adventure for all of us to explore the territory in a way that expands ordinary hiking into a quest for the spirit of places that are part of our daily surroundings.

A fragrant curtain of coastal sage covers the slopes of the hills above and below the path, offering a powerful invitation to leave our urban cares behind. Many a person has used this plant to purify, leave one mind state and enter another, set aside distractions from being fully present; but it's unique that the wild plant, actually growing, marks the beginning of a journey. It's a perfect portent for our day.

# Sage: Plant Ally

The scent wafts into the air and clings to our skin as we run our fingers along the length of stems covered with delicate gray-green needle-shaped leaves. For ceremonial use in Native American sweat lodges and purification practices, it's burned, and the smoke infuses the lungs, skin, and hair. We take its fragrance into our own lungs now just from its perfume on the air, and with our fingers carrying the aroma, we can bring ourselves back to the present moment any time we're distracted as we continue along the way. Remembering its past, we connect through the plant to a lineage of the users of sage that knows no familial or national boundaries. We remember the Romans who used it in their baths to ease aching muscles, remember Europeans who scattered it with other herbs on their floors to freshen their rooms and cook with it in their kitchens. Through the diverse lineage of the plant,[2] Kirby Cove welcomes us.

## TRY THIS: Discover sage's power through its fragrance

- When you discover wild coastal sage along the path, move into the sensory space it offers.
- Without picking it, loosely encircle a stem of sage in your fingers and let it run through your hand.
- Again and again, "comb" the scent from the plant with your fingers. Notice how the air is filled with its generous aroma and welcome it into your body with every breath. Take generous breaths. Breathe from your belly so that the perfumed air fills your body.
- Rubbing your cheeks vigorously with scented fingers, envision the tiny sage molecules wafting into your nose, opening the capillaries in your lungs, and fog-meandering through your body.
- Invite the fragrance to displace any thoughts of being somewhere else or any concerns that might be troubling you. Allow yourself to become fully present, releasing concern over issues that exist elsewhere, tasks that have no place in this moment. Given the invitation, the fragrance takes over attention and senses.

We continue down the path, walking in relative silence by prior agreement. Instead of dialogue that might pull us away from being fully present, a focus on our senses keeps us in the moment. Footsteps crunch along the gravel of the descending path; calf and back muscles brace slightly against the downward slope. Because we are quiet, the characteristics of the site have a chance to speak and be heard. We're going down and around, becoming sheltered from the wind, turning in a big half-circle toward the restless water of the cove. The descent invites us into ourselves, a brief respite from responding to others' needs or social expectations.

## Radiolarian Chert: Participating in Conscious Evolution

Mahogany plates of radiolarian chert begin to appear along the cliff wall to the right. Two hundred million years ago, single-celled microorganisms floated on the surface of the ocean, generated by sunlight. When they died, their skeletons sank to the ocean floor in what Rachel Carson has called "the long snow-fall." Reddish dust from far-off deserts also accumulated there.[3] Trillions of those tiny lives are compacted here with that ancient dust into the stratified bands of sedimentary stone that make up the cliffs beside us. Now here *we* are, taking part in a different stage of the layering that continues through the millennia. Tectonic plates still confront one another, faulting, folding, shaping; continuity of life persists and transforms as new conditions are created.

Radiolarian chert at Kirby Cove, on the Marin Headlands.
Photo by Sandy Miranda, 2005.

From the top of the cliff, each stripe descends backward in time, a reminder of the ancient origin of the hillside. Ages are piled on top of one another. Rocks of the Marin Headlands traveled in that long-gone time from the middle of the Pacific Ocean, near the equator.[4] Rubbing a stone fallen from the wall, my fingers are coated with the powdery dust of radiolarian skeletons—ashes to ashes.

Yet, the solid cliff doesn't exist apart from each of these separate motes. Piled on one another, many layers are visible to us at the road level, and countless others support the cliffs below the surface. The cliff towers over our heads here, a hillside that incorporates uncountable numbers of lives on the planet into something of substance, something that contributes to the shape of the earth.

The cliff reminds us of the agonizingly slow incremental steps that shape changes in human consciousness—that it, too, was created cell by cell. So we sit with our backs against the cliff, rubbing our fingers very slowly over the surface. As our fingers buff tiny grains of sand, or unseen plant or animal material, we let our minds drift to a challenging situation we struggle with in our own lives—a person or an experience that has elicited from us an attitude we don't want to continue to carry. We replay it in our imaginations and sample different endings.

## PERSONAL JOURNEYS

Peggy: *One of my MO's is about being right—finding the right path. But no matter what we do, it's all right, as long as we don't think it's the answer for the whole world. I tend to get into that state; I think, "This is the answer." But I thought of these little creatures. Maybe they lived their lives actually fighting each other, or eating each other. They didn't think, "How am I going to contribute?" They were struggling to stay alive—and then they died. And* this *is the contribution they made! We all make it, one way or another, just by being fully who we are. So I see I can't hold on so tight to my ownership of the right way, needing things to happen right now in a certain way.*

Marguerite: *When I worry about my grown kids not being safe with the changes happening to the planet and the economy, it's really scary. I get stuck in anxiety about what's going to happen, and I want to keep nudging them to work harder or get it together. But I have to let go of that and just realize that there are going to be major transformations coming down, because there are so many people in this country who are in the same boat. I spend hours worrying about them, energy and attention that I put into a situation that I really can't control....A better way for me to be is to take that attention and involvement and put it where I personally feel most turned on to being alive. Keep turning toward Life. That's what I would hope for them, and to count, I have to do it myself.*

Kayla: *I was so anxious about my daughter, and what I finally came to was that what was important for me was loving her, and my desire for connection. In order to have that, I had to let go of trying to make her anything I wanted her to be, and just love her the way she was. It's amazing how things changed, because I was able to do that. It's not like I did it and it's done. Each moment I have to remind myself of that, and that brings it back to me. I love that—I can't focus on the other person; I have to focus on me. What's the feeling for me? What do I do that's alive? Right now, it's my singing. I love the group I'm singing with; the songs are so wonderful. I feel that coming into my heart, into my voice, right when I need it. All of a sudden, I start singing a song. It's that love stuff. It's in the music, and nature does it, too. Being out here, and getting in touch again. Whenever I get in touch with my connection, that I am connected, it doesn't really matter....That sense comes up in me so easily that I have to do something—that if I don't everything is going to fall apart. So that's what I can do—really hold that place that everything is not going to fall apart, and even if it does, it's OK. Because then there's a next. Look right here, there's all this death of these little creatures. And it's OK.*

## TRY THIS: Take a tiny step in evolving consciousness

- Make yourself comfortable, seating yourself at the base of the radiolarian chert wall next to the path.

- Begin to breathe slowly and deeply, feeling the air moving into your chest, into your belly. Relax your body, and as you continue to observe or feel the layered hillside, let your focus soften.

- Think of a relationship or situation in your life in which you repeatedly feel anger, resentment, envy, or some other troublesome emotion.

- Remember a specific exchange in the relationship or situation that leaves you with unpleasant feelings about yourself or the other person. Replay it from the beginning—whether it began with an action or comment from one side or the other, what the response was, how it ran its course, how it ended, and what followed.

- Imagine yourself ten feet distant from the action and replay the same event. Be aware of the context, of who else might have been nearby, or what both of you were involved in during those moments.

- Move back from the event in time—a few minutes, an hour—remembering what led to the event, exactly when you experienced the unpleasant reactions or feelings, how your body felt, what happened to your thinking, what was done or said.

- Notice whether your body responds with any of the same reactions at this moment. If you feel warmth or tension, imagine yourself breathing out the heat and the muscle tightness in a fine mist of breath that sends the tension-laden molecules onto the topmost sedimentary layer of the cliff, taking its place on the debris of centuries.

- Repeat it, letting go of the image, the feeling, and the physical sensation, until you are breathing evenly, calmly, with the air flowing deeply into your belly and limbs with each breath.

- Follow the theme of that issue backward in your life—other people, other homes, other jobs. Each time, as it comes to mind, blow the image to the top of the hillside. Let your own minute flecks of debris join the dusty pile.

- When you've come to the end of the thread of associations, press your hands or your back against the cliff. Remember again the first association; this time allow yourself to meet it breathing slowly, easily, deeply. Spot the moment of the event's beginning, and continue to let your body relax. Surrender to the pile of debris any remaining reactions that came to be part of a painful or unwanted sequence in your life.

- Notice the unbound spaciousness. Sit with the possibility of a different reaction, a different response. A way of handling things might arise that could meet similar situations in a different way. If something comes to you, let the new version play out in your mind's eye. See how you might take care of yourself differently.

- With a deep breath, return to this time and place. Feel your feet or your bottom on the ground; feel the sun, the wind, or the mist against your skin. Notice what you hear around you—birds, traffic, people, wind. Be present, open to whatever this day and place have to offer you.

## Traces of the Past: Exploring Personal Protection

The path takes a turn that moves deeper into the mouth of the cove, and just where the trail makes a hairpin bend, a small side trail leads more steeply down the hillside. We take the steeper trail, and discover, somewhat obscured, the remnants of a cement bunker. This vantage point, high on the cliffs that face both the ocean and the entrance to the bay, makes a logical defense site. The shape of the land, with the Golden Gate's narrow strait only three miles wide, was for several centuries part of the protection against discovery of the bay and of the lives of the native people living in the area. The people succumbed to a more insidious invasion than simple direct assault; illness and different beliefs about what is right, just, and appropriate wreaked havoc on their culture.

Gun and cannon emplacements were eventually strung out all along the fog-bathed headlands to protect the subsequent bayshore communities from invasion by sea. The honeycomb of underground and above-ground military installations put in place over more than a century is a testimony to the conviction of their importance[5]—even though obsolescence dogged the heels of every project, each of them useless in turn.

Later, during World War II lucky servicemen stationed on the headlands kept a sharp lookout for ships from the Pacific, but nary a ship came their way. No guns have ever been fired from Kirby Cove to fend off an enemy.[6] Now crumbling remnants of bunkers and magazines are scattered along the headlands, where soldiers watched, listened, and waited for elusive enemies slipping through the vast ocean. Military men camouflaged many of the constructions with mounds of grassy plantings. Nature continues their work with tendrils of wild berry and invasive Cape ivy.

One hopeful form of protection actually came about through the destruction of a weapon. In a swords-to-plowshares project, Nike (located farther seaward on the headlands) was the first American weapon to be publicly dismantled in the Strategic Arms Limitations Treaty between the superpowers, designed to slow the nuclear arms race.[7] The park that was once a military base now is available to be part of the exploration of our roots in the natural world. The visible evidence here of the evolutionary process invites us to participate in shaping our own evolution—a truly unique moment in human history. Consciousness is no small part of the opportunity.

The scurry line around coyote brush reveals its value to small creatures that venture into the open knowing they can retreat to safety. Field mice freeze in place while the shadow of a passing hawk moves by. Bobcats, deer, foxes, and raccoons come to drink at the streams under the protective cover of darkness.[8] Although most of us don't have to scurry back into safe territory at certain times of day, daytime is safer than nighttime in many human communities. Our own issues of protection vary from person to person, from place to place. Physical, political, psychological, emotional forms of abuse or threat are sometimes not apparent to those around us—or occasionally even to ourselves.

After we explore the crumbling cement structures, we find a small patch of grass, sit down, and pull out our journals. Patria offers writing practices to explore protection in our own lives, and we explore several issues through her suggestions. Although the issues may be straightforward, sometimes we "protect" ourselves from looking at painful truths. Her exercises help us circumvent our own censors, and we scribble our thoughts without pause—not taking our pens from the page but continuing to write uninterrupted and without editing for twenty minutes. Sharing the thoughts brought out in this way surprises us all, and the flowery language makes us laugh.

## PERSONAL JOURNEYS

Marguerite: *What am I protecting? A secure place for my dear ones' retreat and safety....I want to provide a haven safe as a kitchen where soup is cooking, and cheerful music and laughter bubbles out as freely as whooping cough makes its irrepressible sounds...a time and place for people to be without fear, where cheerfulness illuminates the shadowed corners, and Diablo is kept at a distance. The woods are coming to Dunsinane, and the troops need a place to hunker down.*

Peggy: *What am I protecting? It's time for me to protect my body, my health....without my health, I can't be of help to anyone. If I melt into the needs my body is dictating, I will find inner peace myself, and radiate out a sense of safety and protection. So protection involves...attending to my own well-being before attending to anyone else's—like putting on an oxygen mask in an airplane before you put your kid's on. Start at home! Do the work with Self! Protective wings spread from the core of your own being.*

Michael: *What do I need protection from? Thoughts were assailing my inner peace, like SCUD missiles on the desert landscape. (My daughter) Aurora would still be dancing with a smile in 2012 as the monsoon of world change battered the lives of the already weathered in its promise of life to come. I lay in bed in Columbia and wondered how, in all this primal beauty, the intense conflicts could arise, over and over, like waves lapping on the sand beaches of the Indian Ocean. The "Gates of Delirium" was running through my mind, and I asked myself for the 1000th time what it was going to take for all the technological world to have sustainability be as meaningful as headlong advancement. I could see the intricate and delicate crystalline beauty of a Romanesco broccoli being crushed between the teeth of a fat diplomat without so much as a thank you or praise of life.*

Peggy: *What do I need protection from? Tides come and go; my energy and atten-tion ebbs and flows, and I need protection from the expectation that I have to put out, put out, put out. Being able to kick back is a carrot that beckons me, and I need protection from my inclination not to honor the ebbing of the tides of energy, to hammer away toward producing, producing. There's a time for drawing in the sand, like a nesting turtle coming onto the shore and leaving a trail behind it. My legs will carry me to the wilderness, where sun and rain and the raw material of life speak to me, and bring me back to center. The apple from the tree of knowledge tempts me, but I don't need protection from pursuing it, because letting Spirit flow through is just as important a source of knowledge as academic learning.*

## TRY THIS: Explore your own issues of protection on a site that remembers protection

### 1. Weave yourself into the web of earth's protection

- Find a grassy place to sit, with a view toward the entrance to the bay, symbolic portal of safe haven.

- Soften your gaze; without focusing intently, be aware of the shape of the land as it narrows protectively at the Golden Gate.

- Close your eyes. Breathing deeply and relaxing, imagine tiny roots reaching into the earth from every point where your body contacts it. Let every exhalation carry those roots more deeply into the ground, allowing yourself to feel anchored in the land.

- Allow images to come to you—aspects of yourself that need protection, physically and emotionally. On a loop of breath, send the images along the matting of fine roots extending deeper and deeper into the earth. Inhaling, bring the support of the earth back into your body.

- Reach out with your intent as you exhale to the sounds around you—birds calling, the wind in the trees, the faint sound of surf shushing against the shore far below. Inhaling, bring each sound back into your body.

- Take several slow breaths, opening the passages at the back of your nose, so that the air moves freely, easily, and deeply into your body. Pick out the fragrance of the plants nearby, of the moisture in the air. Smell the skin of your arm, of the fingers that may still carry the sage or that have been touching another plant. Again, imagine a filament of intent reach-ing out to weave each thing you smell into your web of connection.

- Move your fingers on the ground, touching the plants within your reach. Feel the temperature, the way the plants emerge from the earth, the shape of stones or anything else around you. Notice whether the ground you are lying on is totally flat or slightly sloped, and how your body might be accommodating to that. See what happens when you change position slightly. Weave the filaments of connection between yourself and everything you're in contact with. With your conscious intention, you're strengthening the fabric of the web of life.

- When you're ready, open your eyes, and continue to be just where you are. Look up toward the sky, and notice if branches or leaves above you form part of the way you see the sky just now.

- Let your intent touch each thing you see. You are weaving each one, and yourself, into the earth's protection, into the web of life.

- Slowly sit up and then gradually stand and walk around a bit, maintaining contact with all the life around you.

## 2. Notice what you're protecting

- Sit down once again and pick up your journal and pen; creating a list, respond with your first thought to each of the following:

| | | |
|---|---|---|
| bird | plant | poet |
| a relative | a room in a house | piece of clothing |
| character trait | a mountain or range | a forest or woods |
| a lake | illness | insect |
| book | attitude | |

- Out of your responses, write a quick paragraph, without stopping, responding to the question: "What am I protecting?"

## 3. Investigate what you need protection from

- Again, write your first response to each word in this list:

| | | |
|---|---|---|
| ocean | vegetable | fruit |
| country | art form | historical period |
| weather | piece of furniture | tool |
| body part | a dance | painter |
| song | child's name | |

- Out of your responses, write a paragraph, without pausing, responding to the question: "What do I need protection from?"

- When you have finished your writing, notice if anything has come up that you would like to weave into the web of earth protection.

- If that is the case, relax and breathe out the thoughts and feelings that have come up about it into the web of connections, a weight to be dispersed throughout the protective weaving.

We return to the path and continue the descent. Fog wisps move in from the ocean ushered by the wind, appearing and disappearing, carrying the fragrance of cypress and pine. The mist trails fleeting fingers over lush green ferns and purple lupine, white milkmaids and bright red Indian paintbrush. Admiring the fog's grace and feeling its whimsical contact with our skin, we fantasize hitchhiking along on its light journeying as it touches the plants and drifts away from them.

Harold Gilliam takes a different view of fog—as part of the ceaseless assault of the ocean on the cliffs:

> "...sending its aerial armadas to carry the attack inland. Thus in the air as well as in the water the bay area is a main arena of battle between the elements. The gigantic land-sea conflict that gave birth to the bay is paralleled not only in the daily struggles between the flood and ebb of the bay itself, but in the summer-long battle between the tides of the air, as well."[9]

As the fog moves past, a pair of vultures becomes visible, swooping in enormous casual loops on the air currents over the canyon. We send our silent thanks to those who cleanse the earth of carrion; their presence reminds us to watch for our own carrion. The stories we tell ourselves over and over, fretting about people or about situations that are not even taking place in the moment, are a form of carrion, distractions to full presence. Watching these high-flying birds, we remind one another to be here, now—this very place, this very moment—and sniff our fingers for traces of sage to help the cause along.

A shoulder-high niche in the side of the cliff has become an altar. It's no more than a foot tall, maybe eight inches deep, and seems lovingly tended. A tiny crescent moon fashioned from a silver gum wrapper dangles from its ceiling, suspended by a thread that twists gently in the slow-moving air. A torn concert ticket stub rests against a small pinecone, and a shiny Lincoln-head penny lies next to it. A bit of colored thread, an interesting branch, a sprig of rosemary appear to have been washed to the ground just beneath the altar by a recent rain; we replace them, adding a eucalyptus button from the path.

Just beyond the altar, the road straddles a ravine carved by the flow of water over the years. Half a dozen similar draws thread down from several hundred feet above us. Above the road, the water's path from high on the cliff can't be seen directly, but it's marked by the intense color and density of joe-pye weed's foliage as it follows the descending line of water. Near the road, vetch sends tendrils along the edges of the stream. The sound of the flow has pleasant associations, conveys freshness. The stream disappears as it travels beneath the road, but as the water continues to descend toward the ocean, hidden from our direct view, we observe its path by the growth of the plants drawn to its company.

We continue down the trail, walking past markers of the headlands' geological story. In the distant past, tectonic plates collided, and the floor of the Pacific Ocean sank beneath the edge of the North American continent.[10] The impact drove layers of sedimentary rock up into striped designs that resemble an expanded musical staff that wavers up and down, as if the earth shape sings its own song, with no need for bird or human voice. We stop, listen to the hill sing its story, with a chorus of birds, planes, wind in the trees, flowing creek water—all verses in the song of Kirby Cove.

## Eucalyptus: Shedding

Trees in a eucalyptus grove on the right side of the road stand ankle deep in their sloughed skin. Near the beginning of the last century, the U.S. Army planted eucalyptus and the nearby Monterey pines to camouflage Battery Kirby from passing ships.[11] The forest it created still gobbles the land around it. Enhanced by a recent rain, the fragrance of this eucalyptus grove freshens the air, inviting us to follow our noses into a new environment.

Amid the tangle on the floor of the grove, huge stands of poison oak guard the trees from intrusion, and we reach up into the forested slope only through sight and smell. Nasal passages opened by eucalyptus's powerful oil, we take in great cleansing gulps of air. Little wonder that it's used sparingly in massage oils—but paying attention to the way it affects us, we let ourselves be taken into its community, and place a small offering of cornmeal at the edge of the grove.

The tree trunks shed layer after layer, exposing so many shades of pale green, tan, and nut-brown that the trees seem almost to be made up of only these layers of thin curling bark. Seeing them makes shedding seem so simple, and we decide to let them guide us in getting rid of attitudes or habits that aren't useful to us anymore. The cleansing aroma of the oil starts to work on us from the inside. We pick up strands of bark and wrap them around ourselves like capes; as soon as we feel their pressure, they remind us of what needs to be pared away.

## PERSONAL JOURNEYS

Marguerite: *It was so amazing, that as soon as I put this thing around me it totally brought me into touch with what I'd like to shed. I want to regain the freedom of not caring what people think of me. I…heard a song and felt like I was dancing around and around, shedding strips and strips, to the point where I realized that I didn't care who saw me dancing. I didn't care who heard the song. I just didn't care. It was like being stripped to my core, my trunk. It brought me back to a time when I had made so many mistakes that were evident to anyone looking that pretending everything was OK was pointless. So I just accepted the chaos I had created, and felt like I had to "Be here now."*

Peggy: *For me, when I put that strip around me I became so aware that I have to shed my weight. I have to shed my weight. It was about being able to move out in the world, do the things that I want to do. I just had this sense of the tree shedding, and the strips going back to the earth. I thought, "Oh God, if I shed this, everything I would have eaten goes back into the earth!" It's a way of giving back to the earth. I've never thought of it that way. But I felt that freedom. I'm so in touch with how I use this, to keep myself not free, to keep myself from moving. It's dealing with my freedom to move. I hold myself back from things because of the weight. And then I realized the effort it takes to hold on to it. Maybe it would fall away if I stopped holding! But there are a lot of other things that would have to peel away, like stubbornness, and attachment to certain things.*

## TRY THIS: Follow the model of the eucalyptus tree's capacity to shed

- Sit on the bank in the fallen bark at the edge of the eucalyptus grove. Notice the community of trees—the density of the grove, the airy, creamy white blossoms or seedpods scattered profusely on the path.

- Pick up one or two wide strips of bark and wrap them like a cape around your arms and shoulders.

- Be as still as the trees, or if the wind is blowing in the upper branches, let your own upper body sway gently with the movement you see.

- Imagine your own torso as the trunk of one of the trees in this grove, and as you exhale, envision your roots extending into the earth, deeper and deeper with every breath. You might want to close your eyes, or soften your gaze, so you are no longer focused on the visual connection with the grove. Listen to the wind in the trees and feel it on your skin.

- Tip your head back, so that your face is turned toward the sun. Imagine that your growth is being drawn upward from the earth, into the branches of your own body, into the leaves.

- Breathe in the freshening fragrance of the eucalyptus; let yourself feel the circulation of breath that draws your life force upward and fills you with a sense of newness, of growth toward the light.

- With the bark strip still wrapped around your arms, move your arms a bit, feeling the constraint of the bark.

- Envision what you might want or need to shed as the trees shed their bark. Is there something outgrown in your life that you want to let go of? Let that awareness come to mind. See or feel what you need to do to release whatever you are restricted by.

- As you envision letting go, feel the sensations, emotions, attitudes that come along with that freedom.

- If the spaciousness is frightening in any way, notice what you are afraid of. Wrap yourself in the bark again, and let it go slowly, feeling the point at which you can tolerate the change. Continue to release it until you are as free of the constraint as you wish to be.

- Be aware of any way in which the presence of the bark as boundary has value to you. Notice how it serves you.

- When you open your eyes and step out of the nest of bark around you, move along the path maintaining that sense of freedom from restriction, completely open to whatever is there to be experienced.

## A Druid's Tree Walk: Planting Ourselves in the Earth

On the left side of the path near the eucalyptus stand, a grove of Monterey pine and cypress begins. Kirby Cove's four-site camping area spreads among the scattered trees. As we enter the grove, a canopy of lofty, dark green branches shields us from direct sunlight. On the ground, the light green of new grasses and miner's lettuce is dotted with the reds, tans, and cocoa browns of mushrooms. Uncrowded, each of these individual trees offers a more distinct identity than those in the eucalyptus grove. Being able to walk among the trees allows us a relationship with them that's quite different from being involved with the trees from the edge of the eucalyptus grove.

Separating, we walk slowly among them as the Druids[12] sometimes do: with each inhalation, we raise our arms, palms up, like the branches of trees reaching toward the sun. With each exhalation we bring our hands toward one another in front of our chests, lowering them, following a path down the centerline of our bodies toward the earth. We envision them sending roots into the earth. Step by step, we become part of this grove as we walk among the trees.

## Listening to a Tree and Talking Back

We want to be "alone together"—a group of individual people relating to a group of individual trees. We spread out, each person choosing a single tree, coming close to meet the tree heart to heart. We place a small offering at its base and ask to communicate with it. When we are confident that the tree receives us, we continue. Our fingers trace the bark patterns, the flow of life reflected there. Noses close to the trunk, we smell the earthiness that's become tree. Finally, foreheads pressed against the trunk, or sinking down to sit with our backs against it, we share stories with the trees, telling our own and listening to theirs.

Pressing my back along the trunk of one of the trees, I follow the pattern of the tree's breathing, its life empowered by the connection with sky and earth. The constancy, the life of the tree present in the one place that is its home, creates an amazing feeling of comfort. My heart slows, breath lengthens, and I feel confident enough to begin to speak and to listen.

### PERSONAL JOURNEYS

Kayla: *Mine was a Monterey pine. I appreciated the patina, the notches where branches had grown and fallen away. There was a lime-green lichen the whole length of the trunk, and it had a big patch about four feet off the ground, where something had happened that had taken off the outside bark. It had bled sap from the patch, but it was dry, and like a healed scar. I felt such respect, such honor, for all its life experiences, and I suddenly felt a release of grief about some of the scars of my own life.*

Peggy: *It was surprising to me when I sat down by the tree. I started talking about the way I live my life without much thought—where it's going, or what I'm doing—and just sort of do what moves me in the moment. I never thought about where it could lead me. That can be freeing, except that I also tie myself to things once they happen, and then I feel bound. But the tree said this message while I was talking—that it sort of lives that way, too. I took what was offered, enjoyed what was offered, and the tree was saying, "I did that, too." This tree, they grow up, and the leaves and the life look like they're at the top. So the tree said, "Everything I did before made me stronger, brought me to the top, and became my base. So you're tall—you might not be the tallest, but you're up there." So all that I did before, that's the base. The tree was so healing for me. It didn't go into my "I did it wrong, look what a mess I've made of my life" routine. The tree said, "No, onward and upward. It's just your strength."*

## TRY THIS: Share your story with a tree and listen to the tree's story

- Choose a tree, and place at its base cornmeal, tobacco, or something else that you regard as an offering. Ask if it is willing to communicate with you. If you don't feel a connection, thank the tree and move to another.

- If you feel received, stand in front of it. Envision the sap flowing through it, and its nourishment from earth, sun, rain, and air.

- Watch the mirrored movement within your own body—your relationship to each breath of air; fluid coursing through your veins; your feet firmly on the earth; your heartbeat.

- When you feel that you are relating to the tree, either sit at its base with your spine against its trunk or embrace the tree while you're standing with your belly and heart against the trunk.

- Without sorting out what you want to say about your life, just begin to talk—either aloud or just shaping the words in your mind and heart.

- Talk as if you were speaking to a friend you haven't seen for a long time. You may find yourself talking about something that's happening in your present life—a pleasure or a concern—or you may find yourself describing the life journey you're on—where you've been or where you're going.

- Notice the freedom you have to speak without fear of judgment.

- Listen to the tree's response—its comments on your story, observations, or suggestions.

- Ask the tree about its own journey—its path through life, what it's like to stay in one place, how it responds to what comes its way, hopes or fears, the visitors of all forms that share its space, and how it copes with them.

- Notice what you have in common and what is unique to each of you.

- When you feel complete, ask the tree about what it might welcome from you in appreciation for the time you've shared. You may find yourself called upon for water, for a gesture from the heart, or some action in the world.

- Honor the exchange between you by following through in whatever way seems appropriate.

Beyond the cypress grove, we approach the bluff at the edge of the beach. Huge cement army structures from the early 1900s take us by surprise. Rusted iron ladders and various fittings forlornly ornament them. Trees, brush, and wildflowers are stealthily overtaking them, slowly integrating them into the landscape.

A stream whose water came from the multiple draws along the walls of the cove wanders through the camping area and begins to find its way to the beach. Its banks are crowded with willow, wild berry vines, an assortment of grasses and shrubs. The runaway day lilies were probably planted originally when the Army occupied the cove. A red brick arch over a culvert as tall as a person holds up a portion of the bluff. Along with another arch, long since gone, it was also a military construction, built about 130 years ago.[13] The cove's streams funnel into one stream, which flows through the brick arch onto the sand and finally into the sea.

Nearby, curving steps edged with wooden beams lead to the beach. Immediately, we take off our shoes, relishing the sand seeping between our toes. We approach two enormous constructions of wood, each bound together with rusting iron strips, huge oval rings at the corners. They look romantically like the flotsam of an old wooden ship that's broken apart and drifted to shore. Versions of their real origin float around as plentifully as by-the-wind sailors, the small jellyfish drying on the sand like bits of cellophane.[14] The apparent fragility of the small creatures belies the fact that they are among the oldest forms of life living here now.[15]

A splash of red on the water catches our attention. Bobbing along on the small incoming waves is a branch of bright red healthy-looking chili peppers, looking as if someone had just plucked it from the plant moments ago. Totally bewildered by its vigorous appearance, we nonetheless receive its powerful message. Here at Kirby Cove, anything the world has to offer can make its way into the bay, and this is its port of entry.

We stroll along the narrow beach, separating from one another so each of us can stay with her own impressions, hear the lapping water, the crying gulls. The small stream cuts across the width of the sand and fans out to the ocean. I wade ankle deep through it and on the other side discover driftwood shapes that resemble animals and birds, one that resembles a human form. A lone kayaker hugs the shore, slowly making his way past the beach and apparently out toward the open sea. Salt spray mists my face.

## Stones That Speak: Creating Stories

Scores of small flat gray stones, polished smooth by the waves, cluster together. Long ago, the beach was known as Gravelly Beach. Pillow basalt from underwater volcanoes forms the cliffs at the west end of the beach.[16] Initially green (greenstone), the basalt turns to a rusty red-brown when it's exposed to rain over a long period. Serpentine is also here, and mudstone. Some stones have beautiful designs created by the intrusions of quartz and other mineral deposits. Some are in shapes that seem ready to speak. Picking up one or two that we're most drawn to, we finger them as we walk along. At the far end of the beach, when the tide is out, two shallow caves have wonderful stone pickings. Nearby, the bleached trunk and branches of a fallen tree make a good backrest. We stop here to arrange the stones we've chosen in a circle, and begin to make up a story.

*Sarah picks up her stone and begins to describe the character she sees there: "Once upon a time, long ago, a bearded man sat down to rest while he was on a journey. He'd come a long way and was very tired. Here, you can see how drawn his face is, and his messy beard."*

*Next to her, Kayla picks up the stone next to the "bearded man" and continues, looking to the stone for the next step in the story. "He'd come through a pass and over an entire mountain. You can see the dent in the stone, the path he took over the top, right here. He'd never expected to travel so far when he set out and had come away from home empty-handed."*

*Holding his stone, Michael adds to the story. "Sometimes you're just driven; you know you have to go forward, even if you don't feel much hope. But there's no resolving your restlessness until you've given it everything you've got. That's just what he was feeling when he'd set off. He'd been a teenage father, and all his life, his family had meant more to him than anything. He'd grown up while they grew up. You can see by the shape of this stone how pointed he was in how he followed his path."*

*Peggy speaks up: "One day the man woke up, and he discovered that his children had grown up. They'd been well prepared by the man and his wife to get out in the world, and that's just what they did. Waving goodbye, the three young people stepped across the threshold. Here they are, right here, stepping across the doorway, very cheery and full of confidence."*

*"And what of his wife?" asks Marguerite after staring at the stone in her hand a few minutes. "She'd been a teenage mother and was really curious about what she had missed. So here she is on this stone, going around the bend. Look how that line goes around from one side of the stone to the other. It wasn't that she didn't*

*love her husband. She agonized about leaving. But sometimes there's unfinished business, and you just have to take care of it. You have to find yourself. It doesn't come to you on a silver platter. So she waved good-bye and off she went, making no promises."*

*Ann rubs her stone over her ears, as if it were whispering to her. Finally, bringing it to her lips, she begins. "In the blink of an eye, the man felt as if he'd instantly become old. He felt like his life was over, and he had a choice to make. He could either sit home and mope, or he could get out and see what else the world had in store for him. Here's the fork in the road. And look at this mysterious shadow at the end of this road. That's the one that appealed, because he felt like a shadow himself at the moment. He locked the door, collected his retirement fund, and off he went with nothing else but the clothes on his back."*

*We're back to the beginning of the circle, and the next round begins, picking up the threads of the man's adventure as told by the pictures on the stones. "I regret to say, he had an unexplored side, too—a shadow side. He'd been a Boy Scout leader, and twenty years at the same job without a single sick day, and he was beginning to feel like it was just possible he'd missed out on something, too. So he followed the bright lights, which he'd never done before. See this gold fleck, and the red right next to it? Neon lights. He found himself in a casino, and in less time than you could shake a stick, he lost every cent of his retirement money. There he was—homeless, jobless, nobody to cuddle with in bed."*

*The circle continues its rounds, the man far from rescue. Kayla picks up the story line with a new stone. "From the casino, he went to the shore of the ocean, not far from where we're sitting. A shallow cave against the side of the cliff had a little seatlike ledge at the back of it. He sat down on it, resting against the back wall of the cave. The seat was the color of this stone, with a little ledge like this, and flat on the top side, just like this one is."*

*Michael continues, "While he sat there, staring at the ocean, the cave began to rumble. 'Oh no,' he thought. 'It's an earthquake!' But just at that moment, a submarine started to emerge from the water, and he realized that the shaking was the vibration of the submarine! You can see its outline, all gray, with the green stone just the color of the water all around it."*

*With another stone, Peggy finds a story ending, just in the nick of time. "'Yikes!' he said. 'I see what's happened to me! I got all shook up over nothing! The unexpected is just going to keep on happening, and that's what adds pizzazz to life! I'm going back home and dig in my garden. [Look, you can see the rows of vegetables he planted.] Then I'll sit on my comfy front porch and wait for the next submarine to emerge!' And he did. And he's still there waiting. It may be a long wait, because it's inland. I believe his wife is still around the bend."*

## TRY THIS: Invent a group story with the characters and story line inspired by stones

- As you walk along the beach, look for a stone that could be a story stone—something with an interesting shape or markings. It could also be a shell fragment, or a piece of polished beach glass. Ask the stone if it's willing to come with you for a time. If you don't feel received by it, put it down and look for another.

- Each time you find one that you're drawn to, see whether it has more to say than the one you're already holding. Repeating the check-in with the stone, be sure the new one is willing to come with you. Choose one to keep with you and put the other down.

- Continue down the beach; at the far end, make a circle of people, with stones on the sand.

- When someone is inspired by the shape or markings on the stone (s)he's chosen, the story begins, based on the sight or the feeling of the stone in hand.

- Continue the storytelling in order around the circle; it keeps the flow going better than each person jumping in as inspired. It doesn't make any difference if the story line takes off on a totally different tangent. Just let it flow.

- When the story's complete, talk about the difference between your original connection with the stone and the place that it took in the story. A stone—and a person—has many potentials; how they are played out is very much a function of the community and the story it creates as a group.

- Leave the stones on the beach, arranging them in a pleasing way. Decorate the grouping with driftwood, shells, and any other interesting bits of seaweed or plant material, a thank-you to the beach. Others may use it in a similar way and they will tell a different story crafted from the same raw materials.

Retracing our steps, at the stairs we wipe the sand from our toes, put on our shoes, and climb to a bluff overlooking the westernmost end of the beach. Using a fallen segment of a tree trunk as an altar, people put on it found objects from the beach—a button, driftwood, a length of curly yellow twine, some of the red peppers, beautiful stones. With the log altar between us and the water, we make ourselves comfortable. From this vantage point, we can see the choppy water of the treacherous Potato Patch Shoal just outside the

Golden Gate Bridge. Colliding currents send sprays of water into the air as the North Pacific powers into the bay over the shoal.[17]

Even though we're near major population centers, there is a sense of wilderness. Visiting midweek, we are the only human visitors to the site. Across the bay, Land's End faces the ocean, and buildings cover the rolling hills of San Francisco; between that bastion of civilization and our vantage point, the Golden Gate Bridge holds the world at arm's length.

Kirby Cove and Golden Gate Bridge. Photo by Sandy Miranda, 2005.

## Meditation: Heart of the Water

The narrowed neck of water between Kirby Cove and Baker Beach symbolically marks a point of exchange that in actual fact continues as deeply into the bay as the area of Suisun. Salt water and fresh water trade their wares. Streams and creeks come from the Santa Cruz Mountains into the bay; rivers come from inland, other streams from Marin. All carry the traces of our lives here in the broader bay area—traces of how we live on the land, the impacts of our choices, the way we honor or dishonor the water that passes through our lives. All this comes to the mouth of the bay twice a day. The fresh water from the communities that surround the bay returns to the sea, like children coming home from school. "Look, Mother, this is what I have done. Look, Mother, this is for you." And whatever the bay carries to Mother Ocean, she receives, accepts, integrates, and carries to all the creatures who call the ocean home. She moves it along and shares it with the other shorelines she touches, and finally returns with the gifts that the people of the other shores have offered.

Here at the edge, where fresh water and salt water mingle, where the land gives way to the ocean, we decide to immerse ourselves in water in a different way. Inspired by the water's flow from one state of being to another, it seems the perfect place to practice a transformation in ourselves from one state of consciousness to another. To touch the sacred, we must move into another level of reality, experience the unseen but no less real realm of nonordinary reality. We prepare to travel on a mystical journey to the heart of the water.

The Chumash people believe that we have ten senses, and that the five related to imagination have been lost.[18] Given our intention to move into new ways of communicating with the natural world, we want to experiment with uncommon approaches, want to find ways to allow the lost senses to emerge once again. Supported by the presence at the Golden Gate of nature's twice-daily transformative processes in the ebb and flow of the tides, the exchange of salt water and fresh water, we talk about how to use this impetus to guide an experience of the deepest essence of water, its heart, its spirit.

In indigenous cultures, a shaman's journey into an altered state of consciousness is usually initiated through some form of percussion.[19] He or she can follow this auditory trail during the journey and on the return to ordinary reality. While in the nonordinary reality produced by the shift in consciousness, she or he might travel to one of three realms—the Lower World (reached through some envisioned opening into the earth), the Upper World (its portal possibly the branches of a tree, and experienced as more ethereal), or the Middle World (the spiritual dimension of ordinary reality). The point of entry is a place that exists in both the world of ordinary reality and nonordinary reality and is a personal point of reference used over and over again. A tree stump, a well, a cave, an animal burrow, the headwaters of a river—all are possibilities for journeying into the Lower World, the most common destination. In these realms, a shaman works with helping spirits who may take the form of animals or human teachers.[20]

Focusing on the domain of water, we borrow two aspects of the shaman's work for our visualization process. As we discuss an appropriate point of entry into another level of reality, various water-oriented entrance points come up—a tide pool, a hole in a rock at the edge of the beach, the exposed roots of a tree on the bank of a stream, a pool at the base of a waterfall. Each of us calls to mind a particular place she's experienced in the past and creates in her own mind a vivid recollection of it.

We sit in a circle and agree on a common process everyone will share to create an individual experience of water—its heart, its essence. We hold our intent clearly and go in mind's eye to a point of entry. I create a rhythmic drumbeat, and the visualization begins. Wind and drum dance together, creating overtones and harmonies that help people journey safely; a thread of sound travels with them. Tumbling, sliding, falling through a tunnel entry into the Lower World, we open our senses to whatever there is to be experienced about the identity, the heart, the essence, of the water. Each person follows her own path.

After about ten minutes, I tug the thread, striking the drum four times and then drumming rapidly to create a path of sound to guide their return. For a few minutes, we're all quiet while we readjust to being here on the bluff at Kirby Cove overlooking the Pacific Ocean. Then people begin to share their experiences.

## PERSONAL JOURNEYS

Marguerite: *I found myself on the back of a selkie,[21] entering the water from a sandy beach on a dark night, with the full moon absolutely blood red. I went very deep, slid off, and began a gentle undulation, moving with the movement of the water. Small particles of sand reflected light from an unknown source and floated away—octopi, squid, pulsing water creatures moved by without seeing me, and I had the sense that I was no larger or more visible than the grains of sand. There was a pulsing sound that went with the pulsing sensation of the water, and I felt like I was feeling and hearing the heart of the sea.*

*I realized that the sea holds the primary material of the life of the planet, but the entire planet is an organ of the universe. The earth is connected to the moon and the sun, and to all of the other planets, and all of them are organs of the enormous living body of the universe. I felt observed, but like an insignificant cell. I moved from macrocosm to microcosm, watching the creatures of the sea as cells in the organ that's the earth. I felt like a cell floating in the universe, not just the heart of the ocean, and realized that my actions, my choices, my existence affected the health of the ocean, the planet, the universe. It was like being a cell under a microscope.*

Sarah: *My point of entry was a waterfall. At first, the drum and the water seemed to merge, like the drumbeats were falling down with the water. I just listened for a while. Then I became the water, slipping into all kinds of places only water could go. It was a wonderful feeling, just slithering into places no creatures with bodies could fit into. I felt so free. I was water itself, falling over a waterfall, under the ocean, and over mossy rocks, and sending sprays of sparkling water into the sunshine.*

Kayla: *The drum seemed to be telling me, with an actual word, to go "down, down, down." And I did! I felt like I descended to the source of the water. On the floor of the ocean, water was bubbling up, making huge bubbles of sand bulge up. Then they'd burst as the water came from some underground source deeper in the earth. I didn't go deeper; it was kind of like I was at the place where water became what it is, took on the form that it has. Past that, I don't think I would have recognized it.*

Ann: *I'm a very literal person, and I don't exactly know how to have the experiences that others seem to have. But I've always enjoyed the physical sensation of floating in water, so I just let my body remember that experience. It was like being a streamer of seaweed. I wasn't going anywhere in particular, but my body felt totally flexible.*

Michael: *I felt I was going down a whirlpool. Everything was bumping around. Things I could recognize went into the whirlpool too, but everything started swirling around and mixing together; pretty soon everything—including me— became shredded particles and just spread out until I couldn't see anything but flecks in the water.*

Carol takes from her backpack a large crystal, a starburst of small crystals pointing in many directions. She carefully positions the point of a nail she's brought along, and using a rock as a hammer, shatters the crystal, sending the fragments flying. She invites each of us to take one, a personal crystal that will make the journey around the bay with us and will represent our individual intent as we visit each site. She proposes that the group bury one crystal at each place we visit, inviting the beautiful gems to call forth the powers of the place and to strengthen the web of connection we create among the sacred sites.

Scooping out a small hollow, Carol places Kirby Cove's crystal in the earth. We add treasures that we've picked up during our walk—a fragment of the eucalyptus bark, a small cone from a cypress tree, a shell fragment from the beach—each contribution honoring something that enriches our own relationships to Kirby Cove. We cover the little depression with earth and leave with the sense that some small part of our own attention and appreciation remains.

Here, walking in silence, we've begun a new way of moving through the world using breath and intent, diverting the distraction of internal dialogue about situations or people not present. We've begun to sniff out connections with other life-forms, parallel behaviors in our own lives. We are paying attention when nature speaks and exploring new means of communication. Surrounded by beauty, we've launched our adventure.

Directly across the Golden Gate, Baker Beach is still in sunlight, while the old remnants of the Franciscan Complex shoreline already bring dusk's shadows to Kirby Cove. We connect the two places, weaving filaments of attention between sunlight and shadow, celebrating the bonds of relationships between the beaches and cliffs on opposite sides of the Golden Gate. The rhythmic sound of the waves washing the beach sets a pace for climbing the hill toward our cars. The seagulls' calling fades as we move farther from the beach, but the moist cool air carries the ocean's presence with us.

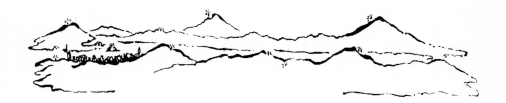

## Chapter Two

# RING MOUNTAIN:
# Petroglyphs of Fertility

It's been raining hard throughout the night; just before dawn, the downpour slows, finally petering out into drops released from the eaves, door frames, and jasmine outside my bedroom window. I lie in bed for a while enjoying the water sounds—and relishing the prospect of a trip to Ring Mountain, a particularly intriguing place to visit after a rainfall because of its unusual geology. A meadow close to the Corte Madera Channel is a lucky heir to a number of springs whose existence is tied to the jumble of rocks on the upper slopes. Because a mass of rock separates serpentine from the sandstone below, rainwater can't pass through the area easily—and it emerges in innumerable small springs that "ring the mountain." (The mountain was actually named for George Ring, a county supervisor around 1900,[1] but the ring of springs lends a much more interesting connotation to the name.) Especially after a vigorous rainfall, the water bubbles up under your footsteps in rebellious spurts of uncontrolled joy. Anticipating it pulls me out of bed and into a sense of childish freedom. I call my friends, and within hours we are under way.

## A Land Grant

The little mountain, just over 600 feet in altitude, squats on the Tiburon Peninsula, which juts into San Francisco Bay slightly northeast of the Golden Gate. We park on the road near the entrance that faces San Quentin Prison. Even though the Ring Mountain Preserve begins on the uphill side of the road, I've always considered the narrow strip of marshland on the cove side of the road to be part of the mountain. Whenever I hike on Ring, I like to pay a visit to the edge of the water in the Corte Madera Channel. It's primarily a mat of cordgrass, dotted with fennel, coyote brush, pickleweed, salt grass, and gum plant. The fragrance of fennel is so delicious that I can forgive its presence as a non-native plant. Native cordgrass is another matter.

The root system of cordgrass is about five times larger than its aboveground biomass[2] and has undoubtedly changed the function of the wetlands in the ecosystem. It's an odd experience to walk on this "floor" of plant material. It reminds me of the tule reeds that have been used so extensively by natives of many continents for everything from baskets to clothing, mats, boats, and duck decoys. At one time many miles of the bay's shoreline were lined with tules. It was a Coast Miwok "wonder plant" used for a virtually endless number of household items and building materials. The young shoots could be eaten raw or cooked.[3]

Stepping on the cordgrass mat links me back to a similar cushioned step I took onto a tule island in Lake Titicaca, which straddles the border between Peru and Bolivia. There, contemporary people still relate to plant material very differently. The Uros Indians, who are native to the lake, lead their entire lives on islands created of tules. Never coming to shore, they have only very recently permitted limited visits from outsiders. Living on these islands gives them moment-to-moment awareness of the link between their existence and its sources in nature. My footfall on the resilient cordgrass here at Ring Mountain brings me briefly into that remembrance, and I drop a small cornmeal offering in gratitude.

No such isolation protected the culture of the Native Americans here at Ring Mountain. In the late 1700s and early 1800s, the Coast Miwoks in Marin—vulnerable to diseases, suffering from depletion of their food sources, and overwhelmed by the power of Spanish weaponry and customs—were gradually incorporated into the Spanish culture.[4]

By 1834, Ring Mountain was already part of one of the Mexican land grants. Although at one point the land was a cattle ranch, it is now virtually the same as before the Hispanic occupation.[5] During the period of Spanish and Mexican governance of California, colonization of the frontier was supported by land grants that were usually rewards for service. Throughout the west, an actual gesture of possession was part of the process.

In New Mexico, for instance, the person acquiring the land had to "physically step on the land, run his fingers through the soil, and make a public commitment to live on it, cultivate it, and defend it…with his life." To secure land that today changes hands for millions of dollars, the prospective owner of those early days only needed to pull up grass, throw stones, and shout to the four directions three times, "Long live the King, and may God protect Him!"[6] At the end of the Mexican-American War, the Treaty of Hidalgo in 1848 supposedly assured that the United States would honor the land grants. In fact, the expensive legal process of burden of proof for ownership was laid at the door of the (usually) Hispanic grantees.

## Plants and Peoples

The geologic feature that has most affected the plant life of Ring Mountain is the serpentine, which forms the upper slopes and the ridgeline. The unusual chemical composition of serpentine creates soil conditions that foster plant life that grows nowhere else. Several processes may have brought it to rest here, among them movements of the earth's tectonic plates. Turbidity currents—undersea flows of muddy sediments triggered by earthquakes—deposited graywacke (the most common rock in California's Coast Range) and mud-rich shales at the base of the mountain.[7] When first deposited, they sat atop the older serpentine, which may have squeezed any way it could through the compacting mass of the Franciscan sediment.

A short wooden footbridge begins the actual trail; just past the bridge, wild crabapple and plum trees scatter tiny white and pink blossoms on the path. Small brown birds jump about on pogo-stick legs. Pausing here, we clarify our intentions for this visit to Ring. Making an offering of sacred tobacco, we ask permission from the Spirit guardians to enter the sacred space. Damp petals falling from the trees blow toward us on the breeze, and we feel that permission is granted. As we had hoped, each step we take brings water from underground to welcome us.

Wildflowers have already begun to bloom. Before summer is over, a number of endangered species will have made their appearance. Best known is the Tiburon mariposa lily, one of the serpentine endemics that blooms in early summer and has so uniquely evolved on Ring Mountain that it grows nowhere else.[8] The Miwok people harvested the bulbs of this and other lilies for food, using a digging stick, sharpened to a point and hardened in fire. Harvesting in this way tilled the ground in which the plants grew and ensured the return and expansion of the crop.[9]

Many other varieties of flowers appear. Tiny white milkmaids, yellow California buttercups, yellow lupine, tidy tips, linaria, blue dick, blue-eyed grass, and wild onion are some of the earlier arrivals—lovely splashes of color against the vibrant green of the meadow grasses. A number of native grasses also grow on the lower slopes. Small mammals make their homes among them, and little birds bob on and off the tips of the coarse grass stems, finding plenty of food.

The narrow wavy-edged leaves of the soap plant are scattered profusely over the slopes and mesas of California and Oregon. It's another "wonder plant." The root lathers well for use in all kinds of washing jobs, from dirty hands to hair to clothes.[10] Slowly cooking the plant removes the soapy taste. The leaves can be eaten raw and were used by the Miwok to wrap acorn bread as it was baking. Soaproot was used as medicine for rheumatism and sores. The juice was used for attaching feathers to arrow shafts. Finally, whole villages engaged in cooperative fishing, and crushed soaproot bulbs were thrown into dammed pools to stun and catch fish.

The path forks off, leading us through ankle-deep grass toward a shady line of trees on the bank of a small stream. California laurel, buckeye, and oak create a soothing outdoor space, a sense of open-air containment, where many hours might have been spent by the Miwok people coming to Ring Mountain. We find a mortar hollowed out in a large boulder, the result of Miwok women grinding acorns and grains for countless hours. This site is not very large and was probably used either by a small group of people or only periodically.

At our feet, black earth is flecked with thousands of minute shell fragments. Middens such as these exist in many places in the world. From their contents, archeologists have inferred cultural and historical information about the communities that created them. Here, the midden holds remembrances, visible even on the surface, of community feasts on the oysters and clams taken from the channel just a few hundred feet away. Offering up these water-borne delicacies, the marshland left no one hungry; pelicans and other seabirds, coyote and bear, foxes and people—all shared the bounty.

Many middens have been excavated without sensitivity to the concerns of native peoples, who do not welcome disturbing them in any way. However, just looking at the surface of the rich soil inspires us to make a simple time travel journey.

## Children Linking Past and Present

Laughing screams of children at the nearby Marin Country Day School bridge the decades and centuries; their cheerful play might just as easily be the sound of Miwok children playing by the stream or in the nearby field. Then as now, children played "house," experimenting with their roles in life and learning how to survive.[11] Balls today are often made of rubber or plastic; two centuries ago, balls were just as popular but often made of squash, pumpkin, or of softer materials such as rabbit skin or soaproot fibers.[12]

Tiny fragments of mica and minute garnets embedded in schists are scattered on the ground around us. They become the dancing stand-ins for the children in their play areas, both past and present. Their voices call through the winking stones. It could be then; it could be now. As we relax and finger the sparkling stones, memories and fantasy images drift through our minds. We call up images and sounds of our own childhood play, then turn to imagine the ways the Miwok children might have played in this place...

## PERSONAL JOURNEYS

Kayla: *I love to hear children laughing and playing without fear—just letting their joy spill out, getting a little wild, and letting go in a way that's so trusting and confident. I lived in Chicago growing up, and on hot summer evenings we played games like "kick the can" in the streets. That was the first image that came to mind. Playing house under somebody's front porch. Chalked hopscotch patterns on the sidewalk. Sidewalk skates with keys on strings around our necks. We didn't miss the country because we didn't know it. Nature still came into play because we all relished playing in the light of long summer evenings. It made it special. When the streetlights went on, it felt very special to still be able to play outside, like stealing time. We hated to be called in.*

*I had an image of visiting my cousin when he moved to the country, catching fireflies and playing under a column of windbreak trees; croquet on the grass. You can make your pleasure with familiar objects, whether it's a tin can or a tennis ball. Imagination, curiosity, taking chances—it's all part of childhood everywhere. Then the sound of the kids in the field brought me back to this place. I imagined standing on the sidelines in the shadows watching a ball game, very much like soccer. The jostling, the shouts of play, were no different from our own. Later, images of throwing sticks into hoop targets came to mind. In the shaded bower of the midden, close to mothers, children arranged patterns of stone. Now and then someone hid a special stone behind her back, and another pointed, guessing which hand held it. It was so familiar. Language, words, were totally unnecessary to feel the rapport with them.*

*When I think of the Native American children who lost everything that was familiar and free—language, family, ways of doing the most common things—when they became part of the mission life, it feels like a tragedy that leaves a permanent mark. That's happening today, of course, in many places. Our own children live in a world where other kids are being damaged by wars, and those damaged kids are the ones that ours will have to make peace with. How will that happen? It's a problem for all of us.*

## TRY THIS: Link past and present through children

- At the midden, sit in the shade next to the stream. Close your eyes and listen to the children playing in the schoolyard.

- As you hear the sounds of universal play, remember your own childhood, your own games and friends. Who was your best friend and what games did you play in your neighborhood on long summer nights? Did you live in the city or the country? Did you go to a camp that took you into nature? What were your favorite toys? Remember...

- In your play, how did you practice being a grown-up? Remember...

- How did your mother and father play with you? What do you know of their own childhood play?...of how they entertained themselves? Visualize them, or your grandparents, in their communities and families before the era of TV. Imagine them, hear their voices...

- Before the time of Spanish intrusion into the Miwok way of life, children who were encamped with their parents on the mountain did what children do everywhere—they ran and jumped in the warm sun, played "house" as they tried on their relationships to adult roles, learned to hunt by catching field mice. Imagine them helping with chores, hunting with the men when they're a bit older. Imagine a child's life on this mountain.

- In your own childhood, you may have had an experience of abrupt change. Your family might have moved to a new environment; you might have found yourself a stranger surrounded by children different from you in their play, their behavior. You might have come from a foreign country, spoken another language. Some other kind of change might have happened in your family. How did your parents react, and how did they guide you? How did you cope with the helplessness of a change you could not control? How did it change you? Remember...

- In the late 1700s and early 1800s, the Miwoks in Marin were incorporated, often abruptly, into Spanish culture. Imagine children of six or seven catapulted into a new lifestyle, bereft of the freedom of their former lives, sometimes even used as servants.[13] Imagine their bewilderment, their pain, their fear. Imagine...

- Be aware of the ways your family's past—their accomplishments, adventures, tragedies, principles—affected the lives of you and your siblings.

- Is there something about your family's experiences and attitudes that affects your childish sense of freedom today, your willingness to play and to explore?

- Remember the people in your childhood who helped you feel joy and curiosity—perhaps relatives, friends, or teachers. Move into the innocence of childhood as you prepare to continue exploring Ring Mountain. What can you tap into—or let go of—that would expand your exploration of the mountain?

- Open your eyes; bring yourself back to the present moment in this lovely grove of trees, ferns held onto the bank of the stream by the exposed roots of the trees, shell fragments of the past in the rich black soil of the midden, the sound of water burbling over the stones. Feel yourself held and protected by the site, by the mountain, by the day.

## Water Carrying Essence

Continuing uphill, the path approaches the stream a short distance above the midden. The water is clear, and for a few moments we watch it swirl around small stones and natural debris. The water's rippled surface reminds me of the skin of an elder whose wrinkles speak of the life the person has led. Watching the patterns created by the movement around the stones, we talk about the impact of our own presence here. We intend to leave it unmarked; at the same time, we want to be part of this sweet life on Ring Mountain. A simple solution emerges: we invite the water to carry with it something of our essence. Bending close, we scoop up water and pour it onto our wrists; it drips down, rejoining the stream, so that a hint of our presence here will go with it out to the cove, then to the bay, and finally to the Pacific. Over the centuries, the water will be taken up and will return again and again as fog, or perhaps as a wild rain like the one that veiled my vision on my first visit to the mountain.

## Sentinel Boulder

Months earlier I had read an article from the Sacred Sites Foundation that mentioned a "feminine" stone on this mountain, with carvings thousands of years old. The carvings are similar to petroglyphs at known fertility sites elsewhere in California.[14] Eager to find them, I couldn't wait for good weather. In spite of gusting winds and fiercely blowing rain, two friends joined the quest, and we went to Ring Mountain.

After driving to the trailhead, we struggled to make our way uphill against unbelievable gusts of wind-driven rain. Visibility was a scant fifty feet and closed in as we followed the muddy path upward. The fields were soggy with days of rain; water not only poured down on us but also welled up from the ground with every step. Dozens of springs just beneath the surface surged up willy-nilly, most refusing to be herded into the several streams that led all the way down the mountain. Feeling this much water beneath us and around us opened the pores of our skin and of our imaginations—all the more so because of a recent long period of California drought.

Suddenly a huge stone column loomed before us. We stopped, awed by its presence; standing like a sentinel, it claimed the territory and demanded to be taken into account. Swirling fog repeatedly enshrouded it, then released it. The boulder stood alone on the hillside, rising out of a cluster of more rounded stones at its base. Bushes jutted out from crevices between the column and the stones, and the limbs of trees on its far side embraced it. Drenched but jubilant, naïve and cavalier, ready to find what we sought and willing to override the obvious, we were convinced that we had found the fertility stone—never mind feminine—reputed to be on Ring Mountain.

Upon reaching the boulder, we were shocked to discover a housing development nudging up to it not ten yards away. We were quite shaken, having come through such an intense experience of weather only to find ourselves looking into someone's back yard and hearing the protective barking of a large dog. The proximity of human habitation clearly expressed the challenge we all face—how to maintain our connection with nature with increasingly dense population pressing in on all sides.

We decided to return home, waiting to explore the fertility stone when visibility and weather conditions were better. Before we left, the clouds around the boulder enveloped us, as well, alternately enfolding and releasing us. We danced and sang to the rain, to the joy of water pouring over us in a land whose inhabitants are always nervous about the possibility of drought.

Warm and dry at home, I felt disbelief creep in. I reread the article from the Sacred Sites Foundation. It described the stone's "rounded shape" and "feminine nature—breasts, vulva, pregnant belly." It seemed a stretch to think of our discovery as "feminine." While the base of the formation had several clusters of rounded boulders, the primary one pointed distinctly upward—much more phallic than feminine. Our search was not over. And the boulder was not the only interesting part of the mountain that awaited us.

## San Quentin: Eating the Shadow

Now, a number of visits later, the sky is brilliant blue after a spring rain. White clouds fly overhead. Climbing higher, we look down on the Corte Madera Channel and the marsh that lines the cove. Across the cove, the buildings of San Quentin Prison face the mountain; behind us, the silhouette of Mount Tamalpais forms the horizon. I wonder if the inmates can see the "sleeping maiden," as it's often called. I'm struck by the contrast between the experience of the men inside San Quentin and the ebullience that being on the mountain always creates in me. Climbing higher, I recall a sculpture of a padlock facing the prison that once sat on the shore at the base of the mountain. I remember sitting to meditate, sending waves of compassion through the keyhole of the padlock, reflecting on freedom and confinement. The sculpture encouraged me to pay attention to the people whose life choices brought them to lose their freedom, and the fact that some might be there through a miscarriage of justice.

Although the sculpture is no longer there, the memory of it makes me think of the men across the water. My friends sit with me on a small mound; we're aware that 6,000 prisoners occupy a facility designed to hold 3,317.[15] The wind blows lightly. From this vantage point of safety and freedom, we can honor without judgment their pain, the pain they may have caused others, the anger and humiliation that flows among them. We envision with compassion the men who share this place in the universe in a way that's very different from our own.

## PERSONAL JOURNEYS

Ann: *My own son spent time in prison, and it broke my heart. You can't imagine how frightening it is to have the situation totally taken out of your hands, not be able to do anything, even though there was probably nothing more that I could do. To sit here, just being calm and holding my heart open, feels like very good medicine for me. And it feels like the most powerful action possible just to create a healing atmosphere around that place. You want to forget them, or pretend that pain doesn't exist, in them or in yourself. You don't want it to be true. But here it is. They're there and we're here. It seems unfair; but choices have their consequences. I can't say I think the experience will change anyone. Doing what we're doing is a different way of confronting it.*

Marguerite: *I was raped many years ago, and the man who attacked me ended up in prison. I felt angry and sad at the same time—angry because of what he did to me, and sad because I can't imagine that anyone who would do something like that hadn't been deeply hurt himself. But that doesn't give anyone the right to hurt other people. I had this crazy desire to visit him, to tell him I understood, but it really wasn't the right thing for me. To do this today somehow is the end of a chapter. It was a way to express the compassion I felt and still hold the boundary that I don't deserve violence because of violence done to him.*

## TRY THIS: Eat the shadow

- Stand facing the Corte Madera Channel, with San Quentin across the water. As you look around you, let yourself absorb the peace that's present here. It might come from the beautiful view of the Corte Madera Cove or from the San Rafael Bridge spanning the bay. It might come from the scudding clouds or from the lazy flight of birds overhead. It might be the sun on your skin or the wind blowing your hair. Feel your body relax; open to the natural world around you.

- Spread your arms wide as you inhale, as if you were opening them to receive a huge gift. Tip your head back, so that you're opening your heart cavity from the sides and from above. As you exhale, bring your hands to your heart and take in the beauty around you. Fill your heart and your whole being with peacefulness, with the pleasures of sound, fragrance, and sight that encompass you here. Do that several times, until you feel quite filled with nature's bounty.

- Sit comfortably on the grass and close your eyes.

- Imagine a mouth in your belly—see the lips, the teeth, the tongue. Notice whether the lips are full or narrow, whether the teeth are perfect or a bit askew.

- Focus on any feeling of unrest you carry within you—irritability, anger, any emotion that keeps you from being as peaceful as you'd like. Imagine feeding the mouth with those heavy thoughts and feelings. Let the mouth eat those feelings—watch the lips close around them, the teeth chew them up, and the tongue carry them down your digestive tract. Imagine composting them. Our feelings, like everything else, are a form of energy. Mother Earth has a composting habit and is quite able to accept that dense energy and make use of it. Here in this beautiful place, send the heaviness you carry into the earth to be recycled; take in the lighter energy that nature's beauty feeds you. Leave your compost for the plants and flowers that grow on the mountain's slopes. Take in the beauty and contentment you're offered here.

- When you're ready to move beyond your own issues, begin to think of the people in San Quentin. Let their anger, frustration, hopelessness, confusion be chewed up in the mouth of your belly, without identifying with these feelings. Take their pain into the mouth in your belly along imaginary strands that reach from them to you; chew the pain up thoroughly and send it as compost to the mountain. Use your breath to help this process—inhale as you take in the heavy feelings, being careful only to envision them coming into the mouth in your belly. Exhale as you send them into the earth.

- Before you take in more from the prisoners, inhale, filling yourself again with the life force around you. When you exhale, send strands of that lightness and peace back to the prisoners.

- When you feel complete, take a few more deep breaths, filling yourself with the mountain's life force in all its forms. Open your eyes and enjoy your freedom, the beauty, and your relationship to the mountain.

We cross the creek again over another small wooden bridge and experience a different sense of being on the mountain. There are markedly different plants here, and the terrain is much more open. It's a doorway, a transition on the mountain. If we were hiking as people often do—talking about politics, people in our lives, our jobs—we might never notice the changes. Walking quietly, paying attention, we notice the differences.

## A Geologic Portal: Schist Modeling Diversity

At this point, the plants, the stone, the shape of the mountain mark a subtle gateway. The wind moves around us differently as we climb higher on the mountain and are more affected by the air currents of the Tiburon Peninsula. All of these forms of life and expressions of the elements have their unique signature, part of the distinctive communication of this doorway. The sensory presence is very different from the spring-filled meadows we've come through. The transition marks our own shift to a heightened awareness of our presence together on the mountain.

A large boulder of schist marks the beginning of this rather bald section of hillside. Schist is easily split into flakes or slabs. It characteristically contains more than 50 percent platy and elongated minerals, such as mica. Granite stones found in the Sierra contain three to five different kinds of minerals, while the schists on Ring Mountain are made up of twelve to fifteen. Each rock's mineral content is distinct from the others on the mountain. It seems that nature has given us a perfect mirror for the diversity of our own human community, where people have come to live from all over the globe. In the safety of the open field, with the inspiration of the complex stone, we prepare to explore the hidden agenda each of us brings to the day.

Sitting in a quiet circle, we gather our thoughts as we focus on the mountain's stones. I light a sage smudge stick. We pass it around the circle, each person smudging the person next to her, preparing one another to become fully present.

We invite the image of diversity represented by the schist to guide our dialogue. Here in one stone more than a dozen different minerals coexist. We pass it around the circle, letting it designate each person's turn to share important thoughts or concerns. People usually move through shared experiences assuming common denominators of attention, feelings, perceptions, and reactions. This assumption may or may not be accurate. Events we share are often colored by the weight of totally unrelated issues we carry with us. In this circle, we explore them as hidden distractions, sharing any thoughts that might be persistent or intrusive, so that they can be set aside for the day. If there's something important happening in our lives, this is a time to speak of it. We let our differences be revealed, bearing witness to one another, with no need to respond, fix, or pass judgment, only to hear one another.

The power of this unusual stone reminds us that even with differences, it is possible to exist in community, sharing events that carry different meanings for each of us. Nature provides a practice ground: in these circumstances, external threats are minimal. This particular group has minimum overt diversity—one lone man with a group of women, one lesbian, one woman with native ancestry, one woman born outside the United States, some differences in socioeconomic level and in religious upbringing. And yet, because of the relative homogeneity, differences not so apparent may be more striking.

With respect for privacy, we agree not to discuss the comments outside of the circle. The meditation we've just practiced, letting reactions and emotions pass through us as energetic compost for the mountain, can now be part of the way we listen to each other—witnessing, and letting go of the content that we hear. As the stone passes from person to person, each feels its texture, traces the variations with her fingers as she speaks, and discloses as fully as possible, paying special attention to the places where she's inclined to hold back.

When everyone finishes, we move slightly apart, so that we can introduce ourselves individually to the mountain. We take up rattles, or clap two stones together, creating unique rhythms; one by one, we begin to hum. Sounds emerge, uncharted syllables or actual words; bodies bending and dancing, we present ourselves to the mountain, holding our intent in our hearts. The separate chants stop and start again as we become more immersed in the movement of our dancing, becoming more and more fully present on the mountain. Dancing and chanting, we hone and express who we are and our reasons for coming to Ring Mountain.

**TRY THIS: Speak your true concerns and opinions with the support of Ring Mountain schist**

- Find a stone that has complexities of shape, of content, of texture.
- Examine it closely: trace its outline with your fingers; notice its indentations and individual characteristics.
- Touch it to your eyelids, your nose, your lips, your ears.
- Touch the stone to the skin of your face, and trace the outline of your face, your arms and hands—part of the physical container of your being.
- If you are alone, or when your turn comes in the circle, speak aloud about the issues that weigh heavily for you day to day, the thoughts that are with you when you first awaken and those that punctuate your daily activities.
- When everyone in the circle has had a chance to speak, do a small ceremony to anchor the effect of sharing in this way.
- Through movement, rhythm, voice, or gesture, offer your full presence and attention to the spirit of the mountain. Be fully here, now.

## Moving with Beginner's Mind

After some time, we fall silent. We form a circle, coming together with a sense of shared and individual purpose. A sense of companionship partners with autonomy as we begin to walk toward the vertical boulder. We move with "beginner's mind,"[16] moving forward with openness, willing to experience the mountain in a new way. It's an attitude of freshness, of attention to being fully present with the mountain. We smell the wind-borne fragrances from the grasses and the flowers, feel the changes in temperature and wind as we move across the contours of the mountain, watch the shadows of clouds as they move across the sun-drenched hills. Moving slowly gives us time to discover the mountain's languages.

Nothing is pushed. In our desire to be in authentic relationship to the mountain, we simply try to stay conscious of ourselves and our surroundings.

We stop next to the sentinel boulder and share our observations and feelings. Its shape, position, and size create in all of us an impression of focus and power. Debbie mentions its guardian character, a protector of the land and the life of the mountain. She remembers someone referring to it as the "Indian Warrior." Ann reflects on the shape, thrusting strongly upward, inspiring in her an intention to connect with the highest principles, with integrity.

# Creating a Mesa: Gathering Power Objects

In many native traditions, a shaman works with a collection of objects that represent his or her personal power. This is sometimes called a *mesa*. The objects may have been given to the shaman by a teacher or may have become "loaded," or empowered, through the individual's work with the objects. A *mesa* is kept safely in the shaman's possession, wrapped in a beautiful weaving, and may never be seen by another person.

Nearly everyone cherishes objects that represent connections to a beautiful place or experience—stones, shells, other items that symbolize an event or relationship. These objects are potentially power objects that might be used to strengthen a person's sphere of connections to a family or community, or to deepen personal spiritual work. Many people have objects in their workplace that serve to inspire or amuse them and others. On top of my computer a Kali finger puppet observes my work; given half a chance, Kali, the Hindu triple goddess of creation, preservation, and destruction, helps me cull irrelevant information from my writing. One friend of mine has a stone from a journey to a sacred mountain in Peru, where stones are revered as full of life and capable of healing. Another has the Tarot card of the Chariot, symbol of self-discipline, of having a sense of direction, a plan. Some might keep a picture of a loved one on a desk, or some memorabilia from a trip to a special place. These ordinary items may be useless or unimportant to others, and yet they can motivate their possessors, provide great personal meaning, and remind them of why they do certain things.

When an object is used in shamanic work, particular attention is paid to its intrinsic power. Each object has a relationship with and has been affected by its place, with the events that have transpired during its existence. A stone, for example, may have been struck by lightning or otherwise uniquely shaped by the elements, or may have lived for centuries washed in the water of a river or stream. Shamans who live on the "barren" upper slopes of the Peruvian mountains emphasize the importance of building relationships with nature through stones. Particular stones are called on for the power they accrue through their experiences and relationships. They may become part of a ceremony to gather the wisdom, strength, and action needed to support a goal, such as healing for an individual, or to support a community project.

In ceremony, the shaman and the community align their intent, feelings, and actions with the power objects. Aligning strengthens their connections with the forces of nature and with the powers of nonordinary reality. No important tasks are undertaken without first creating these working relationships, an acknowledgment that whatever we accomplish is done in partnership with other dimensions of the web of life. To empower ourselves as a group as well as strengthen our individual purposes, we will create a group *mesa*, linking it with the strength of the vertical boulder.

Just outside the boulder's inner sanctum (a narrow niche into which we'll climb to work with it) is a flat stone. On its surface, I spread a Peruvian wool weaving. Depicted in the weaving are the three worlds, reminding us that even as we move through ordinary reality, we are connected not just to the physical world around us but also to other dimensions—the ancestors, the world of Spirit and the beings who inhabit the inner earth, and the universe itself. Folded inside the cloth is another smaller weaving, wrapped around a special group of stones—my first *mesa*, given to me on one of Peru's sacred mountains, Ausangate, by shamans who were my teachers. I place the bundle on the stone on top of the larger weaving. Lighting a slender stick of incense, I prop it next to the bundle, its subtle fragrance perfuming the air. This helps to focus our attention and serves as a communication and offering to the weaving, to the objects that will become our group's own *mesa*, and to the spiritual teachers in all of our lives.

Our ceremonial actions emphasize that we do nothing that is not a function of our joint relationship with Spirit in all forms, whether that is the Spirit of the sun's energy, the weaving, or the life of the earth itself. The relationship between our intent and the objects in the ceremony gives them significance. When archeological bundles are found that were part of a spiritual practice centuries ago, they no longer hold that power because they are separated from the intent of the practitioner. Now, through our actions, we purposely call our own intent into play.

Each person has brought an object connected to the goal she wishes to fulfill. Forming a circle around the weaving, we spend some time in silence, visualizing our goals and their relationships to the objects that we'll place in the *mesa*. For some, the focus is on the mountain itself—for example, concern for the expanding presence of invasive plants that choke the water's flow in the marshland. For others, the goal lies elsewhere—a piece of writing, nature education for children, or conflict mediation. We yearn to feel and celebrate our connection to the web of life, to envision how our intent might participate in it. A *mesa* can be a wonderful tool to experience that connection.

Imagining the end result, still in silence, each of us touches our power object to our belly, our center of power, and makes a commitment to whatever action will be needed to achieve our goals. Touching the object to our hearts, we silently recall the strong desire to bring about our goals, feel the passion required to accomplish them, and open ourselves to feeding and strengthening those deep feelings. Bringing the symbols to our foreheads, we affirm to ourselves the will to bring about our intent and the willingness to allow its form to be shaped as the process unfolds. Body, heart, and mind join forces with the world of Spirit, reminder that we do not work in isolation.

Each person blows on her chosen offering, then places it among the other objects in the *mesa*. Someone begins to sing,

> "You can't stop the Spirit.
> It's like the mountain.
> Old and strong,
> It goes on and on."[17]

Soon everyone is singing; the sound weaves on and on, carrying us on a wave of joy and involvement. Our *mesa* becomes a tool of our intentions, created with music and heart. Finally, we wrap the cloth securely around the power objects and tie it with a gold thread that symbolizes the sunlight present in everything alive. We are touched in ways that are beyond words or consciousness.

## Stone Ally: Empowering Intent

Climbing over some small boulders, we reach an intimate space between several short trees and the tall boulder. Peggy holds the *mesa* against the stone. We all envision our power objects and the weaving connecting to the endless strength and presence of the boulder. In a slow procession, we each take a turn aligning our spines with the boulder. In turn, we envision our connection through the stone downward into the earth, then upward from the stone to the sky. We absorb the power of nature and are empowered by the focus we've contributed through the mesa. We are weavers, weaving our strands into those of the natural world.

The solidity of the stone, the sense of its eternal presence, reassures us that the goals we've set are part of a larger "weaving." Other people, other forces, support our intent and our actions. We leave the space and return to the stone where we created the *mesa*. We compare our experiences of the *mesa* and the stone. In the process, we've become a tighter group, feeling the nameless connections that come from sharing a powerful experience and offering ourselves totally to the moment.

## PERSONAL JOURNEYS

Marguerite: *As a group, we just jumped a level. It was such an unusual experience. Who could imagine it? We put our desires together, without even saying them out loud, and we're in the same pot...what I want to do is being supported by the good will of everybody else, even if we never talk about it. I put a ring into the* mesa *that was a symbol of completion for me; it's about the righteous end of a relationship that I need to leave behind me, and I know that I can finally move forward.*

Debbie: *The solidity of the boulder felt like it was making my backbone stronger. It strengthened my will power to take care of myself physically. I actually did hurt my back at work, and if I want to ski again, I have to take myself in hand and make my body stronger. It's not going to happen any other way. It's up to me, but I feel supported if I make the effort. It will happen. I know it will.*

## TRY THIS: Create a group mesa, a collection of power objects

- Select an object that has deep meaning to you, something that is a talisman or that is associated with a goal or relationship that's important to you at this time.

- Carry it about with you for several days, so that your fingers and your eyes can come in contact with it often (in your purse, your car, on your dresser, the windowsill over the kitchen sink).

- Each time you see or touch it, think about exactly what you want to have happen. Think about your motivation, what it would mean in the lives of those you are close to, and what effect you are seeking.

- Let the thoughts come up and let them go. Invite your unconscious to keep shaping your intent. We seldom have an idea that doesn't benefit from being massaged into a more clearly defined expression.

- Notice subtle changes in your thinking or feelings that may come about each time you return to the object.

- When you come together with friends to create the *mesa*, bring the object you've been working with.

- Create the *mesa* on a small piece of fabric that you'll be able to fold and handle easily as you work with it. Rest it on something beautiful or that has some significance to you.

- Your emotions, your mind, and your physical actions combine with spirit to manifest intent in the real world. With your friends, create a sequence of actions, movements, or gestures that will accompany and honor each of these aspects of your contribution to the *mesa*. (In our ceremony, we did this by touching our power objects to the centers in the body that represent physical action, the heart, and the mind.)

- Take turns placing the objects in the *mesa*, so that the unique signature of each goal is given its moment in the ceremony.

- If someone begins a song, support the spirit of that song by joining in the singing.

- Each object is in relationship to the others in the *mesa*. Enfold the *mesa* in the fabric you've chosen in order to honor this new connection among the human beings and the objects they've contributed to the *mesa*.

- Bring the blended power of the group represented in the *mesa* to each person; bless one another by stroking each person with the *mesa* itself. At the same time, you're imbuing the *mesa* and its contents with the essence of each individual person.

- If there is a relevant aspect of nature (such as the boulder on Ring Mountain), incorporate that into the ceremony.

## Turtle Rock: A Swirl of Ancient History

The trail meanders over a rounded hilltop. From the top of the rise, we see that the trail passes through a wide treeless bowl in which rests an enormous solitary blue-black boulder. Turtle Rock, as it is called, is a remarkable example of metamorphic blue schist, a jumble of minerals. There is a circle on the ground in front of Turtle Rock that seems tramped down, the demarcation emphasized by thousands of tiny golden yellow flowers. The circle's precise form indicates that it must have been created through human use. As we approach, we spread out and walk it, marveling at the number of people who could celebrate here together.

As we walk around Turtle Rock, we trace our fingers over the patterns of flowing molten stone, a remarkable depiction of a geological journey through time. The boulder was formed when debris from far-off mountains fell into a divide between subduction layers. The debris ended up in a trough, where it was pushed, bent and shaped by pressure, and finally spewed to the surface as Turtle Rock.[18]

Swirls of motion are visibly suspended in the stone: blueberry-colored rock twists and turns; orange and tan lichens paint its surface. Small chips are strewn on the ground behind the boulder. Turning them over and over in our hands, we watch the sunlight catch bits of minerals. Iron pyrite looks like tiny fragments of gold, while the near-translucent layers of mica have a diamond silvery hue. Other stones on the ground nearby are mottled with rich browns, tans, and greens; they look like "Tarot stones," stones that tell a story. The grace of the tumbled, flowing rock has been caught for all eternity.

We wonder what we might learn from Turtle Rock about the challenges we face as people from so many different cultures come together and attempt to live harmoniously. On this particular day, the issue of how to live harmoniously amidst intense pressures takes on even more urgency. The United States is at war with Iraq and we are hard pressed to discover how to effect a peace that will halt it.

Probably twenty feet high, the boulder has one vertical side that's used as a practice slope by rock climbers. Another side slopes gradually upward, with shelflike levels that are easy to ascend. The top of the boulder is large enough to hold us all. We each lie down in a pocket or dip, cupped hands of the stone that receive us as if we were attaching ourselves to the womb lining of Mother Earth. The sun surrounds us with light and we cover our eyes with neck scarves to shield us from its intensity. On the back of Turtle Rock, we begin a journey to the beat of my drum, into the heart of the rock, asking for the wisdom to live together harmoniously with human and nonhuman brothers and sisters, even amidst intense pressures.

## PERSONAL JOURNEYS

Marguerite: *A group of schoolchildren arrived at the boulder just as we began to drum and journey. I just kept on, letting myself think of them as one of many pressures in my journey. I followed my guide down into the heart of the rock, and a voice asked, "What makes you think of yourself as a separate entity? You are conscious cells in the body of the Mother. You are part of a flow that's still happening. You may have a sense of autonomy, but that is not so. If you stay conscious, you will be able to help shape the new form of the flow. Speak with integrity, speak your own truth, and you will have a creative part in the evolving.*

*Don't be attached to staying in the same form, because you won't be; everything is in continuous flux. Bits of yourself go off in different directions and are seeds of change elsewhere. Don't resist what is irresistible, but you* can *hold your purpose. It's* your *part of the becoming. Miracles will happen."*

Ann: *The lesson from the stone is that what happens to one happens to all. Things get picked up and moved with the flow into whatever is nearby. You can't create a good scenario for a few and think that it's going to solve the whole problem. White kids in a gated community may be safe from some dangers, but we're all part of the same society, and there's no way that what happens in Hunter's Point [a federal superfund site, and San Francisco's most contami-*

*nated property] isn't going to affect the world we all live in. So surrender. Know that we're part of the same unfolding. Do what you have to do to make it the best that it can be for all.*

Before we leave, each of us sprinkles a cornmeal offering on Turtle Rock in gratitude for the inspiration.

## TRY THIS: Journey to the heart of the boulder

- Observe Turtle Rock from all angles and various distances. Be aware of the aspects of it that draw your attention—shape, texture, evidence of the effects of temperature, and so forth.

- Choose a time when you can be with the boulder without likely interruption or distractions—early morning, evening, weekdays, stormy weather.

- Sit with it in silence for a while and let your own presence be known.

- Look around you; notice the context—the soil, the other stones or boulders in the area. Be aware of stone "families," partnerships with plants. Watch the movement of the clouds and feel the way the wind moves.

- Feel the texture of the boulder's surface, the presence of minerals or other stones embedded in it.

- Make an offering to the stone (sacred tobacco, cornmeal, a strand of hair, chocolate, wine). Ask the stone's permission to work with it.

- Settle in comfortably and close your eyes.

- Form a question or request. Consider what this particular boulder may have to offer you because of its own life experiences. The response might come in a visual image, a vision that changes and unfolds, specific words, sounds, or music.

- Begin a steady rhythm with a rattle or drum to aid your concentration and eliminate potential distractions.

- Imagine yourself entering the boulder, going toward its heart, its depths.

- Pay attention to everything that happens. If you don't understand what you are experiencing, ask for clarification.

- When you feel complete, thank the stone and return to your place on its surface in ordinary reality.

- Assimilate the information you've received by writing the journey down or sharing it with your companions. These communications are gifts from the world of Spirit. You might discover that you are being asked to do something that you as a human being are able to do that a stone could not. You have the legs, the voice, the hands to be the executor of certain actions important to the natural world.

Opposite Turtle Rock is a grove of laurel trees that offers inviting shade. We head in that direction. It's a charming setting, lacking only the people and the picnic for an in vivo replica of Manet's painting *Dejeuner sur l'Herbe*. We fulfill the missing elements. A gentle wind blows the leaves and scents the air with laurel.

Our ultimate destination on Ring Mountain is a petroglyph rock. Its ancient markings are similar to those used elsewhere in fertility ceremonies of centuries past. Sitting in the shelter and safety of the laurel grove, we share thoughts about the successes and errors of our parenting styles, challenges and rewards of being a parent, and memories of the way we ourselves were mothered. We share intimate stories about our childhoods and our current lives. Debbie is not a parent and reminds us of the importance of nurturing the many other forms of creativity.

We remember the disruption of the Miwoks' family patterns, of families everywhere who endure the ravages of wars. We feel challenged to continue giving hope and courage to innocent children caught in the midst of chaos. Finally, we leave the shadows and head back into the bright sunshine.

## Fertility Petroglyph: Healing the Mother's Lineage

In a hollow between Turtle Rock and the highest point of Ring Mountain lies yet another boulder, quite hidden until now, and from this vantage point rather unremarkable. Paths converge on it from various directions. As we descend a steep slope in its direction, Kayla begins to sing, and soon we join in:

> "The river she is flowing, flowing, flowing
> The river she is flowing
> Down to the sea
> Mother, carry me.
> Your child I will always be
> Mother, carry me
> Down to the sea."[19]

We circle around the rock, moving clockwise, looking closely at its surface. The presence of poison oak at a foothold one might be tempted to use to climb the boulder is forbidding. It's not a rock to be dealt with in this way. Subtle shades of lichen, brown, rust, and gold, make fingerprints on its surface. Sparkling mica, and cobwebs suspended in a few small crevices, lend to its texture. Small plants make brave efforts to assert themselves here and there.

On the south side, a deep cleft splits the stone. We easily understand why this has been chosen and revered as a symbol of the feminine. The very shape of the stone, with its full curves and pronounced vulva-like cleft, speaks of the female body.

Petroglyph Rock on Ring Mountain, Tiburon Peninsula.
Photo by Paul Feder, 2005.

We closely inspect the many rounded or ovoid carvings that are pecked and scraped over the surface of the stone. About six inches long, often paired, they are thought by some to have been made between five and eight thousand years ago, although most estimates are about half that.[19] Petroglyphs made in the same manner ("pecked curvilinear nucleated," or PCN, designs) exist throughout the north and central Coast Ranges of California, from Humboldt to Santa Barbara Counties. The densest concentration is in Marin and South Sonoma Counties. The territories of the Hokan-speaking people (ancestors of the Pomo, Esalen, and Chumash tribes) and the Penutian-speaking people (ancestors of the Miwok, Maidu, and Coastanoan) apparently share this same style of petroglyph. However, the extent of shared sites or overlapping territories is unknown, so the identity of the artisans of the PCN petroglyphs is not clear. But the Penutian speakers have claimed the Marin area for at least three thousand years.

Hokan speakers relate this style of incised groove petroglyphs to "fertility" ceremonies and suggest they may have been carved by couples wanting children. There is a similar schist boulder in Humboldt County, called the "Gottville Rain Rock," that is reported to have been used to influence weather.[20] Some believe that the ceremonies were for rain and good crops, others that they involved fertility of the people themselves. Pairs of incised patterns that look more pendulous than round are believed by some to signify a plentiful hunt.

While there are differences in interpretations of the markings, there is no disagreement about the importance of protecting the carvings. They are badly weathered, but far worse than nature's slow and relentless drubbing is the heavy damage inflicted by vandalism. Some pieces have been chipped out, others scratched and defaced. I feel washed by shame at any association—even through simply belonging to the same species—with someone who would deface something so remarkable.

The rock was not identified by contemporary society until 1970; the amount of damage inflicted since then is astonishing. Since the Nature Conservancy fully acquired the Ring Mountain Preserve in 1984, a series of efforts has been made to stem the vandalism. Different approaches with signs were only partly successful; now, with the Marin Country Open Space District serving as guardians of the site, a small fence has been erected, close enough to allow people to see the markings but not to touch them. While the fence isn't big enough to deter anyone who really wants to attack the site, it does create a pause long enough for conscience to kick in.

Just outside the fence, we make an offering of cornmeal, honoring the stone, honoring the mothers. Backing away a little, we sit on the ground to focus again on the shape of the boulder rather than the carvings. Our talk in the grove is much on our minds. The desecration brings up errors in parenting made out of ignorance or out of pain and carried all through the lives of both parents and children. Often deep physical and emotional wounds inflicted on parents as they were growing up are passed on from one generation to the next. We raise concerns for the culture, for the whole of civilization, as war expands and harms both children and adults.

We decide to journey in two directions. First, we will travel back in time seven generations, seeking healing of the personal lineage carried by ourselves as mothers—and by our mothers and grandmothers. Then we'll repeat the process, moving seven generations into the future. In the bright sun, facing the boulder, we begin to rattle.

When the journey comes to an end, I feel stunned. Each of us sits quietly, deeply moved, several crying. After a time, we come into a circle and share our experiences. Profound personal shifts have occurred in the presence of this powerful stone.

## PERSONAL JOURNEYS

Marguerite: *When we started to rattle, I didn't close my eyes all the way; I wanted to see the stone but not in a focused way. I could see that opening, and I felt pulled into it, like a reverse birth. I started to feel very helpless and vulnerable, overwhelmed with the need to trust myself to my mother's body. I don't think I've ever appreciated the sacrifice a mother makes in pregnancy and birthing. I felt so helpless, and I began to pray to my mother, thanking her. I felt so nurtured, so protected, while we were doing this. She was a really tiny person, only sixteen when I was born.*

*I remembered dancing with my mother even before I started school—watching her sewing, making beautiful pottery. She saw my brother killed in an accident and went into a shell of protection—physically present, but I don't think she could feel anyone's love for her, ever again. On this journey, I could understand her pain, that she needed to protect herself, and I could forgive her for the secret pain she carried that distanced her from me.*

*Looking for my grandmother, I thought of those nested Russian Maitrika dolls, with my mother inside my grandmother, me inside my mother, and my daughter inside of me. My grandmother told bedtime stories by the hour and recited poetry by heart. She worked really hard her whole life, and today I forgave her impatience with my laziness. Then in my vision, she, my mother, and I are all enfolded within my great-grandmother, whose husband was killed in the Civil War while she was pregnant with my grandmother. She became a typesetter at a newspaper, an unheard-of job for a woman in that time. Imagining her was the beginning of my memories of strong and courageous women in my lineage. It's not seven generations, but this much feels solid and real. I'm part of a lineage that I really feel here.*

*[On the journey into the future] I started out remembering the birth of each of my kids, and the place I was in personally when I became pregnant each time. None were planned; in those days, we weren't worrying about population, didn't have the luxury of birth control pills. They were born close together, and by the time the last one came, my marriage was in trouble. I ended up raising them alone for six of their childhood years. I remembered making choices that felt like life or death to my soul, knowing even then that it would be stressful for all of us. I went back to school to finish my degree. There was constant pressure, and I was never enough to go around. So while we were journeying, I just let myself see that and acknowledge that it was true—no hand-wringing, just seeing that it was so, and the impact on each of them. I asked their forgiveness and sent my support, my*

*confidence in their capacity to heal. I remembered our joyful times, our camping and singing, and knew that those good experiences were also part of what they got from me, part of what fed them. We were really close dealing with adversity; I felt my love blanket them.*

*Then I started to think of my grandchildren and realized how fiercely I clung to my freedom after my children grew up. Other grandmothers dote over the kids, have pictures of them, and tell stories about them. But it's been hard for me to be really available to them. I watched that reality as we journeyed, and it made me think that I'm not going anywhere that I need to go in a hurry, that I can make different choices about spending time with them. We kept rattling, and I saw unfold a scene like Ebenezer Scrooge's "Christmas yet to come"…the generations of kids who follow my grandchildren's. I saw our culture being shaped by a family life that's lost its intimacy. Events are unfolding that I don't have control over directly, except in relation to my own family. I'm appalled at the thought of street children and others affected by my own culture's styles and greed. I watched my part in all of it and saw myself step away from some life choices that suddenly don't seem to matter as much as they did. I saw that it's a matter of choices. I have to step up to the plate.*

## TRY THIS: Make a healing journey for the lineage of the mothers

- Sprinkle an offering of cornmeal or sacred tobacco in front of the petroglyph stone.

- Seat yourself at a distance of about ten feet.

- Rattles in hand, set your intention to journey along the lineage of the mothers for seven generations.

- With eyes open and focus softened, watch the stone as you begin to journey. There may come a time when your eyes want to close. If that happens, just let them.

- Remember your mother. If at some point she behaved in a way that caused you pain, remember her actions or her words.

- See yourself as a separate being, watching and listening to your mother communicate through words or actions something that may have no relevance to you. What is it about her own experience that she is inflicting on you?

- Let images come to you based on what you know of the way your mother was raised. What were the circumstances—the culture of the time and place, the situation your grandmother was in?

- Knowing what you now know as an adult about your mother, what would you say to her?
- Be aware of how you continue to live it out, perpetuating the pain for yourself or others.
- How would you protect yourself, and how do you protect yourself now as an adult from similar treatment? Aware of your capacity to protect yourself now, is there any genuine way that you can forgive the pain she caused you?
- If you are unable to forgive, allow yourself the role of witness to your mother's life and situation. True witnessing has power.
- Move through the lineage of your grandmothers, to the seventh generation (or as far as feels genuine to you), remembering their families and communities, their beliefs and standards. Even if you don't know the details, let the image of nested Russian Maitrika dolls carry the symbolism of the mothers.
- When you feel complete, stop rattling and open your eyes fully.
- Observe the fertility stone.
- Do what you're drawn to do.

The impact of these very personal journeys has been strong. The work has been so powerful that we agree to return another day to journey again through the inspiration of these carvings. We find ourselves in an intense inward space. Someone begins to sing as we move slowly down the mountain, the trail circling back toward its beginning.

Along the way, we stop once more in the shelter of the laurel grove to plant a crystal from the cluster Carol divided at Kirby Cove. With this ceremony, we honor our experiences on Ring Mountain. When we meditate from our homes, the power of the crystal may amplify our memories and add vitality to our connections here. We pass the crystal, each person naming her most important event on this mountain. When it returns to Carol, she wedges the crystal into a rock crevice at the back of the grove. We continue our descent down the mountain.

The spreading branches of a very old oak tree near the path beckon us; we veer off and climb it. The low limbs are so enormous that there is room for all of us. Ironically, the climbing grounds us, and our songs become cheerful and free. Laughing, joking, calling out to one another, we feel an unspoken kinship born of the intensity of our day. We are sisters, sitting in the lap of Mother Earth.

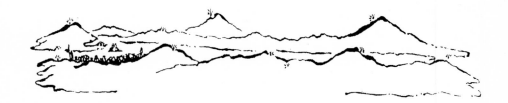

## Chapter Three

# MOUNT TAMALPAIS:
# The Slow Breath of Stone

The full moons in the fall are my favorite. Long dreamy twilights extend the lingering twilight to farmers bringing in their crops, or to lovers falling under the spell of the "hour of power."[1] The orbits of the sun and moon are on the same plane, and when I watch those harvest moons rising, I can imagine that a huge running leap would take me across the void and into the arms of the man in the moon. So I make plans to camp at Steep Ravine on Mount Tamalpais with half a dozen friends; if we're lucky, the moon will lay down a silver path for us across the water during the night.

We arrive midday on the mountain. Before we settle into our campsite, we go directly to one of our favorite places—a section of the Matt Davis Trail that leads through dappled woods of bay laurel, oak, and Douglas fir. A sharp right at the Pantoll Ranger Station takes us to a small lot along the right side of the road—where we luck into one of the few free parking spots. We park the car and walk across the road to the trailhead.

Getting away from ordinary life isn't simply a question of distance. It's as much about attitude and your reasons for getting away. Talking about life's passions, or politics, or religion while walking a trail can energize or relax you. But conversation can also block out the opportunity to be aware of, and to respond to, your surroundings. When I want to sink into this awareness of nature, I prefer companions who will not have a hard time with silence. Different expectations could become overt or unspoken irritations. On this hike, I've come with friends who meditate together several times a week. They are comrades thirsting for a brief retreat, whose ears perked up when I mentioned the full moon in November. We all need some downtime.

# A Portal in the Woods: Shifting to Presence

The canopy of small oak trees provides an arched entrance into a subtle adventure. Passing under the low-hanging branches, we pick up the path as it aligns with the shoulder of the mountain. Shortly we find ourselves in a small sunlit meadow, where we pause and make an offering of cornmeal to acknowledge the mountain; we're grateful for the chance to be here.

The path through the meadow is quite level, hugging the hillside sloping upward to our right. Moss covers the boulders and earthen banks. Even in autumn, the world is very green. Fallen Douglas fir cones and acorns texture the path, adding crunch to our steps. The acorn crop has been particularly abundant this year. We feel the cool air against our bodies and smell the fragrance of the trees surrounding us. In just moments, we leave the outside world behind.

At the meadow's far edge, the path disappears into some woods. As we enter them, we move from the bold to the subtle, from light into shadow. This portal, this shadowed beginning, serves as an invitation to switch our consciousness from casual observation into something out of the ordinary. Something's speaking, but we won't notice unless we pay attention to the moment.

A portal into expanded perception can appear in various forms: a change in the shape or quality of the terrain; an alteration in the plants that grow in a certain area; a different weather or wind pattern; or an unusual stone formation. This portal leads us to consider how to be as receptive as possible to what awaits us. We want to pay full attention to this special place, to how our bodies, minds, and hearts respond to it. We decide to commit ourselves to quiet and observant walking.

## TRY THIS: At the portal to the woods, shift to mindful presence

- As the Matt Davis Trail crosses the sunny meadow preceding the woods, stop for a moment. Look around you, open and expectant. Feel what there is to feel and see what there is to see.

- Notice that when you enter the woods at the far side of the meadow, the trees will surround you, enclosing you in a different sense of space and light. This portal extends an opportunity to be present, helps you awaken.

- At the portal, make an offering of cornmeal or of something that has meaning to you, asking permission to be here.

- How do you want to be present here? What are you asking of your body and senses in order to be fully present? What do you need from your emotions and your attitude? From your mind? Let each aspect of yourself be part of your intention to be present.

- As you move through the portal into the woods, you are passing through a doorway into new sensations, new wisdom. Experience the woods for its own sake, as if you were meeting a new friend; stay open and receptive, focused on this time and place.

- Walk in silence so that you can be attentive to the woods. Do not expend effort identifying the names of plants. If you know them and the name or characteristics come to mind, notice the meaning that knowledge carries for you. Whether or not you identify them, experience them through your senses as directly as possible.

## Walking Meditation: Letting Go

Where the woods begin, the trees are scattered thinly over the hillsides. Sunlight filters easily through their leaves and branches. The alternation of sunlight and shadow begins to affect my state of mind and my body. In the play of light, I'm aware of the rapid shifting of my eyes as they attempt to adjust, first to shadow, then to light. Tension in my body ebbs and flows with the shifting, and as that tension comes to consciousness, I surrender the strain, let go, and relax. My breathing deepens and slows. The distractions of my mind's ordinary diddling slide down through my feet, into the earth. Thoughts of unfinished business, incomplete communications, and unshared feelings leave me. I am more fully present.

### TRY THIS: Turn fretting and distractions over to Mother Earth

- As you walk through the woods, breathe deeply, taking in the fragrance of the trees. Adopt a pace that allows you to move comfortably, enjoying the movement of your body.

- Feel the shade and patches of sunshine on your skin.

- Notice any distractions that arise; if you begin to think of someone who is not here, or begin to mull over some concern in your life, be aware that it is taking you away from being fully present.

- Let those issues, any worries or troubles bothering you, come fully to mind; notice where your body is tense around those thoughts, and as you pass through the patterns of light and shadow, allow the moving light patterns to help you release the strain.

- The light plays on your eyes; small fingers of subtly shifting light patterns dance and help your body relax and let go.

- Allow the unfinished business of life to travel down your body and move through your torso. Your hips swing more and more freely with every step.

- Let the heaviness of your feelings tumble down your legs, into your feet, and into the earth. Compost any heavy energy; let it recycle into Mother Earth, who takes into herself our every single act and thought.

- Let tensions and pressures drop away; as you clear space in your mind, body, and heart, the beauty and pleasure that is here for you will refresh you.

## Running Water: Purification

Even now in dry November, a slender stream issuing from a small waterfall crosses the trail. For centuries, water has been used in baptisms to symbolically purify or cleanse the spirit, marking an initiation into a new state of being. Intent is the water's partner in this transformation, and anyone can engage with it in this way.

We step across the stream. Noticing for a few moments where in our bodies we carry trauma, sadness, or guilt, we kneel just above the path beside the water's flow. We dip our fingers into the current; ripples on the water's surface move around our hands, just as the water creates patterns around the stones of the streambed. Swirling our fingers near the stones, we feel the water's slight pressure against our hands. The sensation hints of water's power to shape whole canyons of stone; we know it can deal with our issues. Taking turns, we baptize ourselves, bringing a few drops of water to those wounded places in our bodies. We envision the pain and sorrow being carried away by the water.

### TRY THIS: Purify yourself with running water

- Sit beside the stream where it crosses the trail. Close your eyes; listen so closely to the sound that you begin to trace its movement around and over stone in the streambed, its tumble when it drops slightly from one level to another.

- Be aware of moisture in the air. The temperature is cooler here beside the water. Imagine the pores of your skin opening to replenish the moisture of your body. Relax.

- Let your thoughts drift to any heaviness that your body carries—trauma, sadness, guilt. As you do so, notice where your body carries those memories and the way it holds tension around them.

- Open your eyes and watch the movement of the water around the stones. Remembering water's power to shape even stone, baptize yourself in this way: bring a few drops of water to those parts of your body that hold tension; envision the pain being carried away by the water.

- As you envision those memories being swept downstream, move slightly so that the sunlight filtering through the tree branches touches your head. Imagine sunlight filling the places that have been emptied of the pain they held earlier.

- Breathe deeply and let the light fill your entire body.

Continuing along the path, we soon move from the cool woods into intense sunlight. It's a dramatic doorway into a different sense of the mountain. We play with the transition—walking back a few steps into the shade, then crossing the line again into sunshine, paying attention to the ways our bodies respond to the increased light. On a chilly day, we might notice and welcome the warmth; if today were warmer, we might move more reluctantly from the protection of the woods into open contact with the sun. These subtle physiological changes affect our responsiveness to the world around us. Noticing them brings our attention to receptors that might operate without our awareness and participation. We can then choose to stay open to whatever we receive.

Today, however, the balmy temperature is relaxing; the sky is clear, and visibility is very good. The path curves and parallels the ocean maybe three hundred feet from a cliff. When a small grove of bay laurels nearer the cliff comes into view, we take a path that veers in that direction.

## Close Observation: Dream Preparation

To the right of the path, about one hundred steps away, a small Douglas fir grows from a crevice in a metamorphic shale boulder of about my height. I'm drawn to the boulder; although I don't want to interrupt the time with my friends, I can't simply pass by without honoring its pull on me. As the others continue on toward the laurel grove, I detour into the field and come close to the boulder.

Walking completely around it, I particularly notice the way the tree grows so intimately from the boulder, seeming to be totally dependent on it. My fingers explore the boulder's texture and the lichen growing on it. I stroke the branches of the tree, then sniff both boulder and tree mightily. Picking one needle from the tree, I crush it between my teeth; its tangy flavor and fragrance leap out. Honoring the attraction this union of boulder and tree holds for me, I sprinkle cornmeal at the places where they join one another.

A surprising discovery hints of someone being deeply touched by his connection to this place. A small bronze plaque, maybe four inches across and three inches high, is modestly attached to an inconspicuous face of the stone. "DAD," it says, "I'm sorry it took so long. Your loving son, Roger." It speaks to me of regrets for neglected gifts of the heart, of opportunities for intimacy ignored and later regretted. I have no idea what really transpired between the two men, but the trace of others' connections with this lovely place touches me deeply.

Long ago, a shaman instructed me to memorize a stone. I spent long hours with it until I could draw the stone without looking at it, feel it in my hand without holding it. Now, my eyes devour this boulder; I take a photo to assure myself that I can correct my memory of it, if necessary. Drawing a few quick lines on a piece of paper gives my hand and fingers a kinesthetic memory. Other details come to my attention as I sketch, and I add them to the drawing. The boulder's power grows for me. As my intentions crystallize, I ask permission of the boulder and the Douglas fir to work with them in my dreams.

With mixed feelings, I finally leave the boulder to rejoin my friends. We sit for a while in the shelter of the fragrant bay laurel, enjoying the view. Turkey vultures swoop leisurely over nearby ravines. The small grove has space for us to sit apart, wrapped in our own thoughts and observations. A lizard darts into view a foot or two from my right knee, then stops abruptly. He begins a series of push-ups, jerking through them like a little cartoon figure. I'm aware of another lizard appearing from a crevice in a rock to my left. It darts forward and stops. The first lizard dashes forward over my outstretched leg and approaches the second lizard. The push-ups, often territorial, might be signaling something else this time. The lizards link, apparently mating, and do a stop-start circle dance on a flat patch of ground just to the left of my knee for a minute or so. They are totally oblivious to me. Just as suddenly as they came together, they separate and head off in opposite directions.

I relax into the company of my human companions. We pass around snacks as we share stories of the mountain and myths of the local Miwok people. The tales help anchor us to the mountain in a different way and begin to turn our focus toward clarifying our personal intent on this particular journey.

## Mountain Stories Feeding Our Intent

As the highest point along the coast between Big Sur and Mendocino, Mount Tamalpais has long been a focal point in the landscape.[2] Its silhouette, referred to as the Sleeping Maiden, is a well-known landmark in the Bay Area. European ships sailed this part of the coast in the mid-1500s, and sailors from a Spanish galleon that was shipwrecked at its feet in 1566 must have hiked the base of the mountain at the very least. Curiously, no direct mention of the mountain was made until 1792, when the British explorer George Vancouver, sailing by, charted it and drew its profile.

No one is quite sure of the origin of the name *Mount Tamalpais*; however, it appears to derive from the Miwok language. For a long time, it was referred to as Table Mountain or Table Hill. But Old Californians called it Tamal Pais.[3] The Miwok word *Tamal* has several interpretations—"coast," or "west," or "coast people" or "west people." *Pais* was "hill" or "mountain" in the Miwok language, so perhaps *Tamalpais* meant "west(ern) mountain" or "coast(al) mountain."

In the 1930s the Mountain Theatre was constructed on Mount Tamalpais by the Civilian Conservation Corps. The first theater director, Dan Totheroh, had heard of the Legend of the Sleeping Maiden; but unable to find anything specific in his research, he made up a legend himself. The result, *Tamalpa*, became the official play of the mountain.[4]

The legend concerned Ah-Shawn-Nee,[5] the mountain witch, who erected an Altar of All Evil to block the path of humankind to the high dwelling place of the Great White Spirit (sic). When a brave came to the mountain seeking the great gift of healing for his tribe, Ah-Shawn-Nee enlisted her daughter, the mountain siren Tamalpa, to enchant him. Ultimately, Tamalpa is overcome by remorse for her deed. Unable to break the enchantment any other way, she eats a deadly herb. She is covered forever by a purple blanket woven by the Four Sisters of Destiny. And so the mountain's silhouette reveals for all eternity the outline of her shrouded form.

Myths go through transformations as they're passed from one storyteller to another or from one context to another. Sometimes this happens just from the use of a different word or phrase. At other times, the transformation is purposeful because a particular thread of the story feeds another need. The original *Tamalpa* play has evolved in exactly this way.

One example of this occurred some years ago. A man dubbed the Trailside Killer roamed the trails of Mount Tamalpais, the Point Reyes National Seashore, and a park near Santa Cruz between 1979 and 1981 before being caught and convicted of seven murders. Four of those murders, the victims all young women, took place on Mount Tamalpais. People were afraid to walk on the mountain even in broad daylight. Then a dancer, Anna Halprin, stepped forward, transforming the story of Tamalpa in an effort to work with the fears of the community. Halprin's work offered people an opportunity to embody and dance the feelings and issues that were important to them. She gathered a group of people together to create a dance reclaiming the mountain. Basing their work on the myth of Tamalpa, they danced to awaken the sleeping princess—who, it was now said, had vowed to sleep until peace came.

An annual event continues to this day on the mountain, focusing on a different issue of current importance in the community. A day of storytelling, dance, and song gives new life and form to the Sleeping Maiden.

According to the Miwoks, Coyote, the Creator, considered the mountain sacred. The summit area was terrifying and at the same time revered;[6] if any human were to transgress that sacred territory, the people believed the transgressor would not return alive. The presence of many grizzly, black, and brown bears might have had something to do with that conception.

Historian Lincoln Fairley describes another untraceable story, concerning the trader Jacob Leese and a Miwok called Chief Marin (who may have been a composite of several chiefs).[7] Marin, it has been said, was the bravest of all men. When no one would accompany him, Leese set out to climb the mountain alone. Reaching the summit, he placed a large tree in the form of a cross so that it could be seen from the lower slopes. Marin, not to be outdone, climbed the peak and left his shirt on the cross.

My favorite Miwok creation myth describes how Silver Fox and Coyote created the world. I love the model they provide—tenaciously carrying out their intent through dancing and singing, putting their hearts into a joyful partnership with one another and with the powers of nature. Silver Fox and Coyote hold the unwavering expectation that connection and intent are part of the natural unfolding of events:

> Alone in an empty world, Silver Fox turned her feelings of isolation into a plaintive chant. 'I want to meet someone, I want to meet someone,' she sang as she meandered through space. At last her longing was answered by the appearance of Coyote, who began to accompany her in her wanderings. But

Silver Fox had bigger ideas, and soon convinced Coyote to join her in bringing the world into being.

They shaped the Earth by their passionate singing and dancing; when it was big enough, they jumped down onto their new home. Continuing to sing and dance, they stretched the Earth, shaping it into valleys and mountains, rivers and lakes. All the trees, the plants, the animal people and bird people, took form through their exuberant joy.[8]

Taking a cue from Silver Fox and Coyote, we begin to talk about what we want to experience during our exploration on the mountain. We pass a talking stick, thinking aloud in turns about the possibilities before us. We find that we share certain general goals. All of us want to deepen our relationships with the natural world and to discover the qualities that each site contributes to the possibility of developing those deepened connections. The specifics of what will happen will depend on what we find and on our openness.

All of us are looking for changes in our approaches to nature that will deepen our capacity to receive the communications that we sense are always available. Several have special needs for a respite from stress, from day-to-day pressures and responsibilities. They want to enjoy whatever simple beauties of sea and mountain present themselves. Some want to have an adventure.

From our vantage point we see the physical relationship of the mountain to San Francisco Bay and the city—and with it, the sweep of coastline and mountains to the south of the Golden Gate. It's inevitable that parts of our exploration will concern the mountain's origins in relation to the sea.

## Reciprocity: Making an Offering, Anchoring Intent

I have a personal desire that started when I was last in Peru. The sacred places of the Andes are very powerful and profound teachers for me. At the same time, I admire and envy the way the people in those mountains weave sacred nature into every part of their lives. They are constantly aware of the reciprocity, the give-and-take that sustains all of nature, including their very existence. Living in an urban setting, I notice that the connection fades for me when I don't make deep and direct contact with nature often enough. When I returned to the United States, I vowed to identify the ways in which nature around the bay supports my daily existence and to pay more attention to the constant presence of Spirit. I knew that it would mean making choices about how I spend my free time, developing habits of focus and intent, and evolving new relationships with familiar places. As I describe these intentions, a ceremony comes to mind that I participated in with Andean shamans, a ceremony laced with the exercise of focus, with attention to relationships within and without. We might explore and enhance our own approach to the use of intent by using their ceremony as a model.

Among the people who are descendants of the Incas, offerings called *despachos* are created when a request is made to the world of Spirit. Sometimes the offerings are made simply to express appreciation.[9] The *despacho*, executed with great attentiveness, is usually done in community, accompanied by much laughter and pleasure. (After all, you wouldn't extend a somber invitation to a party, and if you're inviting the involvement of the world of Spirit, it makes sense that the invitation should be as enticing as possible.) The celebration includes the kinds of things that would make anyone want to come—good food, good drink, and good company.

All life on earth is maintained through reciprocity, through which knowledge and power is bestowed by all beings in nature. This gift must be reciprocated by sharing one's own highest and best knowledge and power with others. The descendants of the Incas believe that the continuous recycling of natural power and knowledge helps to maintain the balance between heaven and earth. In accordance with this lesson in reciprocity from the natural world of the Andes, the Incas began to share knowledge with people outside their lineage.

An example of reciprocal functioning involves awareness of the needs of nature and responding to them with attention and care. When the air is properly taken care of, human beings will continue to have what we need to breathe. When the waters of the planet are not polluted or wasted, we will have what is sufficient for our needs.

The creation of a *despacho* addresses the Spirit world. At the same time it is an acknowledgment of personal responsibility—human actions and intentions are necessary to fulfill any request being made. A *despacho* is an acknowledgment of the human role in that reciprocal relationship. Through the process of its creation, human involvement and responsibility come into alliance with nature's processes and with the presence of Spirit that flows through them. The forces of nature, which are more potent than any one individual's will or action, empower the petition, because the community is coming into conscious and appropriate relationship with the natural world through focusing attention on the alliance. It is a process that helps align priorities.

In preparation for the ceremony, coca leaves are gathered or purchased. The shaman chooses three leaves that are as perfect as possible (no insect nibbles or tattered edges). He groups leaves of similar size, all with the same side up and pointed in the same direction, stem end down. His assistants kibitz through the entire process about the quality of the leaves and how well matched they are in size. The leaves are symbols of the conscientious attention to three dimensions of human participation necessary to achieve the desired end: one leaf represents attention to the motivations of the heart; another speaks to the physical actions of human beings necessary to accomplish the request; the third involves the mind's capacity to envision the outcome and the power to hold the intent.

The *despacho* is put together on a foundation of a small square of paper—sometimes Christmas wrapping, sometimes newspaper—but whenever possible, the paper is fancy (papers with Disney's illustrations of Donald Duck or Mickey Mouse are a treat, but plain white will do in a pinch). A fragrant bed is created consisting of brown sugar (to sweeten the offering), incense (to draw attention, as well as to give pleasure and to honor the Spirits), and sage (to purify the offering).

Twelve groupings of three leaves are placed on the paper. Each person blows his or her personal intent into each leaf bundle before it is positioned on the paper by the shaman. This imbues the *despacho* with the life force of each participant, bringing them into a more personal and active involvement. Each three-leaf grouping is an offering to one of the twelve major mountains in the Cuzco vicinity. The process places the participants squarely into the context of the natural world that surrounds them and affirms the interconnection of their own life force with those of the natural world.

When the leaves are in place, they're "fed" with small decorations of colored candies, animal fat, rice, corn, chocolate, and whatever other treats are available. The paper foundation is folded to enclose the offering and burned to carry the prayers to the Spirits.

Adapting the offering of a *despacho* to our local bioregion can help us form a perspective of the natural world that creates and sustains our lives—the watersheds, the weather patterns, plants, birds, and animals. Here, instead of the twelve mountains of Cuzco, we call on Kirby Cove of the Marin Headlands, and on the six major mountains that surround San Francisco Bay. Before our journeys around the bay are complete, we will have visited each of them. Today we'll name and honor them in ceremony: Kirby Cove, Mount Tamalpais, Ring Mountain, Mount Diablo, Mount Hamilton, Mount Umunhum, and San Bruno Mountain.

We scatter to hunt down good bay leaves, bits of moss, and a variety of interesting objects on the ground. Unloading the treasures from our pockets onto a colorful Peruvian weaving spread on the ground, we poke among them to see what sort of an offering we might be able to put together.

A piece of handmade paper fashioned from wild mushrooms by artist Lynn Marsh holds the offering. We assemble seven groups of three bay leaves; the care taken in choosing the leaves, as perfect and uneaten as possible, as close to matching in size, helps focus our mindfulness. We think about our hearts' desires in being here, about our intent in circling the bay, and consider what is personally called for physically from each of us to achieve what we seek from our journeys.

Some bits of California sage will purify the offering, incense will add an appealing fragrance, and a few crumbs of sugar will sweeten the gift; we place them on the paper. A small yellow ribbon we add to the *despacho* represents the yellow banners flown from the summit of Mount Tamalpais by California women when they first won the right to vote at the turn of the century.[10] Here, the ribbon becomes a symbol of the freedom we've gained, and the dedication and involvement it takes to maintain it.

We take turns blowing breath and intent into each group of leaves, then carefully place them on the paper. The offering is decorated as it might be on the table of a birthday feast: flowers, moss, a beautiful leaf, and small candies and chocolate we share around the circle as we work. It's cheerful, visually appealing, fragrant, and, with a little wine sprayed through our puckered lips onto it, as beckoning an invitation to the Spirit world as we can create.

Folding the corners of the paper over the leaves and decorations, we tie it with gold thread, symbolizing the sun, whose power sustains all life on the earth. We carefully burn the offering in a large abalone shell. In part, our purpose in creating this ceremony on the mountain is to acknowledge the great gifts we receive from nature, to express our gratitude, and to acknowledge that we have a responsibility to maintain the healthy balance of nature. It's the first step in assuming our place in the web of life: nature survives through a cycle of reciprocity. Our offering affirms that cycle.

## PERSONAL JOURNEYS

Debbie: *Helping to make the* despacho *changed what prayer is for me. The setup, calling on the mountains that surround us, is a here-and-now reminder. This is where I am; it's the stage, the props, and the scenery of how this play of my life is unfolding. Paying attention to my own body, heart, and mind with the three leaves, each time connecting them to another mountain about what I'm wanting to see unfold in my life today, was a very important reminder of the web of life that we're all part of. It sank in that it's my own actions and attitudes that will help me make use of whatever the world around me has to offer. Connecting with nature is not just a passive walk in the woods.*

**TRY THIS: Create an offering to honor your connection with nature**

- On a bluff overlooking the ocean, the hills, and the canyons of Mount Tamalpais, find a comfortable spot to sit. Begin to get acquainted with where you are, extending your awareness in all directions.

- Look around you at the conformation of the land; follow the horizon's outline with your finger, as if you were tracing a path along the horizon itself.

- As your hands extend to this activity, imagine a filament, a thread of your own energy, moving from your torso and out your arm and hand, connecting you to the area that you are observing.

- Enlarge the context, identifying the mountains or places of power you believe hold the energy of the entire community of living beings around you. It might be the seven locations of *Circling San Francisco Bay*; there might be other places important to you. Let your images and experiences of them come to mind.

- Begin the preparation of your offering by roaming the trees; find three perfect bay leaves of a similar size for each of the sites you've chosen.

- Return to the spot where you were seated earlier and begin to assemble anything you have brought from home that might contribute to an offering—foods or drinks you enjoy, something beautiful, flowers from your garden, special paper or a page from your journal. Seeds or twigs you've found in the woods might find their way into the offering as well.

- Lay the foundation for the offering, even if it's the paper bag that held your lunch.

- Place California sage on the foundation to purify it; add something sweet—incense or a sweet-smelling blossom or seed, whatever communicates "welcome" to you. You are preparing a context for your own contribution—the intent of body, mind, and heart—to the offering.

- As you place each bundle of three leaves on the bed of the offering, visualize your physical energy, your emotional connection, and the desired outcome, as well as your capacity to hold your intent. Decorate the offering with symbols of the natural elements (earth, air, fire, and water), symbols of male and female, and whatever beautiful or tasty additions may be available from the hidden stores of backpack and pockets.

- Fold the corners of the paper securely; either burn the offering, if there is a safe way to do that, or bury it in an unobtrusive place.

# Serpentine: Umbilical Cord to Mother Earth

For the first time, we have some serious uphill walking to do; several paths lead southeast and upward, toward Rock Spring. Ours is the steepest path toward our destination. We walk and stop, walk and stop, catching our breath. I once heard (but have never been able to verify) that the coastal Miwok had a tradition of walking or running Mount Tamalpais in order to give energy back to the mountain. True or not, we decide to offer our efforts for that purpose; we conclude that pausing often—to appreciate the magnificent view of the Pacific and rolling hills and valleys, or simply to catch our breath—helps consecrate our movement through paradise.

Suddenly, the terrain is very different. On the horizon, a moonscape of serpentine scree gives off a gray-green glow. As the grassy hillside merges into the serpentine, swirls of coral-colored stone mixed with cream and shades of pale and darker green rock present a startling contrast to the woods, to the bluff, and to the hillside we've climbed. Larger boulders are strewn here and there on the serpentine blanket of smaller stones. A path cuts upward through the stone rubble toward the center of the formation, where a huge boulder reigns over the stone community.

Serpentine formation on Mt. Tamalpais. Photo by Paul Feder, 2005.

Here, the scene is desolate—only a spread of stones, and no sight of soil beneath them. Serpentine soils, even when they are present, cannot easily support many commonly occurring plants because their chemical composition has little potassium, calcium, or sodium.[11] On this stone formation, there are no trees or even small plants. Casual observers might hurry away from such a stark presence, but we pay close attention to this messenger from inside the earth.

Poised at its edge, we sit quietly. After a long, still time, Geoff pulls a didgeridoo from its case and begins to play, his circular breathing as constant as the stone. The deep, slow notes seem to be responding to tones that have been sounding for millennia, his music answering a song suspended in time. When he finally puts the instrument away, we continue to listen and then begin to touch.

We search out and trace with our fingers patterns of flow and movement in the stone. The texture is very soft, like the surface of a burn scar on a human being. It's easy to imagine serpentine sliding to the surface like a bar of wet soap, moving past stones of other textures. The mountain is part of the debris pushed up during the development of the Franciscan Formation, some 80 to 150 million years ago.[12] In the process the serpentine here has been transformed from oceanic crustal rocks and moved to the surface near a thrust fault.

Usually, when people speak about nature and the web of life, images of plants and animals come to mind. But here, the life of the stone is palpable.[13] A time traveler from the depths of the earth, the stone has met intensities beyond imagination. Far from being simply inert material, the stone stores the experiences of eons within its cellular structure.

In speaking of the five capacities of imagination lost to us, the Chumash describe one of them as the penetration into other worlds' dimensions; another is the capacity to perceive and understand what you are experiencing in those other worlds.[14] We talk about our desire to access other modes of communication, in whatever form they might occur. Wishing to be receptive to forms other than language, we open ourselves to the possibility of new physical sensations, or perhaps the effects of subtle differences in an electromagnetic field.[15] This formation of stones that remember supports our quest for those vanished senses.

An otherworldly quality quiets everyone; the air holds a soft gray-green aura. In an unspoken agreement, we find separate places on the formation, occasionally moving from one spot to another; for a long while we remain still and open, in private contemplation. Seated amidst the serpentine, we journey through time and space inside the earth.

**TRY THIS: Travel along serpentine's umbilical cord to the earth's belly**

- When you first encounter the serpentine formation from a distance, stop for a while, taking time to observe the relationship between the hillside of which it is a part and the stone itself.

- Notice the relationship of the formation to the shoulder of the mountain, to the summit, to the sea, to the way the clouds move overhead.

- As you approach the serpentine, be aware of any changes in your perception of it or your feelings about it.

- When you reach the formation, walk its borders, noticing what its boundaries are like.

- Observe it from all perspectives, pausing at any places that particularly draw your attention.

- Run your hands over the surface. Notice where the edges are flat and smooth and the flow of stone is evident.

- Wander slowly over the surface of the spreading serpentine, exploring, feeling each footstep's connection. Match your breath to your footfall. Allow it to move down your legs, out your feet, and into the earth.

- Let the stone lead you to a place that is willing to interact with you. Make a cornmeal offering there; introduce yourself and tell the stone why you are here.

- Let your body tell you how to be in that spot in the most receptive way: sitting or lying down; eyes open or closed; rattling, singing, or being still. Stay open to whatever thoughts, sensations, or feelings come to you.

- Surrender to the stone. Notice what surrender feels like—your muscles, your mind, the sensations of your body.

- Be open to whatever and however the stone communicates with you. Don't force the communication; just be open. You might pick up a stone, turn it over, look at the markings or shape; let images parade in your imagination, or songs, or phrases, or stories...

- Blow on the stone, burn incense, or sing. Honor the exchange, affirm it, anchoring it within you.

- When you're ready, move to a part of the formation that faces the ocean and supports your spine when you're seated. Keep your eyes open and let your gaze soften. Don't try too hard to see; just allow yourself to be present. Breathe slowly, feeling what there is to feel, seeing what there is to see.

- When you feel complete, thank the stone. Leave the serpentine and find a spot to be alone for a time among the clusters of bay laurel and oak that dot the hillside. Be with the mountain and with yourself in whatever way feels right.

We make plans to reunite at the serpentine. People move to nearby clusters of trees or to a particular place on the stone formation. One woman finds a wonderful spot near the serpentine patch—a boulder that curves around, creating a miniature cave. At its entrance, one small tree grows; next to it a cavity in the form of a bowl holds "stump water."

After a while, we gravitate again to the serpentine. Lynn begins to arrange a spiral of stones on a backdrop of larger stones. Others join her, and before long the simple spiral is complete. Without comment, she begins to walk through it, circling quietly toward the center. She pauses a few moments, then retraces her steps to the beginning. Peggy follows, and one by one, we pay silent homage, connected by a serpentine umbilical cord to Mother Earth.

Leaving the serpentine, we follow the path that parallels the coast. The hollowed ghosts of long-dead oak trees stand on a hill to the north, ancient sentinels guarding a grove of their green-leafed sisters. The stoic presence of these elders is tattooed with hundreds of small holes where the birds have sought living treasures. Now, squirrels secret their hoards within the cavities.

The oaks on the mountain ridge form a dignified outline against the horizon. Stillness pulses from the heart of the grove. Sitting in a circle, we pass around a crystal no bigger than a thumbnail. As it comes to each person, we share our individual experiences of the serpentine and of our separate places on the mountain. Each sharing is a deposit made to a common memory to be held within the crystal. Afterward, Carol buries the crystal, now linked to us and to its "family" of other crystals that we leave on each mountain in our circling of the bay.

## PERSONAL JOURNEYS

Marguerite: *I feel stripped of pretense, of pretending even to myself. So much of what I think I want to have and do seems ridiculous. I'm embarrassed at how caught up I've become in the culture I feel such scorn for—not so much the having, but the running around looking for answers, or the way of being. I went through a whole series of reactions. First, I was ashamed to realize how driven I am to experience more and more. When I saw that and just kept sitting, eventu-*

*ally I felt like a heavy load came pouring off me. Desperation that I wasn't even aware I felt dropped away, and I just kept sitting.*

*I didn't want to move; I knew I would move away from something very important that was happening to me that was scary and a relief at the same time. Scary, because I had this sense of things being stripped away, and I didn't know where I'd end up. I felt like I was dropping familiar patterns without even knowing what they were, and I couldn't quite imagine what would be left. I felt brought down to my core. When I already have what I'm looking for, it's a pretty pathetic way to live to be caught up in searching for more. I have enough. I do enough. There is enough for everyone, but only if we stay with the core of who we are.*

Peggy: *When we first got here, I couldn't believe what I was seeing. This is a place I've been before, a long time ago, and it turned my life around. I came to San Francisco to visit a friend; it must be twenty-five years ago. We toured around, went to Muir Woods, and then drove up the mountain to look at the view. When we walked up that hill over there, I looked out, and I thought, "This is it. This is where I belong." When I went back home to New York, I quit my job and moved out here. This is where I've been ever since. This is the spot where I knew I was home.*

Sarah: *This stone is so ancient and still going through changes. It gives me hope that no matter what is happening on the planet, whatever happens to everything that's familiar to us, we are the seeds of the future.*

## Bay Laurel: Plant Ally

Before we leave the grove, I share a gift I've brought from home—tiny vials of essential oil from the California bay laurel—to work with in the coming month. In ancient times, leaves from another genus and species of laurel (*Laurus nobilis*) were used for the crowns and wreaths of heroes and poets.[16] The Delphic priestesses were said to use laurel leaves to induce a state that would promote clairvoyance and prophecy. The leaves are still used in soups and stews. The California variety, *Umbellurlaria californica*, is considered by most people to be too strong for cooking. Too vigorous a sniff of the California leaf can produce a blazing headache, but the oil is used sparingly in a variety of medicinal preparations. Both varieties are used to keep closets free of insect pests.

During the course of our day, we've been weaving in and out of bay laurel communities. We will use the fragrance of the oil later to help us recall memories of a place or a day, or help invoke dreams of the mountain.

## TRY THIS: Dream with the California bay laurel plant spirit

- After you've returned home from a visit to Mount Tamalpais, prepare to dream with the help of the laurel plant. Put a very small amount of its oil on your wrist or nose before you go to bed.

- When you go to bed, eliminate potential distractions to dreaming; think about the events of the day and promise yourself that you will set any unresolved issues aside until the next day. Jot them down, if it will help you release them.

- Direct your attention to each part of your body, inviting each muscle group to relax. Start with your toes, and go to the top of your head.

- Formulate your dream request in the simplest, clearest statement. You might program the dream about something at which you want to succeed; the laurel is associated with a long tradition of celebrating winners. If you have had time to visit the boulder with the tree growing from it, this could be an opportunity to ask for its input about partnership.

- Hold your dream desire as you drift off to sleep.

- Repeat the same process with the same dream request for a full week. If programming your dreams is new to you, remember that it's a bit like teaching a muscle a new exercise.

- Keep paper and pen by your bed and write down anything you remember as soon as you waken. It might be the briefest of images or sounds but let the process build on itself. Even if the dream doesn't seem to answer the question asked, record it. By writing it, you might discover something not initially apparent.

## PERSONAL JOURNEYS

My journey, bringing in the memory of the tree growing on the boulder: *I see an old-fashioned iron bank shaped like a log and a boy and a girl on either side with a saw that has a handle on each end. The saw rests on the log between them. A tall, gaunt woman appears and takes a small collection of coins from her pocket. She looks at the coins carefully, selects one, and inserts it into a slot in the iron log. The boy and girl respond, briefly see-sawing back and forth as if sawing the log.*

*When they stop, the woman looks at them for a moment, then reluctantly pokes through her coins, finally choosing another one. She inserts it into the bank, and again, the boy and girl briefly saw the log. With less delay, she selects another coin—a penny. Even as she inserts it into the log, she's getting ready to feed the log again when the sawing stops. This continues for a few more rounds.*

*When her penny supply is exhausted, she puts in a nickel, then two dimes, then a quarter. As the coin value increases, the duration of the sawing action is extended and she is less tense. Her hesitation fades; by the end, she's completely caught up in the impact she's having. When she puts in her final quarter, the bottom of the bank suddenly falls open, and a huge pile of coins falls into her lap.*

*I awaken—and as I write down the dream, I realize that I've just been waiting for some kind of grace to come to me. I have to keep feeding what I want to have happen; if I don't, no treasure will fall into my lap.*

## Steep Ravine: Camping Decisions

After retracing our steps to the car, we drive down to Highway 1, turning south one mile before Stinson Beach. A few minutes down the road, we come to the padlocked gate of the Steep Ravine campsite area. The combination to the lock had come with the reservation confirmation—a precious piece of paper because of the popularity of the site. Reservations must be made months in advance. Although there are other wonderful camping areas on the mountain, this is my favorite because it's so close to the ocean. A twisting road descends about two hundred feet to the parking lot. A camp host is always in residence to supervise the two cabins, six environmental camping sites, and two large group sites. We place our confirmation letter on the dashboard.

Each campsite has its unique appeal. One is set apart from the others, two are closer together, offering less privacy but more opportunity to be close to friends. Further down the trail we find a third possibility that is more interesting to us—a pair of sites open on three sides but set back and protected. This is a configuration that allows our group to spread out a bit and yet still be close enough to connect with one another along a conspicuous path.

A wheelbarrow near the door of the camp host's cabin helps us transport camping paraphernalia to the two sites we've reserved. The trail passes small cabins perched on the cliff; they look like they're out of a storybook, simple and inviting. Peering in through the window of an unoccupied cabin, you see a sparse interior—a wood stove, sleeping platforms, a table and benches. They have no running water indoors, and primitive toilets are outside. Each cabin faces a beach. Long waves swoosh onto shore unbroken by any large boulders under the surface. The water rears back, pulls up into a long turquoise wave, and strikes the beach with a wild splash of white foam.

Beyond the cabins and the six small environmental campsites are two larger sites reserved for groups. We see backpackers carry in their equipment while we trudge forward with our laden wheelbarrows. We reach the last pair of smaller campsites and wander between them, matching our tents to the best terrain.

We'd already decided on our tentmates—based on amount of restlessness, snoring, and need for solitude. Dellalou, Hera, and I share a luxurious four-person tent. Dellalou's touch of home is a flowered pillow with inch-deep lace. Hera has a white down comforter, twice recovered, that was once her mother's. I have an orange air mattress—and since I've forgotten a pillow, fold my blue fleece jacket to do the job. Each site is equipped with a four-legged wooden cabinet to keep food away from marauding animals, and we stash everything out of temptation's way. In spite of having decided to support one another's dietary issues, tiny splurges, cracks in the diet dike, appear from nearly every backpack.

Each of us takes off independently to discover a comfortable lookout spot from which to watch the sunset over the Pacific. Solitude in the midst of friends is one of the gifts of this particular camping trip, nourishing us in a very special way. It dispels the vague uneasiness that women often experience alone in nature—a disquiet that has nothing do with bears, snakes, or bugs but rather another aspect of nature—the possibility of an encounter with a menacing human being. Seven mothers give one another the comfortable sense of space to explore our own worlds and still are ready to protect each other. I'm astonished and embarrassed at the relief it brings.

## TRY THIS: Find compatible camping companions

- Before leaving on a camping trip, talk with possible companions about expectations. Things will move more smoothly once you arrive. Share about any special needs or habits you can think of—nighttime roaming, talking in your sleep, snoring, early waking.

- Agree on a way to signal your need to be alone for a time. For some of us, asking for this time is not always easy.

- Supporting one another's dietary issues is a good idea, as is the joint decision whether or not to splurge and have delicious desserts. That way, everyone is equally guilty or virtuous.

# Traces of the Past: The Death of a Whale

Traces of events continue to resonate long after they take place. Last year when I was camping here with my friend Meg, we saw something very unexpected on the rocky beach below the bluff. The body of a small whale was beached in a cove formed by huge boulders between the base of the cliff and the pounding ocean waters. It had been there for some time, and the odor was dreadful. The whale's gray skin had rubbed off, exposing its bruised flesh. The

rawness of the scene intensified the impact of the death beyond that of the carcasses of birds or fish occasionally found along the beach.

Other people had been here before us, and perhaps twenty small cairns
(piles of stones) had been assembled on the beach, silent witnesses honoring
the life and death of this creature. We sat with them, wondering what could
have happened that brought this juvenile whale to an early death.

Rather than retreat from the odor and the sight, we participated in this
important event while not completely understanding it. Drumming, we honored the whale's life, envisioning its journeys in deeper waters, its connection
to the pod, to its own community, the ruptured relationship with its mother.
It was slowly surrendering its own form as small crabs and other creatures nib-
bled enthusiastically at its body. Whether or not this particular death came
from natural causes, it was a powerful reminder that all is not well in the sea.

## TRY THIS: Honor a life that has passed

- When you find an animal or a bird that has died, sit with it.
- Close your eyes and envision the way the bird or animal led its life.
- Imagine its birth—a live birth or an egg cracking open.
- Let a picture unfold of its relationship to its parents—how it was nour-
  ished, how it became independent.
- Envision its relationship to the land. Remember how it moved—wings
  spread picking up an air current, fins pushing through the water, slender
  legs stepping carefully, sensitive mouth foraging, or sharp beak ravaging.
- Notice any yearning to communicate, any sensation in your body, any
  words or songs. Let physical sensation translate into the vibration of a
  sound, a word, a syllable.
- When you open your eyes, try to move in the way the animal did. Feel
  your body bending, stretching, flowing forward. Dance in honor of the
  fleeting life of this creature, and if you feel the urge to sing, chant, or
  hum, give yourself that freedom.

Remembering helps extend a sense of community, the recollection of a
shared history. There isn't even a single bone left on the beach below, but the
whale is still here for me—a trace of the past encoded into my brain. As the
images fade from my mind, an overlay to the memory is being added; I hear
someone striking a singing bowl. On this trip each of us carries a Tibetan brass
bowl that sings out when it's struck with a beater. From our separate vantage

points, we hear one another's bowls singing out sparely and randomly—acknowledging the moment, the community, and our separate space.

As the sun dips lower, we gradually find one another on a nearby bluff. We hope for a sighting of the famous green flash that is sometimes visible from a slight elevation just moments after the sun goes down. No luck, but the sky is beautiful, all the same.

## Time Travel: The Path of Distant Ancestors

Twilight blankets everything with a soft glow, a wordless reminder that everything is connected. I invite my friends to do a bit of time travel with me, letting this special "hour of power" support our voyage. Lying down on the grassy bluff, they close their eyes and listen. I drum and share the mountain's history, feeling all the while like my own grandmother telling a bedtime story:

> *Make yourself comfortable; move stones and sticks until you can lie comfortably on the earth, and let your attention drift with the clouds passing overhead. Breathe easily and deeply, letting each exhalation settle your spine against the earth, as if each vertebra were sending a tiny root into the mountain. Let your eyes close if they want to. Let your mind drift through time, following the path of the words, and as it comes to you, remember and weave into the tale your own history.*
>
> *There is a legend about the mountain from the 1930s, a Euro-American's invention of a pseudo-native tale enacted in the Mountain Theatre. The story says that the mountain is a sleeping enchantress. Her perpetual sleep came about through her love for a young brave, on whom she had initially cast a spell to thwart his search for the gift of healing for his people. Overcome with remorse, and with no way to undo her own magic, she sacrificed her life to free him. Viewed from nearby, the mountain's outline reveals her silhouette, feet pointed toward the sea. She's covered with a purple blanket woven by the Four Sisters of Destiny.*
>
> *You have a lineage that goes back to the time when that story was told. Your family told its own stories. It might be that you remember a legend of a place near your childhood home—a hill, a valley, or a plant that inspired a story. Remember it now...*
>
> *The last report of the trapping of a grizzly bear on the mountain was in 1880. You have a lineage that goes back to that time.*

*An ancestor was alive on that day. Perhaps your own ancestors hunted for some of the food they ate and might have had a different sense of appreciation and respect for the animals that provided that food. Or it could be that they reacted out of fear of the wildness. It could very well be that those ancestors were alive to tell you their stories when you were a child. Maybe there's a story you remember now...*

*The Europeans began to settle Marin in 1817, and within decades, the Indians were decimated. You have an ancestor who was alive during that brutal time. Your ancestors might have been part of the changing face of the United States. They might have been among the Native Americans considered invisible or inconsequential even as their homelands were being overrun. Or they might have been among the immigrants who crossed the country when it seemed to most would-be settlers that the land was uninhabited. Perhaps they were still in other countries, anticipating new lives or sanctuary in America. The lives of your parents and grandparents were shaped by their feelings of movement, of change, of the possibility of new beginnings. Remember what you've heard of your own family's migrations...*

*Twelve hundred years ago, the oldest redwood tree alive today sprouted in Muir Woods at the foot of Mount Tamalpais. Your lineage goes back to that day, and while you may know nothing of that long progression, you might be aware of the general area of the planet that sprouted your own family's roots...*

*Seven thousand years ago, the Miwoks, migrants from Siberia, lived on the margins of Mount Tamalpais. The courage to strike out into unknown territory, taking a risk to improve a family's or a community's chances, represented a challenge to survival. Your lineage goes back to that day, and you may have a sense of your own tribe's challenges, its struggles against the elements in whatever place was homeland and in the territories they traversed, of the sacrifices made to unfold their destinies...*

*Eighteen thousand years ago, the last global ice age peaked, and the sea level was thirty miles west of Mount Tam. Your lineage goes back to that day—a time when brains and bodies responded to vastly different challenges, a time when the senses were called on in very different ways. Imagine the taste of water so pure you can bend down to drink from any stream...Imagine your salivary glands responding to the distant fragrance of a plant you're searching for, leading you forward until you find it...You carry within you the dormant traces of those powers...*

*Sixty-five to a hundred fifty million years ago, the uplift of plate movements formed Mount Tam. You have a lineage that goes back to that day, a lineage that you might not recognize as your own if you saw it. What was the shape of humanity or its precursors? Float through those centuries, those early forms of existence that preceded human form, and be aware of your consciousness on the planet...*

*Follow the beat of the drum, and journey back from those most ancient beginnings of your earthly heritage. Gather the threads and gradually come forward in time, through the forming of the mountain, the ice age, the epoch of the Siberian migration, the genesis of that ancient redwood, the time of transition from primarily Indian to European presence here, the stories of the ancestors, the presence of other animal life on the mountain. Gather the personal power that has come to you through your ancestors, the power that has accumulated in your being today and throughout your life. You are a confluence of all that is past, all that exists in your present life, and all that will come to be...*

*Like every creature on earth, we are a concentration of the powers of nature in whatever form our lives take. Everything that sustains us comes from Mother Earth—and in turn, whatever we are and do feeds energy back to Her. As your breath flows in, fill your body with all possibilities.*

*As your breath flows out, send your intent into the earth to return the gift of life to Her.... When you are ready, open your eyes. Be aware of the day moving through its cycle, carrying us toward the evening.*

We drift gently back to the present and slowly make our way back to the campsite. We gather at the table near the fire pit. As we begin to spread the potluck feast we have brought, quiet pensiveness gives way to community pleasures. Reserving the firewood for our fire ceremony later, we crank up the propane camp stove for miso soup and coffee water. Dellalou lights the lantern, and Lynn mutes its harsh light by covering it with a square cotton neck scarf. One person will be arriving late, about dinnertime, and although we had intended to wait for her, everyone digs in.

As we eat, we keep an eye on the winding hillside road above us, more imagined than seen in the darkness of the night. Soon the headlights of a car appear. Licking the chicken juice off my fingers, I walk up the trail to the parking area to pilot the latecomer back to our campsite.

Later, dishes out of the way, we move into a circle around the fire pit. Virtually car camping, we've brought luxury along: a light plastic kitchen chair, folding camp chairs, the end of the picnic bench, and stadium seats together make an uneven but comfy circle around the fire pit. The wood leaps into flames with a single match. Every face is beautiful in the firelight, and the pleasure of sharing a circle of friendship washes over us.

## Fire Ceremony

We've been anticipating this moonlit evening for weeks, when we might have a chance to work with fire's power to transform. Our entire circling of the bay is intended to be transformative in a variety of ways; this evening, it's fire that will be our agent of change. A full moon fire ceremony offers a focus to change a useless pattern of thinking that robs us of the energy to move forward in other directions, or to enact something that can move the issues forward.

Fire itself is always transformative. Something with one form becomes something else as fire consumes it—a piece of wood, an animal's body, a pot of soup with flavors blending as the fire works it. We all know ways that we're a bit stuck—attitudes or habits that interfere with stepping into transformation.

Earlier in the day, light and shadow joggled loose some of that debris; the stream's running water carried some away, as well. If we want to be alive to change throughout our lives, different forms of shedding will inevitably be part of that transformative process.

Through a fire ceremony, energy bound in old ways can be freed to move in a new direction. We symbolically release something that no longer serves a useful purpose and claim the energy we invest in that old behavior pattern for a new purpose. Through intent, we purposely set aside a way of moving through the world and claim the involvement with it for something more meaningful.

We've brought supplies for making prayer ties. Dellalou brings out a bowl of cornmeal and places it on the ground near the fire. Marguerite passes out small squares of red cotton material. Jenny cuts lengths of cotton thread. Deep in our own thoughts, we sit quietly. Concentrating on events related to what we want to shift, we assemble the prayer ties by taking a pinch of cornmeal, replaying episodes in our memories as we place the cornmeal in the center of each cloth.

Firmly tying it with the thread, we acknowledge its teaching and the fact that we have no need for the same lesson to revisit us. The process honors the learning in the experiences we're finished with, so that we aren't just running away from something we don't want to face. Rather than thrusting it away in distaste, we honor it. What we know now permits us to let it go.

## PERSONAL JOURNEYS

Marguerite: *I've spent a lot of time in the past mourning something I couldn't change about an imbalance in my relationship. I finally realized it was occupying so much time and energy that I was bogged down and wasn't moving forward in ways that I could be. So I made a list of all the situations and comments that have triggered my anger or sadness about it. I replayed each one as I made a prayer tie about it. Saying thanks for the understanding that came from each one became much more than just the repetition of a formula. It was a real kick in the pants to move forward, very empowering.*

## TRY THIS: Make prayer ties for a fire ceremony

- Make a list of experiences that relate to the same kind of shift you're ready to make in your life, thinking as you do so about what each experience has taught you.
- Gather together some six-inch red cotton squares, a bowl of cornmeal, and some colored thread.
- Say a brief prayer over each of these components of the prayer ties, asking them to take part in releasing a pattern that's no longer useful and helping to free the energy bound in it for a greater good.
- Pick up a pinch of cornmeal, placing it on a cotton square. As you do so, replay in your mind the entire episode—what happened, what you did, how you felt about it, what perspective you have now after the passage of time.
- Acknowledge what you learned from the experience. Express your completion with its teaching, and the fact that repeated lessons are not necessary. Tie it firmly and set it aside.
- Repeat this process, making a separate prayer tie for each experience on your list.
- Sit for a while, allowing anything to surface that's been evoked by the process. Make a prayer tie for whatever has come up.
- Dispose of the prayer ties by burning them, burying them, or throwing them into the ocean.

Now each of us has a small pile of packets, each representing different aspects or episodes of the issue we're dealing with and what we have learned from each of them. It's a quiet time; the only sound is the fire's crackling as it waits to be fed. Debbie's role in the ceremony is self-appointed; she will focus intently on the fire—assuring the quality of the flames, feeding it more wood to keep it strong. Finally, everyone is ready, and we prepare to transform the fire into a sacred fire.

We've brought handmade rattles. Some are fashioned from gourds, painted with animal features, geometric designs, or mythological figures. Others are papier-mâché, kelp bulbs made into whimsical figures, carved wood, or photo canisters painted with symbols of the elements. The sound of our rattles, shaken in unison, delineates the space we occupy as a group and helps create a sacred circle. Because our ceremony focuses on fire's alchemy, we address the aspects of fire in each direction.

Facing the east, I raise my arm and begin a steady rhythm with my gourd rattle, a full-figured feminine shape with gold tinsel hair that catches the light of the moon. In my mind, I see the form of fire I most enjoy that's connected to the east—a red-gold path from the rising sun crossing a lake toward me, the sky's predawn lavender and rose melting before its progress. Remembering our own origin among the stars, our cellular relationship to the sky, acknowledging the unknown, praising new possibilities that we can shape through our minds, our dreams, our intent, I give thanks to the power of a new day to inspire me to think, to feel, and to be each moment seizing the chance to live differently. Although this moment is night-time, I ask the quality of the morning sun to be present in the fire ceremony, to take our offerings, letting the fire be nourished by what no longer serves us, sending its sparks to join the flaming stars and meteors.

Rattling vigorously to the south, Hera whistles and calls to the south's form of fire. She honors the passion that drives thoughts of change into manifestation. Each of us, she says, needs the power that comes from strong feelings, from being enflamed with purpose and intent. She calls for help in strengthening our focus—asks the fire to take our gifts, that it be made stronger by them and that we ourselves will be stronger in return.

In the west, Peggy speaks her appreciation of fire's presence in the beauty of a sunset—the light that brings a touch of magic to everything around us. She calls on those moments of transformed light to help us leave behind the actions and attitudes of the day, knowing that our dreaming minds can create new forms. She asks that special light of evening to diffuse any heaviness in our hearts and to bring us an awareness that we are all part of one Being. She invites the spirits of the luminescent creatures of the oceans to join us and to share with us their capacity to be radiant where light may not exist.

Sarah calls to the north, to the heat in the planet's center, to the lava that bursts through volcanoes, bubbles up to the earth's surface, scours whatever is before it, and creates new land in its place. She offers up verbal images of the aurora borealis, whose lights dance across the skies of the far north, swooping, snapping, crackling. She calls to the hidden light each of us carries within our own being, inviting it to come into the dark night around our fire.

Creating in this way a circle of fire's presence from each direction, we turn toward the fire in the center, continue rattling, and begin to sing. The chant we use tonight was passed our way long ago and has undoubtedly gone through permutations that would make it unrecognizable to those who initiated it, but it bears for us the intent of honoring the power of fire.

One by one, we approach the fire and bring our offerings. We touch the prayer ties first to our navels, acknowledging the need to align our own power and will to be fire's partner in making the change. We touch the small packets to our hearts, wanting the changes to be heartfelt and motivated. We touch them to our foreheads, remembering the importance of holding a vision as our responsibility to work with fire's capacity to transform. We feed the prayer ties to the fire and watch the flames consume them.

Afterward, companionable silence reigns. Later, someone begins to sing. First they're sweet songs; gradually, we make our way through nostalgia, songs from childhood, joking songs, camp songs, risque songs, songs from musicals. We run down as the fire runs down. The full moon casts a silvery glow over the sky and illuminates the terrain with a pale blue light. We open the sacred space we'd created by sending our gratitude to the fires of each direction and head for bed. Nestled into our sleeping bags, we drift off to sleep listening to the waves on the rocky shore.

Around 5 a.m., a strong wind comes up. Our tents are buffeted and squeezed and all of us are wakened. Crawling out into the pale blue moonlight, we find the temperature to be surprisingly warm. We collapse the smaller tents, which are not staked down. Wandering through the brush into a clearing, we watch an amazing moonset, the most incredible of my life. As the moon slowly descends toward the horizon, the light shifts. Bands of soft rose and lavender appear and widen. A gauzy sheen of mist rises from Bolinas Bay, lifting very slowly, embracing the moon, absorbing it into the bands of color. Behind us, the sky is beginning to welcome the day; but we keep returning to the moonlight pouring its majestic beauty into each of our hearts.

## Steep Ravine Trail: Stone Cairns Bearing Witness

Slowly, we move into the day—eating breakfast, packing up camp, and moving toward one more adventure before leaving the mountain. We leave two cars near the entrance gate and pile into two others to drive to the Pantoll Ranger Station where the Steep Ravine Trail begins. Aptly named, the trail is just what its name implies. We plan to hike down the trail, return in the cars parked below, and retrieve those left at the trailhead.

The trail descends through a redwood-shaded ravine, and within a very short time the creek's plummeting roar points up the personality of Steep Ravine. Gravity beckons us to communicate with the ravine; each footstep deepens our connection. We cross a wooden bridge over the creek, round a bend in the trail, and stop abruptly, making an unexpected discovery. On a series of large boulders extending into the creek, a cairn community sits in silent contemplation. Responding to their overwhelming sentient presence, we join the stone figures in meditation.

We sit with the Stone People, enjoy the sound of the water tumbling over the rocks, the coolness of the grove of redwoods sheltering us, the rustle of squirrels and birds in the trees. Both the people who created the cairns and the Stone People themselves communicate with us as surely as if words had been spoken, all of us sharing the tranquil beauty.

### PERSONAL JOURNEYS

Sarah: *It wasn't just the cairns. Everything seemed so alive, so vibrant. I felt transported. I knew that every living thing in the woods was communicating. When I think that this is happening all the time, human beings seem out of the loop, missing something really wonderful. I suppose we shut it off just to survive being overwhelmed by too much happening around us. But it was a great privilege to share it, without any obligation to do anything, protect anything, convince anyone—to just be. It was a marvelous moment shared with nonhuman beings.*

### TRY THIS: Honor a beautiful place by engaging it

- Spend time in a natural place that speaks to you. Simply be open to it; give yourself plenty of time to absorb and appreciate its beauty and the special qualities it holds.
- Take all the time you need to experience its communication to you.
- Before you leave the site, look for elements around you that you might arrange as an act of appreciation.

- Pine cones, yellow leaves, interesting shapes of debris or fallen twigs can be used to form a pattern at the spot that touches you; stones can be piled into cairns. You are using a nonverbal language to convey your thoughts and feelings; the materials you use are themselves a part of the dialogue.

- If you notice yourself humming aloud or in your head, maybe you've been given a song you can take home.

- A spoken or sung phrase might repeat itself over and over; it might become a mantra that can carry you back to this place when you are far away from it.

- Leave the natural world to evolve at its own pace, taking nothing away.

- Let your connection be woven into your memories; return to it whenever you want to replenish the feelings it evoked for you.

As the trail through the ravine gives way to the grassy hillside facing the ocean, I remember a dream I had long ago: In the darkness of space, a weaver holds in listening fingers golden strands vibrating with vitality. The strands come from sacred places on the earth, and as they are gathered together, the weaver creates a golden net to encircle the planet. Within it, a new era begins. Each strands originates in a separate life form at a sacred site. The varied expressions of the life force—including the Stone, the Plant, and the Animal People—create a weaving of unbelievable beauty. Together, they are as powerful as a coat of mail.

In the dream, as I visit the sacred mountains near my home, I touch the origins of the golden threads in each form of life I meet. One by one, I guide the free end of each filament into space, into the weaver's waiting hands. With great concentration, the weaver places them in the beautiful life-sustaining tapestry suspended in the darkness of the starry universe.

I recognize my path—to help weave a tapestry of the life force over San Francisco Bay, over the surrounding land, and over all beings who are part of it.

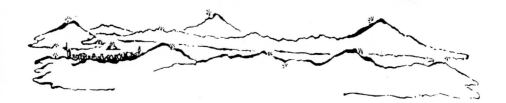

## Chapter Four

# MOUNT DIABLO: Surveying the Web

Deep in the Juniper Campground area a trail begins, winding through open rolling hills. On this spring day, a painter's palette of wildflowers splashes every hump and hollow with vivid patterns. We feast our eyes on the glorious blossoms, taking in the evidence that spring has arrived. Once we've made camp, preparing the nest we'll return to, we walk out of the sheltered oak grove to take in the wide vista. No sight of buildings or traffic mars the view; we've been transported into wilderness far from home, even though the drive is no more than an hour and a half.

The intensity of living in Silicon Valley, one of the most bustling centers of creative and commercial activity in the world, often feels overwhelming. Now, concerns of war and the attendant moral and political issues add to the stress of the plummeting economic fortunes of some and the still-intense workload of others.

This pressure is very hard to switch off, and we look to our journey on the mountain today to support a shift to a more uncluttered mind space. All of us are yearning to listen to our own inner voices and to the natural world, hoping to receive the precious gift that open space offers—an antidote to tension. Each of us wants the opportunity to spread her psychological and emotional wings, and to feel the reassuring connection with Mother Earth. We want to empty ourselves and refill with tranquility and the beauty of nature.

A few moments after leaving the campground, we separate, staying within view of one another but far enough apart to feel that each of us in this moment occupies her own space.

# Vulture's Carrion Quest: Bird Ally

Seated comfortably on a hillside, I follow the flow of the land with my eyes. All around me, the earth is carpeted in emerald green grass. High above us, a vulture picks up the invisible thermals rising from the earth. Master of the air currents, the bird guides my fantasy flight, and I join the "kettle" of maybe ten of them soaring companionably. There is space for me among them, and we circle together on the warm air. They make minimal adjustments of their feathers and wing positions. Their flight seems effortless. Heads bent, looking for meals of rotting bodies of rabbits, mice, or other small animals,[1] they turn their quest into an airborne dance full of grace and apparent pleasure. They are my teachers, and there's much for me to learn about not separating work and pleasure. Buoyed by the air, I relax more and more deeply.

As the huge birds see and smell out carrion, I follow their example. My own carrion today is dread. Ordinary demons are replaced by worries about what it means to go to war, about how to talk with high school grandsons who are about to be faced, quite unprepared in their naïve carefree days of youth, with life-and-death choices that affect their lives and shape the world's future. I dread the destruction of youth's innocence in Iraq and Afghanistan, and the seemingly unstoppable war machine of our own government.

I never spot a vulture actually descending toward its prey, but I know the routine. I've seen them feasting on carcasses of deer, raccoons, and roadkill. Ready to make thorough use of what is already available through accident or natural death, they tidy the environment. My carrion has many forms—emotions, old habits, useless activities that resurface again and again, blocking creativity or courage. Disposing of this garbage would clear my own environment and make way for fresh approaches.

Descending from the kettle of vultures, I come back to myself sitting on the hillside and begin to sort my carrion. On a small piece of paper, I jot down my concerns. There's the everyday detritus of keeping life going—errands that need to be done to maintain household and family. I need to set aside these nagging demands. Promising I'll return to them when the moment is right, I put the list, pen, and paper in my pocket. But aside from the content, the energy of the concerns needs a different treatment. I'm counting on the mountain to help transform those concerns into new visions, actions, and language.

I run my fingers down a tuft of grass, touching the cool soil at its base. Yes, I reassure myself—the earth is here, and so am I. I send anxieties through my fingertips like taproots feeding the sun's energy into soil. Another bit of carrion follows the anxiety—my fear about the future. I let it trickle into the ground.

Mother Earth nurtures both the grass and me; I continue to relax against her body. My hips and two hands make a three-pronged earth connection. I let go more and more, willing the sunshine to fill the places in my mind and muscles that have been holding onto tension and worry. I feel my "wings" expanding, like the vultures who preen themselves in the early morning, allowing the sun to prepare them for their flight on the thermals.

## TRY THIS: Follow a vulture's carrion quest

- Scan the sky while walking on the mountain, watching for a vulture or a group of vultures circling.

- Sit or lie down comfortably. Watch their circling flight. Observe the ease with which they maintain their height, moving on thermals invisible to human beings.

- Greet them, sending them your respect. Ask permission to be guided by their capacity to search out carrion.

- Let your breathing slow, your chest rising and falling as if the thermals support you from within and without.

- Visualize yourself among the vultures, lifted as easily and effortlessly as the birds, carried by the currents of air.

- Let your mind drift effortlessly to the concerns or issues that take you away from being fully present. Just as the vulture consumes carrion, allow yourself to consume your personal carrion, moving it through your being into the earth. As you do so, the blockages of anger, fears, and obsessions release their hold on your body and pass through it.

- Return your attention to the vultures' flight, noticing how they are at ease and vigilant at the same time. Move into your own sense of ease, enjoying the sensations of buoyancy and movement, the odors, the light and shadow. At the same time be poised to handle intruding thoughts or self-talk, all the personal carrion that takes you away from full presence.

- Let those intrusions tumble, like raindrops along a downspout, down filaments that connect your soaring body to the earth. Let your carrion find its way into the earth, compost for another form of life.

- Thank the tireless vultures for their wisdom, for their teaching.

- Return to your own form, refreshed and free to move through the natural world in a more open and receptive way.

Thanks to the vultures and to the earth who welcome my carrion, I've arrived more fully on the mountain. I feel ready to search for the flower that will be my companion in the journey I have agreed to make with my friends. Our intention is to indulge in a unique discovery of a wild spring flower, the harbinger of new beginnings and the continuity of life.

## Flower Power

Sitting very still, I hear the call and response of quails behind me: "Where are you?" And somewhere close by, "I've found you!" Taking that hint, I search for a flower nearby. I'm touched by the frail loveliness of two pale blue blossoms—baby blue-eyes—and move closer to them. So perfectly do they reflect the beauty of the sky that it's hard to believe they've sprung from the earth and not fallen from above. A wash of cloud-white in the center of each flower deepens the sky association. Their presence mirroring the heavens seems ideal for my needs, and I settle in to get better acquainted.

My skin and the still air are the same temperature. I hardly know where I end and the air begins. As my gaze softens, that same melting of separate entities takes place in what I see around me. Pure patterns of color wash over me, unhinged from connection with specific objects or plants. I fantasize that I am becoming the same shade of blue as the sky and the baby blue-eyes, taking on the same tranquility that the flowers exude.

Bending closer to one of them, I fill my field of vision with the blue as I purposely unfocus my eyes. Tiny pinpoints of color—variations of blue, of lavender, of white, of gold—show me their weaving of this amazing drop of sky scattered on soft petals. Becoming part of the weaving, I breathe in the blue of the flower, the spaciousness of the sky. Pale blue is drawn into my chest, into my heart. My body becomes aligned with an embracing sky, and I feel utterly at peace with all that I am and all that is around me.

### TRY THIS: Fill yourself with the beauty of a flower

- As you walk near wildflowers, notice which of them draws you most. Are you responding to the color? The size? The location? The fragrance?
- Notice the flower's environment—plants, birds, trees, bugs—as parts of a tapestry. Open yourself to the whole—perhaps through breath, posture, change of visual focus or mental attention, or all of these.
- Follow the invitation of the flower and approach it.

- Make yourself comfortable, aware that you are part of the field in which the flower is growing. Relax into the field, making yourself as totally at home as the flower seems to be.

- Let your senses open; notice the feeling of the air on your skin, whether there is movement from the wind in the grasses or the trees. Be aware of the fragrance of the earth, of the grass, of the soil, of other plants, and of the flower itself. Notice the calling of birds or other sounds around you. Allow yourself to be completely present in this moment.

- Like a zoom lens on a camera, narrow in from this wider perspective to the individual flower that brought you here.

- Is the flower shaded, in full sunlight, or does it receive both sun and shade at different times of the day?

- Relate to your chosen flower with your whole being. Imagine it experiencing you, aware of your presence.

- Touch one of the petals; feel its texture, its softness. Very slowly, very gently, stroke each petal, combing the delicate threads of softness into your fingertips, feeling your own skin becoming petal-soft.

- Allow the softness to flow up your fingers, into your hands and arms, into your body. As you stroke the petals, invite yourself to embody its softness.

- Notice tiny pinpoints of color in the petals—minute variations of blue, of lavender, of white, of gold, of red or pink in their textured weaving.

- Become part of the weaving of colors. Imagine floating toward the center of the flower, into the weaving of colors; feel your presence among the array of colors, nestled among all the delicate or vivid hues you feel and see before you.

- As you breathe, absorb the beauty of the colors, infused with their essence. Let the flower's perfection live in you.

- Breathing slowly, luxuriously, feel yourself safely and lovingly bathed with the fragrance of the flower. Allow your nose, your throat, and your lungs to open and fill with the pleasure of its fragrance.

- Remember, re-member. Feel your body and memorize the feelings, so that when you want to experience the flower's exquisite presence again, you can do so.

- Offer the flower a partnership—that through the focus of your intent, you will send the peacefulness and beauty it has shared with you to other places and people who may be in need.

- Slowly return to ordinary consciousness, into awareness of your own presence in a human body on the mountain.

Back at our campsite a bit later, a little tender and gentled, we fix some tea and lunch. The shared activity of its preparation grounds us, brings us back into teasing and ordinariness, but each carries within her the quiet mystery of nature's intimate sharing.

## Creating a Thought-Form

After lunch, our next course becomes another nature feast. We come together around one bloom—this time a California poppy—to enhance our focusing abilities. Aware of the give-and-take that sustains the natural world, we want to explore multiple ways of helping to heal a site on the mountain that's been damaged by human intervention. We want to discover how to take the blessings that come our way and pass on the wonderful effects—see what it feels like to share it and discover how to do that. Our morning's involvement with the pleasure and beauty of the flower was the first step—enjoying ourselves individually, enlivening ourselves as a group. Now, focusing on a poppy becomes the next step toward learning to deepen our participation in the process of reciprocity.

To prepare for a meditation consciously extending vivacity to other lifeforms through our now more open hearts, we practice on ourselves, taking turns experiencing the roles of senders and receivers. As senders, we first conjure within ourselves anxious or unpleasant feelings. Holding those feelings, we attempt to send peace and caring to the receivers. As receivers, we notice what happens to our bodies, emotions, and minds, trying to judge the effect of receiving a communication of goodwill or kindness from an unpeaceful place. Comparing notes, we conclude that it doesn't seem rewarding from either direction.

We vigorously pat our bodies, arms, legs, and faces, bringing ourselves back to neutral. Then we tap into the memories of the morning's visit with the baby blue-eyes, taking time to rekindle the connections with their beauty and health. Once again, senders make connections with receivers, this time from a place of peace and kindness within ourselves that is consistent with the message we want to communicate.

Our little experiment makes it very clear that if we want to project peace or loving feelings, we have to experience what we want to send. Learning how to do that in the presence of a flower is far easier than doing it first with human beings. Flower power is more neutral. We can replenish our own wells of optimism by pulling our attention back to nature's nourishment in a flower or something else that feeds us.

Stepping into this process of receiving and sending through intention is a practice of mindfulness. Once more, we probe its components. Sitting together around the poppy, we each choose a particular quality to focus on. Debbie chooses the form of the flower itself, Ann the plant's motion in the slight breeze. Sarah takes the fragrance, Peggy selects the color, Kayla the leaves, and I work with the plant as a whole. We spend five minutes, opening ourselves in the same way as we had done in the morning but focusing on just the one aspect of the poppy we've chosen. We open our hearts to that single aspect of our experience.

Then we move away from the flower to the edge of the field, where there is grass without flowers. We form a circle and focus on the space in the center. Remembering the experience of the baby blue-eyes and the pleasure and appreciation we received, we unfurl those images and sensations toward the center of our circle. Effortlessly, the physical and mental memories fill our bodies with pleasure. Thoughts translate themselves into the sensations of pleasure and of enjoying something beautiful. There is warmth, relaxation, and the feeling of a loving heart.

In the center we've created within our human circle, we build a wordless, formless picture, each of us contributing her own dimension of the full picture. We pool the positive and nurturing feelings that came to us through the intense attention to the poppy in the center. Each person focuses on "beaming" only her individual experience. We are relaxed and at ease, pleased and excited as a wordless tranquility spills from the center back toward us. We're enveloped in a joint creation that none of us can quite name. But the relaxation in each of our bodies, the look of satisfaction on each face, tells the tale.

## Conduits of Healing

During our lunch break, we plan our next experience. Afterward, we move into it silently and individually. We begin to walk the same path we took in the morning; however, this time we veer right when the path splits, toward Mitchell Canyon. As we round a curve, a shocking sight greets us. In the foreground, undulations of the earth create beautiful rolling countryside. But across the valley, outside the park's boundary, an entire hillside has been hacked into ridges from top to bottom. Trees and ground cover are gone, exposing raw rock for hundreds of feet, both horizontally and vertically. In such a pristine setting, with adjacent hillsides so beautiful in their spring growth, the contrast is all the more unnerving. From this gravel pit, part of the mountain has been carted away piecemeal to be used for roads, landscaping, and shopping centers.

Clayton Quarry on Mount Zion, seen from Mitchell Canyon Trail, Mount Diablo.
Photo by Paul Feder, 2005.

Scattering a bit, we each find a boulder to sit against. We plant ourselves in the earth and send down personal taproots, settling in to be here for some time. The sun warms our faces, and the pleasure of it feeds us, sends light into us through our heads, through our entire bodies. Breath flows from sun to the earth's center, back and forth, our bodies the conduits.

A dilemma faces each of us: what realistic positive action or attitude can we take in relation to a gashed hill whose gaping side is not going to reassemble itself? We step back from judgment, focusing instead on what has been revealed to us—a cutaway that speaks of the land we are ordinarily oblivious to, the land on whose surface we walk, dance, and sit; we offer gratitude for a new understanding.

As I believe the others are also doing, I remember the beauty of the flower we spent so long with earlier in the day—the flower that radiated to us its beauty, its health. From my heart where this beauty now resides, I send tendrils of the flower's vivid life to the exposed rock, brushing it with pulses of the flower's life.

The effects of geologic ages are exposed before us, and I let my imagination play out the scenario—materials that rode up from the ocean floor along the oceanic plate and were scraped off by its encounter with the continental plate, pushing the matter up through the process of subduction. When the collision between plates took place, the San Andreas Fault developed to deal with the sideways motion. As compression buckled the land, a massive fold formed. Old ocean floor material became exposed. Softer strata were worn away.[2] The early emergence of the mountain-to-be came about as a melange of metamorphic Franciscan rock pushed up through sedimentary layers. The changes continue, now sped forward by human hands.

Huge portions of the mountain are steeply sloped layers of sandstone. Veins of coal laced the foothills, some mined more than one hundred fifty years ago. Silica sand for glass making, and lower-grade sand for steel casting, were mined at Nortonville and Somersville townsites, not far from where we sit.

Young boys were part of the mines' workforce, children who wriggled through tunnels sometimes no more than eighteen inches high. Remembering, I bear witness to the choices made by human beings, with effects on the land—both positive and negative. Compassion floods through me for the hillside, compassion for the children and the men who worked in the close and dangerous quarters of the coal mines.[3] Pity and anger pop into my mind, eroding momentarily my feelings of peace and compassion. Attention to my breath brings me back; the visceral memories of the way my body felt as I sat with the flowers helps me return to peace. I fill myself again with the images, the physical sensations, the connections with health and well-being, and send them to the hillside.

Undoubtedly, crevices between the stones on the hillside host birds' nests. Birds will drop bits of grass and seeds, beginning the long, long mending of the surfaces. In my mind's eye, on the skin of my arms and face, I feel the memories of fog moving across the valley, dampening the grains of soil and rock, beginning to host the earliest forms of plant life. I send the hillside my encouragement, my faith in the renewal of life, my commitment to make thoughtful decisions about using the earth's energy, my willingness to pay attention to political and economic issues that contribute to decisions to rip the earth in this way.

Most of all, I bear witness to the experiences that the land has endured and do not turn away from its scars. The Dalai Lama reminds us not to turn away from suffering. I send the hillside my loving attention. Instructed hours ago by the flowers, I remember what harmony feels like in my body, renew it as many times as I need to, sending in turn a loving attention to the exposed mountain. I honor the harvested stone carrying to its destination the beauty and strength inherent in its being.

## TRY THIS: Help to heal damaged earth

- Find a site in or near your community that has suffered some devastation, whether through human choice or action or from a natural catastrophe.

- Sit quietly; before you begin to work with the site you've chosen, ground yourself, making a connection with the earth, envisioning roots coming from the base of your spine into the earth, as if you were a tree growing right where you're sitting. Imagine those roots breathing, extensions of your own breath.

- Connect with the universe, imagining branches of your tree extending toward the sky, seeking light, air, and maybe even rain. As you inhale, reach upward with your intention, reaching for that connection; as you exhale, send your breath through the trunk and along the roots into the earth. Let your breath connect you to your presence on the land—this very place, this very person.

- Recall your experience of filling yourself with the beauty of a flower. Let those feelings return to you now.

- Open your eyes and observe the place you've chosen to relate to. Simply see what there is to see, without judgment. Look at it without reference to its function, only seeing what there is to see.

- As you observe it, open your heart and send tendrils of beauty, peace, acceptance, and compassion to the site. Those filaments are threads of what you received earlier through your intention by opening to the natural world.

- Your thoughts may travel to the situations that created the devastation and to its effects felt by other lives. Consider the train of events that followed it and the ways in which the resource was used.

- Witness what you believe to be the motivations of human beings who were involved in the devastation—wealth, power, ignorance, or need. Observe without judgment. Watch the progression of events. Send compassion to all concerned—to the land, to the decision makers, to those who executed the decisions.

- If the devastation is the result of an act of nature, envision the event.
- Watch the power of the element that created it—flood, fire, hurricane.
- Honor the power of the element. Through your imagination, witness its presence in its benign form, as well as its presence as a destroyer.
- Visualize the most appropriate relationship between human beings and that element.
- Consider your own relationship to that element, how you might shift your actions to be in more harmonious relationship to it.
- Choose one change in your own actions that could express a more harmonious relationship with that element. Follow the implications of that choice—the way it would change your life, your relationship with someone in your family or a close friend or coworker.
- Imagine any strain that your choice would make in your own life or in your relationships, and envision how you might handle that.
- When you are complete, open your eyes and acknowledge the gift that's been shared with you by the site you've been visiting.

Later, at our campsite, we sit around the fire pit, talking over coffee.

## PERSONAL JOURNEYS

Sarah: *Ordinarily, when I see something like that gravel pit, first I'm appalled, and then I'm angry at the hit-and-run action—grabbing something from the earth and then leaving it shredded. They walk away, and there it is. How long will it take that place to regenerate? It's like clear-cutting in the forests, or mining in Colorado and leaving rivers running red with toxic waste. But today, I could just be there with it and stay calm. Getting mad doesn't help, and it just makes* me *shredded.*

Ann: *What's even worse to me is to know that I'm part of it. I drive on highways that probably use that gravel. If they use it in drainage pipes, the water from my house uses those channels. It makes me feel totally helpless. I'm part of the culture, and we're all involved in using what those companies take. We use resources without giving it a second thought. Seeing it, at least I'm reminded that's what's happening. Doing what we did, I realize that if I'm part of it, I can be a more conscious part.*

Peggy: *When I come out to be in nature, I'm almost always dealing with lots of demands from work and family. That's just how my life is right now. So I need a place where I can let it all out and not feel responsible for one more thing. But this sequence we did makes me feel like I can go back to my ordinary world with all the demands still there for me and not be so cranky. It's really a challenge to live with this much constant pressure. A gravel pit's not high on my agenda, but being able to be calm when all hell is breaking loose definitely is.*

Marguerite: *I had this weird fantasy that I was waking up the light in the stones, and when that light touched the light inside me, mine began to expand. It was as if we were mating! We were linking, somehow, and out of our contact the renewing plants would come over the centuries that would repair the damage to the natural world. My attention sped up the process.*

## Norns and the Tree of Life

Listening to Marguerite, I remembered an old Norse myth. It's the tale of three sisters whose lifework is the Tree of Life.

> *The Norns, three mysterious sisters whose names translate as Becoming, Being, and That-which-is-to-be, wandered into the kingdom of Asgard. There they came upon a tall and ancient ash, the Tree of Life. Every form of life is nourished by the magical tree, and the women saw that it was in distress. It was rotting; all day every day, creatures scrambled up and down the trunk, poked holes in it, tore its bark, and broke its limbs.*
>
> *Near the tree, the sisters discovered a well—the well of Fate—lined with a magical white clay. Next to it was a cave, where the women settled in to live. Every day they brought the well's special waters to the tree, scooped up the powerful clay and spread it over the tree to guard and heal it.*
>
> *Each day, after tending the tree, they sat to spin the threads of life and death. People came from near and far to seek their advice and council, and to learn how to make the threads of their lives as long as possible. To this very day, the Norns care for the Tree of Life; without their unceasing attention, the Tree would cease to live.*[4]

I suddenly feel like a daughter of the Norns. They search out a miraculous well whose waters help to heal the Tree of Life. My friends and I poke about in the gravelly soil of Mount Diablo and search among the flowers for the heal-ing magic of natural beauty. The Norns observe the wounds to the Tree of Life and bring the healing clay to its roots. We too have come to a wounded branch on the Tree of Life with a magic clay in the form of our involvement with nature's power to heal. We come in hopes that our efforts will also help to sus-tain the Tree of Life.

## Owning Our Projections

Several hours later, we cross the road to a hillside field facing west. As the drama of sunset unfolds, lights from towns along the bay begin to wink in the valley below. We mull over the stigma of the mountain's name. Two hundred years ago, the Chupcan people were among the East Bay Indians who resisted missionization. In one incident, Spanish soldiers believed they had trapped a group of them in a willow thicket several miles from the mountain. During the night, the Chupcan made a daring escape across the Carquinez Straits.

Confounded and embarrassed, the soldiers claimed the Indians could only have escaped with the help of the devil. The thicket, from that time, became associated with the devil. Settlers later transferred the name *Diablo* to the near-by mountain.

Nothing could be farther from the mountain's earlier connotation. The few written fragments of Indian accounts suggest that Mount Diablo was central to the physical and symbolic world of many groups that could view it from their territory. Stories from south-central California describe the earth as cre-ated from a world covered by water. In one version, two islands (Mount Diablo and Reeds' Peak) stand above the water; the creator Coyote and his assistant, Eagle, made Indian people and the world.[5] How did the people carry the ancient knowledge that we now know to be true—that the entire East Bay was once a young sea, itself preceded by an older, ancestral ocean?[6]

In the *kuksuyu*, described as the most sacred and elaborate ceremony of the Central Sierra Miwok, a song is performed during which a dancer enacts an emergence from Mount Diablo: "When they come to possess supernatural power, they do this kind of a dance…." The mountain was a place for healing both the living and the dead. The Southern Maidu regarded Mount Diablo as the place where the dead had to come for purification before entering the land of the dead.

Among the Pomos, medicine people held ceremonies on the mountain. The Wintun people went to Diablo to pray and talk to the Spirit. It is their sacred mountain. The Nisenan from the Auburn area called it Dog Mountain because it was the source of dogs that they caught and traded.[7]

The sunlight fades, and we let the softness of evening overtake us. As we talk about the projections of the Spanish that resulted in such a negative name for the mountain, the story leads us to consider our own projections. Sometimes we hold opinions or act in ways that we ourselves fear or dislike; we may have impulses that are not in keeping with our values. Attempting to divorce ourselves from those opinions or impulses, we may project them, attribute them to someone else.

We decide to do a fire ceremony, entwining our experiences of projection with those of the mountain. Before it's totally dark, we separate and look for small sticks. Preparing the sticks as offerings for the fire becomes a meditation of its own. Spending quiet time with them, we decorate them with symbols of the parts of ourselves that we dislike and would like to dissociate from. We think about people who are difficult for us to deal with because they embody the traits that help us identify our own versions. As we decorate the sticks, they receive and hold our projections. Some people carve or write words or symbols on them. Some attach a strand of hair, ribbon, plant material, or whatever they find to represent their projections. Quietly we prepare for the transformation offered by the fire ceremony, for the opportunity to relate once again to the mountain as a holy and healing place.

## Celebrating Fire

After dinner, we prepare a fire in the pit—a small tribute to a very old ceremonial custom. As we carefully lay the wood, we recall that for the indigenous people of California, the controlled use of fire was key to maintaining balance in the ecosystem.[8] For more than three thousand years, they shaped the landscape with fire. Certain seeds that need drought-like conditions to sprout were scattered after a fire, where they lay dormant until cyclic droughts arose.

Fire was tailored to each type of environment. Grassland, chaparral, and forest fires each had their specific purposes. Acorn harvests were improved by reducing ground-level competition through regular burns. Fire enhanced hunting and helped to control pestilence. Year after year, fire management supported the production of favorite wildflower seeds and bulbs, and twigs for basketry.[9]

The importance of burning was so misunderstood by Europeans that bans against fires were among the first California laws enacted by Europeans to govern the Native Americans. Only recently, after massive forest fires burned so much of Yellowstone Park, has the importance of burning begun to be understood, although it still is not used with the refinement of the Native American practices. The countryside during their occupation here was landscaped as ours is today but with different standards and intentions.

Tonight the air is chilly, and the heat of our small fire is welcome. Before we begin our fire ceremony, we rattle for a while, herding together our scattered thoughts, humming softly, until we feel quite present with one another and the fire. We call in the elements of the four directions. Earth, air, fire, and water are honored for their contributions to every event of our lives. Addressing them, we create sacred space. Speaking to the mountain itself, we ask its Spirit to be with us. We pull close to the fire, and each person shares about the projection she wants to take back. Listening, we recognize threads of our own inclinations in each other's stories. We make no suggestions, don't try to "fix" anyone. We simply bear witness.

When everyone has had a chance to speak, we begin to rattle again, softly singing a song to the fire. As each person is ready, she goes to the fire and kneels for a few moments. Silently or aloud, she offers her projection to the fire, asking that the energy consumed by the projection be released for use in a different form. Some of us mention or think of a specific way we want to use the energy—creating some project or shaping a different attitude toward themselves or others. We are freeing ourselves from the limitations of projections for the sake of our capacity to grow.

When everyone has finished, we stop rattling and sit companionably in the quiet, the fire crackling, devouring our old habits of thinking and acting. After a time, some of us are ready for sleep. Reminding those who stay up to be sure the fire is out or well contained, I head for bed. I'm asleep in minutes.

Some time later, I'm awakened by an urgent voice, "Wake up! Get up *now!*" I rise immediately and find everyone else still asleep. The wind is so strong that tent poles are bending. Sparks from the wind-flamed campfire are flying all around the camp. Alarmed, I call to the others. We stamp out the embers, extending our search to the far edges of our campsite to make sure we've found them all. We totally smother the fire and then secure our tents more firmly. We stand in the open for a few moments, still shocked and dazed. As our adrenalin subsides, we return to the welcome protection of our tents.

Who called? Was it the subliminal popping sound of the fire, or the voice of the mountain? I don't know. But I returned to my sleeping bag bowing to the powers of nature that surround us, day and night.

It could have been a disaster. The mountain is often closed to visitors when fire danger is extreme. Even though the forests held dampness from recent rains, the scare was a message to be mindful and to respect the power of fire and wind to consume and transform. Fire, or a fire ceremony, is not to be treated casually.

**TRY THIS: Prepare a projection offering for a fire ceremony**

- Find a stick that will help you explore a personal projection—one that might have some characteristic that reminds you of a projection you want to transform.

- Tell the stick what you're doing, how you intend to use it as part of your process. Ask if it is agreeable to the plan.

- Once you've found the appropriate stick, make an offering of cornmeal. Sprinkle it over the surface of the stick and the environment that was its home.

- Sit quietly. Relax and allow your attention to become a full-body response. Let the gaze of your eyes soften. Begin to explore the stick with your fingers, feeling the textures, the protrusions, its unique qualities. Use all your senses—smell it, touch it, see it, taste it.

- Let the stick evoke your recollections of a projection, of the persons, events, and contexts related to it. Consider the way the projection is out of line with your own standards or expectations of yourself.

- Continue to explore the stick with your fingers, allowing it to bring up whatever you need to know about this projection. Where did the standards come from? Are they truly your own or are you playing out instructions from parents, teachers, or some other source? Is this a reflection of some feeling of inadequacy?

- Decide whether the standards fit for you at this point in time. Let the stick communicate with you about your projection; be sensitive to whatever your body feels, whatever your heart knows.

- Anchor your understandings, your thoughts, your feelings by marking the stick in some way as you meditate with it—carving some symbol onto it, writing something on it, tying a thread or a hair around it, rubbing it with earth, singing into it—whatever you're inspired to do to connect the stick with your intentions.

- Thank the stick for its help and participation in your process.

Modern living takes us very far from direct contact with the minerals, trees, and other resources that eventually come into our lives in very modified forms. But we're winding our way back, acknowledging that the stick we prepare for the fire is alive, a being in its own right, that it has its own capacity to interact with us.

The stick becomes a partner in a process of alignment with the web of life. When we create a fire ceremony, we will be transforming the life-form of the stick. Through our intent, it can become a vehicle for our own transformation. Thanking it, relating to it as a living part of the environment, helps our consciousness to expand to thoughts of all the tools in our lives and their source in the earth.

## TRY THIS: Deepen connections to the power of fire

- One person takes on the role of guardian of the fire. Her responsibility is to maintain a focused relationship with the fire throughout the ceremony. She maintains a relationship with fire as a living being, feeding it and caring for it to maintain its vitality.

- With full attention, she builds and lights the fire.

- All participants rattle, chant, or sing, until everyone is fully involved in the ceremony.

- Invite the four elements necessary for life to attend the ceremony—air in the east, fire in the south, water in the west, and earth in the north. (The connotations of elements with directions may be different in different groups; it is only necessary that all the elements be represented.)

- Invite the Spirit of Place to be present and part of the circle.

- Seat yourselves around the fire. Rattle together, creating a sound that consciously connects everyone in the group. You are holding the space of transformation for one another.

- One at a time, as each person is inspired, take turns kneeling close to the fire, making an intimate connection with it.

- Touch the offering you created to your belly as you focus on how your actions will be different after surrendering the projection.

- Touch the stick to your heart, as you focus on the feelings and emotions that you are transforming—what they have been, what you want them to be.

- Touch the stick to your forehead, symbol of your thoughts and mental images of what has been and what will be.

- Place the stick in the fire, asking the fire to be fed by your offering, asking it to transform the projection and make its energy available to you in a new and more useful form.

- Watch the fire consume the stick as you envision your personal trans-formation taking place.
- As each person returns to the circle, she continues to focus on holding the transformative space for each of the others.
- When everyone has had a turn and the fire has died down, thank the Spirit of Place for being present.
- Thank the four elements and their part in the ceremony—earth for the material form of the stick, fire for its active role, air for the oxygen it contributed to the flame, water for its part in the growth of the stick.
- Feel the energy of the circle and respond in whatever way seems appro-priate. It may be a quiet time, or it may be a joyous time of feasting, dancing, or sharing.
- Put the fire to bed. Make sure it's tucked in well!

We drag ourselves from our sleeping bags before sunrise after a night's sleep that seems too short for some. Fog swirls slowly through the oak grove of our camping area, and we crawl from our tents into the time warp of a scene from Brigadoon. Acorns and drops of moisture punctuate the stillness as they fall from the tree branches onto the tents.

As the other women collect themselves, I walk among the oaks. Their shapes remind me of mimes striking a pose and staying very still for minutes at a time. Erosion has carried away the soil from around the base of the biggest tree in this grove. Perched on a rise above a steep hillside, the thick gnarled roots grip the ground fiercely, spreading horizontally. The roots create bowls holding fresh water to drink or to mirror the faces of those who bend to look closely.

## Summit Sunrise: Weaving the Web of Mountain Powers

Piling into cars, we drive to the top of the mountain. Ten minutes later, our caravan parks in the lot beneath the stone Summit Building. The wind has picked up. Grabbing mittens and hats, we pull our jackets tightly around us and quickly climb the winding stairs to the building whose small enclosure provides a sheltered 360-degree view.

Relatively speaking, Mount Diablo is not a tall mountain—only 3,849 feet high. But the peak is key to geographical surveys in California, for which it provides the base meridian. Because it's surrounded by low rolling hills and broad, flat valleys, it's sometimes possible to see almost two hundred miles in every direction. From the summit on very clear days, the Farallon Islands might be seen to the west, 25 miles past the Golden Gate. Between the

Farallons and the peak, the view includes the East Bay hills, the Santa Cruz Mountains, San Francisco Bay, San Pablo Bay, and Mount Tamalpais. To the south, 4,200-foot Mount Hamilton is often visible. Mount Lassen to the north, Mount Whitney to the east, and—to a knowledgeable viewer—even Half Dome in Yosemite are occasionally visible. On the best of days, it's said that one can see more than forty thousand square miles from the summit.

Today, tule fog roams some of the valleys to the east. A lavender curtain nudges away the last of the star-studded darkness; pale rose begins to replace it. As sunrise approaches, the interplay between fog and the coming sun fills the valleys with red mist. Sky, hills, and valleys are variations on a constantly shifting coral-colored theme. Red swells higher and higher. When I turn around, I expect to see my friends enveloped in fiery shades, too. The shades of red deepen, successive valleys fill with flaming mist. For twenty minutes, all of California is on fire with the sunrise.

In many cultures, a repeated image of a net or web reflects the interconnectedness of all life. In the Hopi or Navajo tradition, Spider Woman spins her web.[10] In Indian mythology, Indra's palace is covered with a net in which every intersection is marked by a jewel reflecting everything that exists at every other intersection.[11] The Norns of Northern Europe spin the threads of fate, weaving together the actions of past, present, and future.[12] In South America, the Kogi envision the earth as a huge loom upon which the fabric of life is maintained by the ways in which human beings fulfill their responsibility for all life.[13]

As we look around us at the sacred places we've visited and those yet to come, the image of the weaving takes on immediacy and vividness. Our lives, and all the life-forms we're meeting as we visit these sacred places, are part of the web. We are learning to honor them and to discover new relationships with them.

Softly we start to hum and then begin spontaneously to call out the names of the mountains, the birds, plants, and animals we've seen at each of the sites, honoring them as they waken in the dawn light we are sharing. As the flaming sky spreads a mantle of color everywhere in celebration of the coming day, the animal names weave together, our voices rise and fall, and sound fills the air around us. Not only are all our contemporary beings with us but also the memories preserved by the different cultural myths. The Norns are with us, as are Indra, Spider Woman, and the Kogi Mamas. Our web of life extends through time and space.

Finally, the sun itself comes forward. Our voices quiet, the brilliant sky eases into a familiar blue, leaving the fireworks to the sun itself, and the day has begun.

Several hundred feet below the summit, Devil's Elbow—a red chert protrusion that's part of the Franciscan Formation—juts out facing south. It looks like a wonderful place to deposit our gift of the crystal fragment to the mountain. A trail descends from the summit parking lot, but in order to catch the special morning light we drive to a lower trailhead that also leads to Devil's Elbow. The wind is blowing fiercely, and our inclination is to hurry along, but the steep trail has many loose rocks, so we cautiously temper the pace.

When we reach the formation, we scatter among several perches the Elbow provides to continue watching the marvelous new light of day melting into the folds of valleys below us, rolling hills, trees, and open meadows unmarred by habitation. Strong wind in our faces also heralds the day's beginning, and before long, it drives us to find the special niche to secret the tiny crystal from view. Forming a circle in a slightly more sheltered spot several feet from Devil's Elbow, we pass the crystal among us, imbuing it with our pleasures on the mountain as it goes from hand to hand. Carol tucks it into a deep crevice in the stone.

## Joining a River of Stones

As we retrace our steps along the path, we pause at a river of stones that flows near Diablo's peak and runs on down the mountain. I doubt that any water other than rainwater has ever caressed those stones; they cascade recklessly through boulders and down through a narrow ravine. To my eyes, the stones flow of their own accord, no longer nesting on the steep slope. Their journey is so sporadic that I seldom see any movement other than that begun by my own footsteps.

Now, in this moment when I stand at the edge of their flow, I half-close my eyes and imagine jumping into the stream. In my imagination, I make the journey as one of them. I fling myself into the path of descent—jumping off the high places and feeling the exhilaration of parting from my mother, Earth, who patiently and knowingly waits my return, gravity pulling me toward her.

Tumbling, tumbling, the stones pummel my rough edges as we glissade together down the steep slope of the mountain. Not silent, the stones careen together—and as they touch one another, they rebound, as if shocked to encounter one another. They bounce on down the mountain until they find a resting place, halting for a few hundred or thousand years. The mountain reshapes itself. Greenstone and quartz-laced chert color the earth. The stone river heaves with the breath of the earth itself—rising and falling, the stones lifting and tumbling as she breathes through the eons of her existence.

The stones stay in place for a while, holding the memories of the moisture they knew when they were once covered by a sea, remembering the delicious wetness that bathed them, stones and water forever together in spirit. When it is bidden, the microscopic life suspended on the stones over the centuries comes to life. The brilliant sun touches the stones with fingers of light and heat, rain nourishes the cells of life, and the stones' microscopic plant companions are launched into a journey. The stones and the water, the substantial and the fluid, yin and yang, forever woven together. There the mystery continues to unfold; all the secret cells of life held by the minerals of the stone begin to reveal themselves, and infinitesimal plants begin to blanket the stone river.

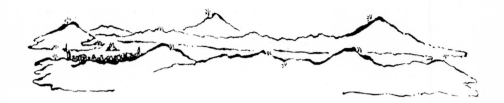

## Chapter Five

# MOUNT HAMILTON: Exploring Our Space in the Universe

It's just before sunrise on Mt. Hamilton, and the temperature of the air is inviting. Later, waves of heat will push us into inertia, so we let nature's tune guide our actions in the moment and drive the short distance from our camping spot at Joseph Grant County Park to Grant Lake. We walk to the lake's edge. A single blue heron, messenger from a rookery in a nearby eucalyptus grove, quietly and intently stalks the reeds at the edge of the lake for breakfast. Smaller birds begin their own morning rituals of territorial calls and food searches in a small group of live oaks near shore. Audubon Society members have placed boxes in the trees, initially to encourage bluebird nesting. Now different varieties of birds use them in sequence. When the bluebird fledglings depart, ash-throated flycatchers or other cavity nesters move in.

The stillness of the morning is broken only by the swooping flight of swallows, the call of a red-winged blackbird, and the quick flash of an oriole's gold-orange breast. The long-legged heron, well camouflaged with its gray-blue plumage, takes a single solemn step among the plants at the water's edge.

## A Heron Walk: Elegant Concentration

About fifteen years ago, the city of Palo Alto held a wetlands ceremony. In preparation, a group of friends and I used an Innuit shamanic practice—we petitioned songs to sing from the world of Spirit on behalf of the birds and animals of the wetlands. We sat in total darkness and asked those we sought to come to us, to send us songs to honor them.

We rattled in silence until someone was moved to begin singing. That person sang over and over the song that had come to her, and we joined in as soon as we could. We recorded each song on a tape recorder and then began to rattle again, waiting for the next song to come. The heron's song was so powerful that it floats into my mind even now, its simplicity and haunting pauses a musical reflection of the sparse movements we're watching here.

> "Quietly standing...Watch the water.
> Quietly standing...Heron."

Moving toward the water, we begin to match the heron's composed progression; it's a long time between the steps it takes, and if we were to move that slowly, we'd be all morning walking the length of the small lake. Instead, we take a step and pause for a few moments, modeling our watchfulness of the heron after its own attentive search for food. Inch by inch, our individual paces slowly move us apart from one another as we find separate vantage points from which to watch the bird at the water's edge. Moving along to find our spots, we keep our eyes on the heron.

The tall bird has an advantage over our technique for observing; the heron's eyes angle downward so that it can always watch the water.[1] Skinny long legs keep the heron's feathery body out of the water. Sometimes it stands on one leg, totally balanced, concentration undisturbed. We continue to watch it as we move, taking care that our steps don't alarm the beautiful bird into taking flight.

The "heron walk" offers us a very physical lesson in concentration. Our breathing slows, and we begin to relate our movements to our breath, each step one breath. Our gestures are more conscious and sparse, and we narrow our focus of attention. The twittering birds seem far away; when the movement from another person registers slightly, it, too, is simply background. We experiment with what we need to do to approximate the heron's attentiveness and balance.

## TRY THIS: Take a heron walk, an experiment in elegant concentration

- Visit Grant Lake at Mount Hamilton. When you spot a blue heron standing in the shallows, become very still, so that you don't startle it into flight.

- Notice how long the bird stands perfectly still between movements.

- Feel your own connection with the ground; wiggle your toes inside your shoes. Be aware of the way your feet are relating to the earth, to your shoes and socks.

- Imagine the long bare toes of the heron, sinking into the mud, helping it to stay balanced in her slippery domain.

- As you think of the heron getting a purchase on the precarious mud or plants, let your own toes and feet relax, finding their relationship to your shoes and to the earth beneath you. Feel the relationship between your foot, the sock, the shoe, the earth—a unit that holds you upright.

- Shift your weight to one foot; as you do so, feel the changes in the muscles of your calves, the ligaments around your knee, the shifting of your pelvis and spine.

- When you see the heron pick up a foot, very slowly pick up one of your own feet. Feel your weight completely supported by the other leg and foot.

- Notice how the heron's curving neck and head move, extending forward as it steps.

- Breathing, send an exhalation down through your torso, your hip, your leg, your foot, and into the ground.

- As you begin to move forward, be aware of where in your body the movement originates.

- Take a very slow, small step forward, putting your foot down so that your balance is maintained throughout the movement.

- Notice how your shoulders and torso feel. If you find yourself tense, take a few breaths.

- Repeat the process, staying relaxed and focused. Notice any changes in your experience. Continue very slowly, without the need to arrive anywhere. Simply own your body and its movements. Concentrate on this moment, this particular place.

The bird never strays from its graceful motion. The neck held in an S-shaped curve reminds me of a hunter with a weapon drawn back. When ready, the heron spears a frog or a fish in a lightning-quick extension of its neck and beak. Sometimes it flips the catch into the air, positioning it as accurately as a tossed Frisbee, then gulps the morsel down as it falls back into its waiting mouth.

After some time, the heron takes flight, the enormous wings moving very slowly. A small fish dangles from its mouth. As the huge bird approaches the rookery, its feet dangle behind it like rudders, turning its flight toward a rickety-looking nest. The heron slows its flight, altering the movement of its wings to push air forward. Its skinny legs would not fare very well in a rapid approach,[2] and this fluttered reversal of wing motion cushions its landing.

After a time, we gather under the shade of an oak tree to compare notes about our experience.

## PERSONAL JOURNEYS

Kayla: *I'm astonished at how hard it is to stand on one foot! And how many muscles are involved to make the shift from one foot to another! My whole body was working, doing this very simple thing. I think of hiking as related to how strong or out of shape the muscles of my legs are. But to focus this way shows me that anything you're doing, you're doing with your whole body. It makes me think that maybe I could take the strain out of my legs if I paid more attention to another part of my body that's involved. At least it would distract me from an aching muscle!*

Ann: *I know there's a whole community of herons up in the eucalyptus trees, but here's this one, all alone, doing its own thing. That's hard for me to do; when I'm with other people, I'm always watching how someone else is doing whatever we're doing together. That bird wasn't being influenced by anything, just focused on what it was doing. I started to feel like I must have Attention Deficit Disorder in my ordinary life. That bird definitely showed me a thing or two about concentrating.*

Debbie: *I'm noticing something that must have been going on all this time, but it's only now that we're sitting and relaxing that I'm aware of it. It's hard to believe there are so many small birds in this same oak tree. Maybe it's because there aren't very many trees on these hills, and they're all bunched together, or maybe it's because there are a lot of insects in the air near the lake, and that brings a lot of birds here. Think of the number of life cycles being played out near the lake that we don't even notice when we're next to it. But the heron exists because the lives of the water critters are living their lives out here, too. They're all connected.*

Once a lagoon, the now dammed Grant Lake is lined with blue-green reeds, slender pink columned blossoms of Water Lady's Thumb, and other shoreline plants. Nestled among the low-rolling hills, the lake is an echo of an ancient sea whose presence powerfully shaped this land. That sea had its own watery predecessor.

## "Melted-Ice-Cream Topography": Supporting Transformation

The ocean we now know as the Pacific once extended over the entire East Bay—"just fish-filled, clam-filtered salt water," says writer Christine Colasurdo.[3] Then, about thirteen million years ago, the movement of tectonic plates that even now continues to shape the California landscape boosted the land upward, and islands began to appear. Eventually, through the relentless pressure of the Pacific Plate against the North American Plate, the Coast Range came into being. When the plate motion changed slightly about three million years ago, the added compression uplifted and folded the East Bay hills.

An inland sea persisted in the area. As sediments eroded from the land that appeared above water level, they slumped onto the floor of the sea, forming sandstones and mudstones.[4] Geologists refer to the phenomenon as "melted-ice-cream topography," and even though the sea is gone, the hills continue to "melt" in heavy rains.

The silhouette of the hills created in this fashion looks deceptively gentle. In the light of early morning or late afternoon, their sensuous appearance tempts you to feel as if you could stroke the toasted grasses on the hills as you would the soft fur of a tawny cat. But overland hiking would soon disabuse you of any sense of a benign landscape, as you would quickly find the terrain to be much more challenging than it appears.

In 1776, Juan Bautista de Anza, accompanied by an expedition that included Fray Pedro Font, discovered the challenges of the topography for himself. Trying to return to Monterey from the site they had chosen for San Francisco, they thought to take a shortcut through the unexplored mountains they saw to the south. It appeared to be a simple day's journey, but once they were well on their way, it became clear that it was very inhospitable country—"very broken," in Font's words. The arduous trip was much longer and more difficult than expected, so much so that they called the ridgelands "Mountains of the Joke."[5]

Our hike brings us to a vista of hills that appear rounded and soft, just as they must have seemed to de Anza. We make ourselves comfortable and survey the view. Images of the events of the ancient past that shaped the land shift kaleidoscopically in our minds, finally returning us to the fragrant toast-brown California hills in front of us. However cataclysmic the events that shaped the terrain, it's fine to be here now. Lying on our backs, everyone makes closer contact with the earth—just being present with the sun, the drifting clouds, an occasional bird soaring by. The longer we lie here, the more relaxed and open to the moment we become.

In the slow-moving warmth of the day, I propose that we use the land's experience of change to inform an exploration of personal change. Perhaps something that's taken place needs to be honored or more fully accepted; maybe something in our present lives needs to shift. We agree to journey in our mind's eye to the essence of this land, the essence that holds the wisdom of the transformations that have taken place here. Afterward, we share our experiences.

## PERSONAL JOURNEYS

Sarah: *I asked for help in shifting out of a stuck place I'm in. I want to become a nurse. All my life, that's been my desire, but I had children very early. My daughter is handicapped, and I had to deal with that for years. Even though she's on her own, I still worry. Every time I get ready to go forward with my own plans, something happens that takes my attention, and my plans are down the tubes. I always feel like I'm dangling over a cliff edge, and let go to help her, all the time that I'm screaming to myself, "No, no, no!" Today I felt like I was looking down from a high mountain. It was like seeing a movie; I saw the changes that have happened to her—her progress and her setbacks—nothing new to me, but somehow I got some distance that I never had before. I saw my own hanging on, trying to earn the Good Mother Award of the Year, and how much my rushing to her rescue is for my own image of myself. I know I'll respond to her again, but I don't think I'll give myself away.*

## TRY THIS: Let the melted-ice-cream topography support a transformation or honor a shift

- Find a slope that has succumbed to the topography. The slump may be ancient, or it may bear evidence of a more recent slide induced by the rain.
- Choose someone in the group to drum for the journey's continuity.
- Lie down with others in the group, making yourselves comfortable.
- Look at the land, at the clouds moving by. Allow yourself to relax.
- Feel the slope of the hillside and let your body relax against it.
- Close your eyes and begin to breathe slowly and evenly.
- Hold in your mind the situation that you would like to shift, or a shift that has happened to you that you'd like to make peace with.
- Explore your personal shift by following the sound of the drum. Ask your personal guide to take you to the spirit of transformation at this place.

- Observe any images and their changes; listen to sounds, words, or songs.
- Any time you feel bewildered by what you see or hear, thank the messenger and ask for clarification or more information.
- As the drum beat changes tempo, signaling that it is time to return, know that you have received whatever you need at this time. You might not be consciously aware of what has been given to you, but clarity can come through your dreams or be triggered as you explore what you do remember.
- Write down the details of your experience.

## A Gathering Place in Community

Human communities radiate from all the sites we've visited in our circling of the bay. But the greater Mount Hamilton Wilderness divides the communities just to its east and west, and plays a unique role in defining them. Mount Hamilton is part of an extended ridge running north and south, and parallels the southern tip of the San Francisco Bay Area. To the west is the area referred to as "the flatlands" by Hamilton Wilderness residents. It's the location of the biggest transformation in California population since the Gold Rush. Then, as now, people flocked to California seeking their fortunes. Silicon Valley and the communities that have grown up around San Francisco Bay have created an inflow of humanity that enfolds cultures and traditions from all over the world. In the culture created by the technological boom, many people work virtually every daylight hour and often into the night. The nature of community and of family interactions is deeply stressed.

By contrast, to the east of the ridge you find "the backcountry," the San Antone and San Geronimo Valleys. Ranchland predominates, and the people who live here often recount family history going back generations on the same land. Many backcountry residents believe that the twisting road with its endless hairpin turns leading from the west side to the summit of Mount Hamilton is a barrier protecting their privacy and lifestyle. Beyond the ranches stretches the fertile Central Valley, where farmers grow a huge amount of produce distributed throughout the United States.

For years state and local officials considered building a freeway that would cut through Mount Hamilton to connect the Central Valley, where housing is less expensive, to Silicon Valley, where jobs are more plentiful. Meanwhile, the two worlds divided by the crest of the mountains struggle with the same problems: expanded communication, easier transportation, and extreme wealth and material success that have no corresponding growth in cultural wisdom to guide their enfoldment into the broader culture.

Passions run high on both sides of the freeway issue. It comes under discussion at the Mount Hamilton Wilderness Association, in individual homes, and also at the Junction Café. The Junction Café is the social centerpiece of the valleys to the east of the summit. Here, three boars' heads decorate the walls, complete with sunglasses and red, white, and blue bow ties. The store is an oasis in time and in the hot rolling oak savanna of the San Antone Valley.

It's cool and rather dark inside, a relief from the bright sunshine that bakes the land outdoors. The wall to the right of the front door is a bookcase filled with hundreds of *National Geographic* magazines and porcelain figurines of prancing animals and costumed children. The hours of the family-run café are dictated by its flow of humanity, comprised of a comfortable community of ranching friends, cyclers, and Sunday drivers taking a break from their explorations of the winding roads. Coffee floats slide down easily as we dawdle and listen to the gossip. Friends tease one another and pass opinions back and forth about the latest political crisis.

## TRY THIS: Write about the hangouts in your community

- Begin with a phrase that names the place near your work or home where you spend leisure time: "I like to go to...and [do]..." The place you choose may be a gym, a church, a coffee shop, an environmental or political organization—any place that you return to often.

- For fifteen minutes, write about it without stopping. Write anything that comes to mind, even if you think it's not relevant. If you run out of things to say, write the phrase again ("I like to go to...") and continue to write.

- Even if you are repeating yourself, don't stop writing.

- Where is that place?

- What do you do there?

- How does it make you feel about yourself? Your community?

- What does it reinforce in you or in your life? Does that satisfy you?

- Is there an in-group you are a part of? How do you feel about being either in or out?

- What is the power of this place in your life?

## Human Imprints

Some people have the distinction, unusual in California, of having lived their entire lives in the same place, in this case the San Antone Valley. When I come to the valley to visit, ninety-five-year-old Helen Hurner sits on the porch of her streamside home reading Fannie Flagg for her book club. In the front yard, a sprinkler slowly revolves on a small patch of green grass bordered by bright flowers. Only within the last five years, when a stroke "set her back a bit," has she stopped riding horses.

Helen's parents had five girls and only one boy, much to the disappoint-ment of Helen's father, who had wished for more sons. Ranching was a passion Helen couldn't *not* pursue, and from childhood she relentlessly dogged her father's footsteps. Her blue eyes sparkle, and she breaks into a slow grin as she describes how thrilled she was when her father finally admitted that girls were just as good as boys.

Helen's story unfolded very differently from that of Sada Coe, whose father Henry also had a ranch in the Mount Hamilton Wilderness. Sada spent many years of her life on the land; she expressed her love for it not only through ranching activities but also through writing a number of books, both prose and poetry.

Sada ran Pine Ridge Ranch alone for a number of years. However, when her father died, he left the ranch to her brother, on the premise that ranching was too hard on a single woman. Her brother sold it to a land and cattle company. After a short time Sada bought it back, operating it again as a successful cattle ranch until she donated it to Santa Clara County to be preserved as a memo-rial to her father and other early cattle pioneers.[6]

During a springtime visit to the ranch, I sit with friends among acres of wildflowers, pondering the pain Sada must have experienced, her courage and positive attitude. What was her secret? How did she avoid bitterness? I'm curi-ous about how she came to hold so positive an attitude after having been passed over by her father for the ownership of the ranch. She was clearly a woman who respected herself and was able to forgive.

We share personal stories of others' beliefs about what is right for us, about how our lives should be played out. We reflect on how we first reacted to those attitudes, how they affected the course of our lives and our feelings about our-selves. We consider the intentions and motivations of those people who were so important in our lives and let surface any unfinished business with them.

After we hear one another out, we write letters to those people in our past. With the perspective of time, with the freedom to follow our own paths, we let them know through the letters what we now understand about them and about ourselves. Afterward, we burn the letters in an abalone shell. As the flames curl upward, we forgive ourselves for inappropriate reactions that may have come from our needs to defend ourselves without having the tools to do so effectively. We accept the well-intentioned motivations and release the effects of their controlling intrusions.

Heaving big sighs, we lie back in the field, filling our vision with the blues, purples, and yellows of wildflowers against the blue sky. Breathing deeply, we are filled with the peace of forgiveness.

## PERSONAL JOURNEYS

Marguerite: *My mother was my biggest emotional supporter. She didn't graduate from high school, but she encouraged me to go to college, even though she couldn't help me financially. I lived at home while I went to college. But when I wanted to get married before graduate school, my mother started drinking heavily. She didn't like my husband-to-be, and as it turned out, she was right about him. My life was hell for a long time, and I had a lot to deal with because of him. But I think if I hadn't gone through it all, I would have continued to be a "good girl" on the outside and wouldn't have found a path to my own free personality. I wish that she could know that I now realize the roadblocks I created for myself, but that so much of what she taught me about life was the very stuff that pulled me through. What I had to cope with made me a more real person, more true to myself rather than accommodating to expectations.*

## TRY THIS: Let go of someone else's blueprint for your life

- Close your eyes and let your mind drift toward someone who had or has a plan for your life. It may be a parent long gone, a teacher, a spouse, even a child. It may be someone living or dead, an ancestor or a mentor/model.

- Visualize the way their plan for you is or was expressed. Was it through disapproval of something you were already doing? Was it through encouragement of something you felt too timid to take on?

- Were there assumptions about worthwhile or appropriate ways to be?

- Remember your efforts to meet or to resist those goals. In what ways were they useful? In what ways were you unable or unwilling to work toward them?

- How did it affect you to either work toward them or turn away from them?

- Allow yourself to consider how others' plans for your life reflected the life experiences or unmet needs of the person holding those expectations of you.

- If it is appropriate, honor the wisdom that you were unable or unwilling to follow. Take the portion that has value to you, and from its seeds, formulate your own goal.

- If the goals imposed on you don't fit your own life path, acknowledge the unmet needs in the other person or the good intentions he or she held for you in trying to encourage your behavior.

- When you open your eyes, write down the other person's goal for you on a piece of paper. Write anything you might have said if you had possessed then the perspective you have now. Include any other communication about your relationship, or anything else of importance.

- Tear the paper into many small pieces and burn them.

- Let the smoke carry your acknowledgment of the person's good intentions and the communication of the goals that are more appropriate for you.

## Grand and Unusual Legacies

On the west side of Mount Hamilton, at its base, lies the 9,522-acre Joseph D. Grant Park, the largest regional park in Santa Clara County. Part of a Mexican land grant in 1839, it eventually made its way into the hands of Joseph D. Grant.[7] Grant was influential in California conservation, one of the founders of the environmental group Save the Redwoods.

The qualities that made him such a powerful person in political and economic realms did not serve as well in creating a happy family. Grant was a man who didn't like to be crossed. He once burned down the house of one of his daughters in an effort to eliminate her wild entertaining.[8] When his only son eloped rather than marry the woman Grant had chosen for him, he had his son kidnapped, then bought off the new bride and sent his son to England to marry a woman of Grant's choosing.

After ninety years of family ownership, Grant's land was purchased by Santa Clara County. Because of its unique habitat, a wildlife management program was instituted on the land to reestablish the threatened tule elk population.[9] It's not a program that is universally appreciated, however. Much of Mount Hamilton is still privately owned, and all the elk have wandered off onto private property; none remain in the park. Some ranchers have been angered by the grazing competition between the elk and their cattle. The program feels to them like a personal assault, part of a campaign to get the ranchers off the land.

James Lick had a different and equally powerful impact on the use of Mount Hamilton's unique geographical position. Lick came to San Francisco days before the discovery of gold at Sutter's Mill. A lifelong eccentric, he intended at one time to build a pyramid in San Francisco as a memorial to himself and his family. Someone convinced him instead to accomplish the purpose of a memorial by building the world's greatest telescope at the summit of Hamilton, a project he was involved in until the time of his death.

At the time of the decision about where to locate the telescope, observatories were usually built in cities. But cities became less and less viable locations as outdoor streetlights and pollution became more widespread. At that time, visibility on Mount Hamilton was pristine, and so it became the chosen location. With not so much as a trail to the summit, a challenging road construction project was undertaken to transport heavy and very delicate equipment by horse and wagon.[10]

Today, as we wind our way up the road, eight policemen on motorcycles accompany us part of the way, no doubt improving their motorcycle proficiency on the curvy roads. The serendipitous escort passes us by. We take our time, enjoying a magnificent view of the valley. Smaller ridges and peaks below poke through the sparkling morning fog. Ahead, the two gleaming white hemispheres of the observatories weave in and out of our view.

Lick Observatory, built in the 1880s, has the characteristics and proportions of an old institution. Enormous polished oak and glass doors open to a marble-floored vestibule and hall. The walls are lined with illuminated photographs of celestial objects that have been taken through the telescope—nebulae, the moon, colorful streaming gasses and swirling clusters of stars. At the end of the hall is the telescope itself, which rests on a floor that can be raised and lowered to accommodate the movement of the enormous instrument.

The observatory is a true memorial. Lick's body was laid to rest beneath the floor of the great telescope. I sit with my friends in the beautiful outside courtyard, where we talk about the impact all these unusual people have had on the mountain. We consider how we would want to be remembered and talk about the people, the environmental and human issues, the places, the pursuits of science that are important to us. One person describes an ethical will she has written—the principles and attitudes toward life that she wants to pass on to her children. At last, we return thoughtfully to our campsite. Inspired by James Lick's radical choice and legacy, we create our own obituaries and plans for how we want to be remembered.

**TRY THIS: Write your own obituary**

- Imagine that you have died and that you are reading your obituary in the paper.

- Recall the people who are important to you. Describe how you want them to remember you and your relationship with them. Include a description of the imprint you want to have made on their lives and memories of special times that you shared.

- Incorporate the dreams, experiences, and/or accomplishments that will fulfill your legacy.

- Include mention of any regrets for unfinished or unmet dreams.

- When you feel complete, read the obituary over. Consider changes you might want to make to bring the course of your life into alignment with what the obituary reveals.

## Journey to the Stars: The Pleiades and Peace

Since ancient times, people the world over have used the stars to guide them in navigating the oceans. Within our lifetime, voyaging canoes retraced journeys to Hawaii from various places in the southwest Pacific using ancient methods of star navigation.[11]

Almost every culture in the world has had stories about the Pleiades, using their movements to help define a calendar and to organize planting and harvesting. The Zunis call the Pleiades star pattern the Seeds, and a continent away along the Amazon, the Tapirape Indians monitor the stars' disappearance as a precursor to the end of the rainy season.[12]

Each year at the first appearance of the Pleiades, the Hawaiian Makahiki Festival begins. In its original form, this celebration had a profound effect on the life of the community. The festival required enforced peace at a time when warfare was dominant in the culture. This agriculture-based society could not be sustained unless people who might otherwise be away fighting were tending their land. Dedicated to Lono, the god of rain and agriculture, the festival demanded that the people focus on pleasing Lono by partying and giving thanks. People rested and engaged in fun and games. As part of the prolonged ritual, everyone was required to rest and relax for four days, followed by four months during which time no one could do more work than was necessary for survival.[13] It's a stunning thought to consider what might happen if we were to call for such a moratorium on warfare and work.

Given the important issues of peace our world is facing, we decide to let the presence of the Pleiades in the firmament be a magnet for a journey to the stars. Since the stars initiated a peaceful interlude for the Hawaiians, tonight we'll invite the stars into our own elusive peace process. We clarify our intent and find we're in agreement that issues of peace take many forms—ranging from the personal to the family, the community, the state, the country, and the planet. We'll be looking for guidance about how we can most effectively seek and create peace. It's the time of the new moon, and the darkness of the sky reveals many more stars than we ordinarily see from our communities, where city lights mask their splendor.

We spread a large tarp on the ground, cover it with blankets, and then lie in a circle, our heads pointing toward the center. I begin drumming, striking seven times to each of the four directions, followed by a sustained rhythmic beat to accompany our journeying. Unlike during most of our journeys, people keep their eyes open, looking toward the sky with "soft eyes," not fixed on any one thing. We hold our intention to go to the stars, asking the Pleiades for guidance about how to encourage, and be part of, peace on the planet. All over the world, dancing and escape play major roles in human relationships with the Pleiades. We're seeking to discover how we might escape from a way of being that prevents world peace.

Being outside under the stars is an unusual experience for most of us. When camping, we usually spend the night inside our tents. Often we have a campfire. We seldom simply lie down and just look at the stars for a long time. What a treasure to engage in an activity that has been shared across all of human existence! Our minds hold the intent of the journey, and as the drumming begins, the stars take us into their fold.

## PERSONAL JOURNEYS

Debbie: *I was "gone" very quickly. It started with light coming from above, from the right side, at an angle, directly to the left, into my heart. A really bright light flooded a scene of things at work, and I was just not responding to anything negative. A rainbow was coming* out *of my heart and going to the stars, in full color. Then the starlight came back into my heart. I think it just confirms what I already knew and was reinforcing me not to feed into negative energy, not respond to it. That whiny, snively energy that just has layers upon layers upon layers and builds throughout the entire world.*

*That (rainbow) came from me, from within my own heart. All this was reminding me to try to exude that light in my workplace, an inpatient psychiatric unit. The busyness gets in the way, but it's stuff that I* have *to do for my job, so I think that the best thing is just to stay as relaxed as possible. If I can just stay as relaxed as possible, things can get done in the amount of time they're supposed to be done in. And the rainbow connection to the stars will feed me the energy to do that, and to stay positive.*

Each person's role or contribution to peace is spotlighted through the journeys. Listening to the others makes it very clear that working toward peace is a daily opportunity, not simply an issue among politicians and countries.

### TRY THIS: Journey to the stars in search of peace

- At the time of the new moon, when the stars are most visible, ask the Pleiades for information about how to encourage, and be part of, peace on the planet.
- Spread sleeping bags or a ground cloth in a place where you can see the stars.
- Choose one person to drum or rattle for the journey.
- When the drumming begins, hold your intent in your mind clearly and simply. Watch the stars with "soft eyes" as you let your consciousness drift from that high place into space.
- Be aware of any sensations, visual images, sounds, colors, the unfolding of a story. If you have questions about what you are experiencing, ask for more information, more clarity.
- When the drummer signals your return with a rapid drumbeat, stretch and flex your muscles and come back into your body, returning to the place from which you launched your journey to the stars.
- Sit up and share your journeys. Look for common threads, common experiences. Identify anything that emerges that could provide a concrete step or act.
- Write down your memories.

## Traveling Companions: A River of Birds

The next day, we return to the network of trails in Grant Park. In the still-cool morning, we begin to walk the Hotel Trail behind the lovely white house once occupied by the Grant family. It's one of the more benign trails, more level than most of the others in the park. The Circle Corral is our destination, about a mile from the gated entrance to the trail. At that point, the trail loops back to return to the starting place.

Walking quietly, we listen to the red-winged blackbirds, whose song swells to a giddy chorus. Hundreds, it seems, are moving in groups of thirty or so from field to field, feasting on the reddish seeds of burdock. The sheer number of blackbirds reminds me of stories of how the sky was darkened by the flight of migrating birds in the Bay Area just two hundred years ago. Dellalou recalls that she's heard of a recent Chinese archeological find related to women with wings. She begins to sing,

> "There's a river of birds in migration,
> A nation of women with wings."[14]

We join her singing, and the lilting melody soon has us swooping from one side of the path to the other, imitating the flight of the birds in the field. The birds seem oblivious to us, but we are celebrating their presence, taking part vicariously in the pleasure of feasting, flight, and freedom.

## Boars and Other Worthy Adversaries

We discover the prints of many creatures in the dusty path we're walking. Feral pigs have crossed the road, and we find grass pressed down where the animals have slithered under the fencing. Deer, bobcat, other hikers, birds—all have left signatures. Katherine stops by the side of the road. Grasping the stems of oat grasses, she braids a cluster together even as they're still rooted in the soil. "Now we'll know we're on the right path home," she says—a whimsy that's delightfully unnecessary, since there's only one path through the field. But she's clearly pleased to find a way to mark her visit without picking anything.

An oriole swoops near the fence at the side of the road, and we soon realize that the bird is distracting our attention by perching on a fence post nearby, then ostentatiously flying to the next post, luring us away from its nest. When we're far enough away, the bird abandons us, continues to forage, and then flutters back to its nest.

A tribe of twelve or thirteen wild pigs comes trotting over the rolling chaparral fields. They root about, boldly foraging in broad daylight, even though they normally roam at night. After foraging eagerly for a few minutes, they seem to melt away into the high grasses. The Spanish introduced domestic pigs in 1769. Much later, in 1925, Eurasian wild boar stock was introduced onto a ranch in Carmel.[15] The two have now met and interbred.

Other rooting animals like the peccary and grizzly bear once roamed these same hillsides but are now extirpated from the region. The wild pigs have since moved into their niche. Even before the grizzlies—some nine or ten million years ago—the East Bay was home to a great diversity of mammals, including camels, three-toed horses, and gomphotherium (ancestors of the elephant). Their extinction is thought to have come about primarily through change in climate with its resulting impact on plant communities. As the Coast Ranges became elevated, a rain shadow was created. The once-mild climate developed more seasonal extremes, and a drier climate intensified.[16]

Boars have carried vastly varying symbolism in the world's cultures throughout history. They have been considered sacred to many cultures, including Greece, Oceania, and India. In Scandinavian folklore, a boar with golden bristles was a gift to a god and pulled the chariot of the sun across the sky.[17] In agrarian-based cultures, where sowing and reaping were primary activities, boars were worshipped. When a boar tribe passed through a field rooting with their snouts, it was as if the gods readied the land for planting.[18] In England, many taverns and inns are called The Boar's Head, and boar meat was believed to bring health and happiness.

Venus in Roman mythology and Freyja in Norse mythology, both goddesses of love, rode wild boars. Until very recently, having as many children as possible was important to individual families' wealth and to the expansion of the culture. This is still true in many developing countries. The boar, who grows quickly and can reproduce a large litter frequently, was a totem to be worshipped and emulated. During times of drought, even if most of the herd dies of starvation, wild boars—and their wild pig offspring—exuberantly reproduce once reliable food sources are again available. Large litters soon replace the lost members.

The connotation of the wild pigs' presence on Mount Hamilton is more in line with ancient Egyptian traditions, which saw the boar as evil, or the Judaic tradition, which considers it unclean. As wild pigs dig up fields and devour grasses, it's easy to understand how some viewed the animal as a symbol of voracity. The pigs wreak so much damage to crops and native plants in some areas of the state that they have become a source of great concern—so much so that California now has an extensive wild pig management program. While tags are required, there are no limits on the number of wild pigs that can be hunted.

Wild pigs have become almost as important a big game species in California as deer. One of the most dangerous animals to hunt, the pig shows a ferocity that invites admiration and presents a challenge to hunters. Its enormous tusks, angled upward, while normally used as tools for foraging, can be deadly weapons in defense, and the tough carapace can block a spear or a bullet. The pigs' fierceness seems to excite an equal ferocity in some hunters, who consider them to be worthy adversaries.

The wild pig, eliciting the archetype of the boar, represents some of these same qualities to our group, but we take their significance in a different direction. We talk about how the most challenging situations in our lives have forced us to grow, to become something larger than we were in order to survive either physically or psychologically. Worthy adversaries exist for some of us.

Some are inner adversaries—behaviors or attitudes that we don't like in ourselves, and that we may have a hard time changing. They may be evoked by a variety of situations—an unfair resolution of a child support issue leaving outrage and anger in its wake; never catching up to the cost of living, no matter how many hours of work are put in to create financial balance; not having time after long work hours to do the creative work that is bursting to be born. Jealousies come up, and feelings of helplessness regarding politics. We want our focus to be not on those external situations but on the elusive path of personal growth that will bring us to a new level in dealing with these challenges. Once we've formulated the intent for our individual journeys, we make ourselves comfortable and begin to rattle, asking the boar to illuminate the challenges given to us by our worthy adversaries.

## PERSONAL JOURNEYS

Peggy: *Several years ago, my husband ended up in a custody battle with his ex-wife. The judge believed lies she told in court, and she won on the basis of things that just weren't true. I found myself filled with outrage and hatred. She won not only in court, but it felt like a bigger win for her that I ended up so filled with bad feelings and even shame at untrue things said about me. I was shocked at myself. I knew that I had to get on top of those feelings, or I'd feel totally defeated. It happened in stages, but the first thing had to do with my commitment to myself not to get stuck there. The final stage happened years later when I went to a forgiveness workshop. I realized that my feelings toward her kept me from being the kind of person I want to be. So I just consciously let go—and committed myself to staying relaxed and open. I gained a lot of freedom, and the capacity to recognize when my own judgmental feelings were getting in the way of my image of myself. In the end, it was a great gift.*

## TRY THIS: Deal with a worthy adversary

- Identify a worthy adversary—a strong person or someone in power who triggers an intense and unpleasant reaction in you. It may be a present challenge, or an old wound that colors your present thinking about yourself or another person.

- Let an image come up of the person or situation. Replay it in your mind's eye, paying attention to where the anger, pain, fear, or upsetting emotion surfaces. Note what is happening at the point when you begin to feel uncomfortable.

- What is being triggered in you? An old wound? A youthful time of help-lessness? Some feeling of inadequacy?

- Begin to rattle, asking the boar to guide your journey in search of a way to take back your own power.

- Follow the boar and the images that arise. Notice the smells, colors, images and directions, motions and sounds. If you find yourself wallowing, going nowhere, ask the boar if there's anything else it can show you that will help you reclaim your power.

- When you feel finished, thank the boar. Return to where you met the boar, to the here and now, in the same manner in which you left. If you met the boar on the road, part with it at that same place. Rattle in a pattern that confirms to you that you've finished the journey—a rapid rattling, a sharp rattling, or a rattle in a pattern of four.

- When you return to ordinary reality, leave the boar an offering. You may have some food in your backpack. When you put it down, turn around and leave immediately, signaling in this way that it now belongs to the boar, with no strings attached.

## Vishnu the Boar: Rescuing Mother Earth

The image of boar hunting is so primitive that it reminds me of the story of Vishnu. The Hindus honored the strengths of even the fiercest forms of nature and took lessons from creatures like boars, which they saw as manifestations of the divine.

> *Vishnu was a warrior god, and highly respected the boar's fierce qualities. A warrior wants a worthy adversary; it's no great honor to best a weak enemy, and Vishnu's reputation was not based on winning battles over the weak. No wonder, then, that once when Bhoodevi, the Earth Mother Goddess, was suffering from human beings' cavalier and selfish choices, Vishnu took the form of a boar to rescue her. Human error weighed heavily on Bhoodevi, pushing her deeper and deeper into the primal waters, until finally she was inundated completely. Undaunted, Vishnu the Boar assumed a gigantic size, wallowed in the primal waters*

*(as boars are fond of doing), and after prodigious effort, retrieved Bhoodevi. As he lifted her above the waters, all the heaviness fell from her, and she was able to begin life anew.*

*But that was not the end of the tale. Vishnu took great pride in strength and power over others (as warriors often become enthralled with violence), and decided to continue to explore boardom. He took a sow mate, forgot godliness, and in the manner of boars the world over, they had huge litters.*

*This did not sit well with the powers that be; the god Shiva, embodiment of Pure Consciousness, saw what was happening and stepped in to jog Vishnu's memory of his godly responsibilities and talents. In this world where violence begets violence, an animal as fierce as a boar needs to be dealt with fiercely, and this Shiva did. He attacked the boar and flayed its pelt, thus removing the amnesia that had overcome Vishnu. Vishnu came to his senses; he returned to embody his formidable role as a god, now with the wisdom of how the wanton pursuit of strength misuses power.[19]*

The wild pigs move voraciously over the field; their large numbers make us happy they're headed in the opposite direction. When they reach a muddy spot, they all splash about, clearly enjoying the experience. We see what it really means to wallow. After a time, they leave the mud and continue across the field. One male tries to mount a sow who seems more interested in rooting than anything else. We watch them until they are out of sight, as they bump playfully (or perhaps obliviously) into one another and jockey for a prime position in relation to the elders. For no apparent reason, a small fight erupts between two of them, but their quarrel ends when they fall too far behind the others. Some invisible pig magnetism keeps them harnessed together; they're clearly a team.

These formidable animals have no concern for the opinions of others. They are just who they are, doing what wild pigs do, and so they offer an opportunity to explore a key issue on the planet today. Personal greed is embarrassing, something most people keep hidden, even from ourselves. We sense that it feeds the imbalance inherent in American overconsumption of natural resources. Our group gets ready to ask the feral pig to help us look at the way greed surfaces in our own lives, to show us its source and its power over us, what we do to hide it, and how it affects other people. Our hope is that we might bring our own part of this major world issue under more conscious control.

## PERSONAL JOURNEYS

Debbie: *Where I really am a hog is with food. I'm sure that's because of my upbringing. I know what it's like to be hungry…A friend of ours recalls a party at his house. I was seventeen or eighteen. He remembers me putting food in my pockets, wrapping things up and putting them in my pockets, to make sure I had enough food. Here I am, 50 years old. I'm thin, not overweight. I would share my Costco trail mix, but that's a lot easier to share than See's California Crunch. When you're born from poverty, it's a survivor thing and doesn't leave. But I've finally learned to share food with friends; and it's very important to me.*

*Then there's the fudge issue. This gives me a migraine, if it's got dark chocolate in it. I can't resist it, though. I'd get up in the middle of the night, and eat it. Clearly, I've got a chocolate addiction. Of course I wind up in the emergency room to get a shot to end the migraine. My partner can't imagine how anyone would do that to their body….But if you're a chocoholic, it's very hard not to eat it. So I just don't have fudge in the house. Once you understand it, you still may have the desire, but you don't need to act it out. You do have to figure out ways not to be tempted.*

### TRY THIS: Journey with a boar ally

- Journey with rattle or drum, asking the boar to help you see what you need to know about your greed—how it shows up in your life, what you do to hide it, how it affects other people.

- In your mind's eye, follow the boar wherever it leads you. Be aware of everything you see and hear.

- Be open to considering whatever you see, but if it confuses you or doesn't seem to fit, ask for more clarity.

- Ask if there is anything else that will help you understand the power that greed holds over your life.

- When you feel complete, thank the boar and return the way you came.

## Summer Solstice in a Sacred Grove

For many centuries, the activities in people's lives revolved around the seasons of the year. In the sixteenth and seventeenth centuries in Italy, ceremonial battles were waged in trance between two groups of Italian wizards, the *benandanti* and the *stregoni*—the good guys and the bad guys. These were not physical battles, but spirit battles fought in a trance state. They were probably a continuation of archaic contests intended to enhance nature's creative forces and those of human beings.[20] The image of this contest, embedded in the wizards' natural surroundings, presents a vivid contrast to the prevalent forms of recreation and contest today, typified by electronic video games.

Our sense of dependence on natural cycles has been masked by the inventions of modern science. Artificial light intrudes into nature's periods of darkness, heating and refrigeration obscure temperature extremes and weather patterns. Earlier, wealthy and poor lived within the same framework. Today people can live their entire lives disconnected from any understanding of the origins of material resources.

When we're not conscious of these cycles, we lose an opportunity to be in deeper relationship with the natural world. Subtle effects of cyclical changes on human behavior and thinking are often seen as inconveniences or irritations. For example, seasonal affective disorders related to shorter daylight hours often affect human interactions without our awareness.

Changes in weather in San Francisco can be quite different from those farther down the peninsula. Visitors to the city are often shocked and disappointed to find that the warm weather they expect in San Francisco is nowhere to be found. Summer is the foggiest time of the year in the city, and it's often chilly and overcast for most of the day. At the same time, people in full sunshine on the mid-Peninsula south of San Francisco may enjoy the sight of white billows flowing over the ridge of the coastal range toward San Francisco.

Paying attention to the cycles of nature rather than the clock when planning explorations can offer far more enjoyment of exactly the same territory. Walking in the summertime at Mount Hamilton is most pleasant in the early morning and late afternoon; at those times of day, you're treated to patterns of shadows and light on the hillsides that draw your awareness out toward the horizon. In the springtime, some of the best displays of wildflowers in the state can be seen in Henry Coe Park in the Mount Hamilton Wilderness. During much of the rest of the year, the grasses on the hills are brown and dried, and may be unappreciated by the non-native or uninitiated visitor.

We have come to Mount Hamilton on the day before summer solstice to witness and pay tribute to the longest day of the year. It's a time to remember the gifts of the sun, and to remember that our own lives are also natural cycles of birth, growth, fullness of life, deterioration, and death. The members of our group span three generations.

The camping sites of Hall's Valley are located under the shelter of oak canopies, which are spread out over rolling hills with wide vistas. Tom, who has observed the solstice and starlit dark nights from Hawaii and from Alaska (where he's lived for many years), begins taking time-lapse photographs of the sky.

On the morning of June 21, we rise before dawn; birds begin their calls to the day at first hint of light. We walk toward the fields near the parking lot, just past the park horse camp.

On a tour of the park several weeks earlier, park interpreter Ron Bricmont had led a group of visitors to a sacred grove, a double line of trees that orient toward the eastern horizon. Standing in this "Avenue of the Sun," he told us, we could expect to see the sun rising over the hillside on the summer solstice. At least three hundred years old, possibly much older, the trees are not designated in any particular way. They appear to the casual observer to be no different from other trees in the area.

Ancient oak in the Avenue of the Sun, Joseph Grant Park at Mount Hamilton. Photo by Ron Bricmont, 2004.

Through many years of astute observation, Bricmont discovered the con-figuration and significance of the trees. Often, information silently held by the land can only be revealed through a long-term relationship with a place, the reward of an appreciative, careful, and respectful approach. A person returns again and again at different times of the day and the year to observe the rela-tionships among the plants, the animals, the land, the weather, and the move-ments of the celestial bodies.

We are not the first celestial observers here, and neither was James Lick. The Avenue of the Sun is undoubtedly imbued with the memory of innumerable gatherings honoring the wheel of the year. We don't know the form other gen-erations have used, but what links us is the desire to explore, recognize, and honor the gigantic web of which our planet is a part, to acknowledge that our lives are irrevocably linked with the rest of the universe. No one knows how many generations of people have used this site, but when we stand between the columns of trees on the summer solstice, we are acknowledging the sun's power in the company of a long lineage of others who also watched and hon-ored the celestial progressions.

Just before sunrise, the sky is overcast. We wait anxiously to see if we'll be able to observe the sun coming over the hill. Scattered clouds drift by, the blue sky straining to show itself. Suddenly the clouds on the horizon are edged with light. For a long while we watch, each silently reflecting on the beauty of nature, the simple joy of being alive to share a new day. Someone begins a soft spontaneous humming. As the brightness increases, we move in unpremedi-tated gestures of welcome, upraised hands invoking the coming of the light. One person begins to sing, "Well-come, well-come," and others weave their voices around the word.

We begin a line dance among the trees, spiraling into a smaller and smaller circle. Dellalou begins to sing,

> "She is luminous.
> She is bright.
> She is shining,
> Crowned with light."

We quickly pick up her spontaneous tune and join her, weaving the sound as our steps bring us closer and closer to an invisible center. When Dellalou reaches the center, she begins to spiral out again. Holding hands, we move in a double circle, with some still going toward the center and others weaving out-ward between the lines. Finally, we've all spiraled in and back out, ending in a circle facing one another, quite delighted with the song, the light, the morning, the cheerful company that spans the generations.[21]

Hera, the baker among us, takes a circular loaf of spicy sweet bread sprinkled with poppy seeds from her backpack. She holds it up, looks at the sun through the open center of the loaf, and cries, "Behold the mystery of the unbroken circle!" She breaks off a piece and passes the loaf to the person standing next to her. As the bread makes the rounds of the circle, each person breaks off a piece, enjoying the delicious food and cheerful company. We eat, thinking of the seeds that became the grain, the grain that became the flour, the flour that became the bread, and the bread that becomes our bodies, thinking of what we will do with the energy it provides us—we, who belong to the unbroken circle.

Nan empties her pockets of flower petals she has brought from home, a confetti bouquet that she showers over all of us. We celebrate ourselves, growing in the beautiful garden of the natural world. As Carol passes a fragment of crystal, we honor the amazing mountain—the grove of ancient trees, which is foremost in our minds; the beautiful teaching of the heron's elegant concentration; and the "melted-ice-cream topography" demonstrating that even the land itself continues to evolve. We remember the very unique and strong sense of community on the eastern side of the mountain and around the observatory. We remember the pleasure and teachings of the animal kingdom: joining a river of birds, encounters with boars calling attention to the value of worthy adversaries. When each of us has contributed our special memories, Carol nestles the crystal at the base of one of the ancient trees in the Avenue of the Sun.

## TRY THIS: Celebrate the summer solstice, longest day of the year

- As the solstice approaches, get together with friends and talk about what summer means to you. Consider how it's different from other times of the year—activities, foods, gardens, the ways you spend time with friends in your community. Remember the pleasures that are only possible in summertime.

- The balance of light and dark at the time of the solstice may encourage thoughts of personal balance—what is necessary, what form it might take.

- Think about what is flowering in your personal life.

- Find stories, myths, poetry, or music to use in celebrating the qualities of the summer season. Include references to the cycles of life, of the seasons, of light and dark.

- Choose a beautiful place in nature to gather with a group of friends. The top of a hill, or a place with a vista toward the east, lends itself to celebrating solstice at sunrise. Gardens are good at any time of the day or evening.

- Entertain yourselves, with lavish use of flowers, herbs, and beauty of all kinds. Celebrate the sun and give thanks for friendships, for new beginnings and the blessings of your lives.

# A Star Party

Several weeks later, we return to Hall's Valley to see what has been obscured by daylight. On the darkest nights, "star parties" are held here. Amateur astronomers bring their telescopes and often give other people an opportunity to share in observing celestial bodies. Their generosity is impressive. Occasionally someone jars one of these delicate treasures, and the astronomer has to begin again to adjust the sighting—sometimes patiently, sometimes with irritation.

Several of them train their telescopes on the Ring Nebula, a dying star surrounded by a circle of particles flying away from it in a spectacular end-of-life dance. Sharing something so profound with strangers feels like being on a lifeboat from the Titanic on a sea of stars, and it's not until the next morning that I begin to understand what the experience has given me.

In my dreams, I'm carried beyond space and time into the Ring Nebula's dance. Floating there, I feel totally insignificant, aware that a human lifetime on the earth is a minute presence on the planet and in the universe. At the same time I'm conscious and have the power to make choices. Insignificance brings a kind of freedom; like the debris floating into space, I release picayune doubts and criticisms that just seem too self-important.

I'm alive, conscious, and fully present. Why not, I wonder, say and do whatever I am in a full expression of being human? Why not? This is it. This is the whole moment of existence. I am alive in the universe.

Mount Hamilton is weaving my own life into that of the universe. Being able to choose gives me a direction, and I feel myself moving as a fragment of the pattern of moving particles around the dying star. I have an odd sense of being part of something vast, and at the same time my consciousness affects the movement of the whole swirling mass. When I waken, I'm totally content. I feel both purposeful and free.

## TRY THIS: Get some perspective at a star party

- Arrive at a star party at Hall's Valley before the sun goes down.
- Camp there if you can, free to leave the park whenever you like.

- Watch the sunset from whatever hilltop vantage point draws you.

- At dusk, walk the trail without a flashlight up to the plateau where people have set up telescopes. Let your eyes gradually adjust to the darkness.

- Notice light pollution from just over the hill in the direction of San Jose.

- Observe how the visibility of the stars varies in different portions of the sky.

- When the sky is dark enough, begin to look through the telescopes. Circulate among them, asking the astronomers what they can tell you about the celestial object you'll be viewing. Even if the vocabulary is overwhelming, let it wash over you, just taking in the vastness of space.

- Observing the light from stars, you are viewing an event that took place many light years ago.

- Where are *you* in so vast a scheme? In your imagination, float through time toward the event you are observing. Float through the space between the stars.

- When you have seen all that you're able to take in, leave the gathering.

- Later, as you drift into sleep, allow yourself to move freely among the stars through your dreams.

- When you awaken in the morning, write down thoughts and images, fantasies and perceptions, new ways of holding the vision of your life.

## TarantulaFest: Fearful Encounters

In the fall, we return to Mount Hamilton Wilderness drawn to another event that both intrigues us and fills us with trepidation. A tarantula festival is being held at Henry Coe State Park to introduce people to this feared yet harmless citizen of the countryside.[22] This is the time of year when tarantulas migrate in search of mates, and they may cross the road by the hundreds. A tiny, virtually blind army, they search with sense receptors not yet fully understood by human beings. Sensitive hairs on the spider's legs detect vibrations from other moving creatures. When it senses prey, it gives chase.[23] These same detectors may be part of the search for a mate. After mating, the male wastes no time in leaving, because the female may actually eat the male.

To human beings, the tarantula's bite is no worse than a bee sting, but to a beetle, cricket, or other small creature, it's a fatal encounter. The spiders of stories and nursery rhymes may have programmed in us responses of fear or aversion. To observe tarantulas free from these responses, most of us have to consciously and purposefully shift away from judgment into the role of witness.

Tarantulas can teach us to face judgments and preconceptions in challenging situations. Faced with this small creature, we have to *decide* to adopt a more relaxed attitude. Tarantulas can sense fear and react accordingly, and yet in reality they are quite fragile. If they are to survive their encounter with us, we have to resist the temptation to shake them off or drop them, and instead just relax, watch, and feel the sensations.[24]

## TRY THIS: Meet a tarantula and be present with something you fear

- During the mating season, go to where tarantulas are known to migrate. You may choose to meet them in the controlled situation of a Tarantula Fest, or you may find a place on your own at Mount Hamilton.

- Sit where you can watch them move, simply observing them.

- Get as close as possible. If it feels frightening, imagine that you are about six or eight inches above your body, observing from a place outside yourself.

- Keep breathing deeply, into your belly, comfortably filling your whole body with breath. Stay relaxed. Extend your hand, letting it hover close over a spider. Follow its movements with your hand.

- Keeping your hand close to the spider, notice when you begin to feel close to this living creature. Notice how that sense comes to you, while you continue to breathe deeply, relaxing.

- When you are ready, extend your hand in front of a spider and allow it to climb onto your hand. Feel the touch of the tiny claws that keep it from slipping as it walks on your hand or arm. Notice any hesitation in its movements, or any change in its behavior as it moves over your hand or clothing. Notice the delicacy of its body.

- When you are ready, put your hand down and let it crawl onto the ground.

Later, we laugh as we share with one another our personal experiences with the tarantulas. We marvel at the power that comes with staying relaxed. Holding the tarantula is an opportunity to practice equanimity in the face of an irrational fear. We share episodes in ordinary life where we might find it useful—doing our income taxes, applying for a job, taking tests. If we can do it with tarantulas, we can do it elsewhere.

## Gray Pine: Reclaiming Honor

A lone gray pine stands next to the path, its feathery gray needles spread wide like fingers over a piano keyboard. The tree offers so little shade that the needles themselves seem simply shadows. Even the tree's name has a shadow of a sort. When the European settlers arrived in California, they looked at the Native American practice of digging for bulbs, nuts, and seeds with derision, scornfully referring to the people as Digger Indians. The name "digger pine" became associated with this tree, which provided one of the nuts the Native Americans harvested by digging.

In actuality, the native peoples' method for digging tilled and loosened the soil, distributing the bulbs left in the ground over a greater area and ensuring that the crop of the following year would be more plentiful. The sharpened digging sticks they used were very effective gardening tools. The gray pine is one of the native pines collectively called fire pines, so-named because their seeds are only released by intense heat generated by fire. Controlled burning was an agricultural practice of Native Americans that helped ensure the availability of pines for future harvests.

This is a tree that survives the challenges of steep slopes, intense summer heat, and very little winter rainfall.[25] It is vulnerable to beetles that cause illness, prone to death through a fungus that produces pitch canker, and susceptible to dieback caused by mistletoe in its branches.[26] Its story is one of survival, of character—and we have our own to tell.

Scattered over the hillside are other gray pines, and we separate to each find our tree, searching for the one that will become a partner for our personal journey. We each approach one, circling its slender trunk, reaching between the skinny branches to touch its bark, observing the variations in color and texture. A children's taunt comes to me, on behalf of the pine tree. In sympathy with, and in defense of, the gray pine, I chant in my head toward those who demeaned it:

> "I'm rubber,
> You're glue.
> Everything you say
> Bounces off me
> And sticks on you!"

We settle in, make an offering, and give the trees our full attention. We listen, honor the tree's history, and extend compassion for human beings—ourselves and others—who have been misunderstood or inadequately perceived. We tell the tree our tale and know that this is a being who can understand.

**TRY THIS: Exchange issues of humiliation and survival with a gray pine**

- Find a gray pine; make a respectful offering of cornmeal, tobacco, chocolate, or wine.

- Ask the tree's permission to hear and feel its story, and to tell your own.

- Sit facing the tree; envision the tree's roots extending into the earth. Follow the roots, the stones, insects, underground dwelling places of small animals.

- Follow the sap on its journey into the branches and needles, the touch of the sun on the trunk, the needles, the enormous cones.

- Feel the soil in which it grows. Crumble it in your fingers; get a feel for the challenge it faces.

- Envision your own roots extending into the soil, the challenges that you may face in your hold on life—economic, physical, emotional—and how you confront and handle them.

- Return your focus to the pine. Breathe in its purposefulness, its intention to survive the challenges. Let that strength flow through you, melding with your will to confront your own challenges.

- Open your mind and heart to the life of the tree, to the lives of those who have been involved with and depended on the tree. Hear and feel its story.

- Consider what it means to be called Digger Pine, or Digger Indian—the effect of being thought of so derisively.

- Remember anything that has been said about you—by parents, by childhood friends, by adult partners—that has caused you pain, shaped the way you perceive yourself or the way you function in the world.

- If there is something you still carry that doesn't serve your way of being in the world, notice where in your body the weight of that judgment rests.

- Feeling the sunlight on your head and your limbs, relax your whole body. Guide that sunlight to the place in your body where the judgment rests, and allow it to be flushed through your roots into the rocky soil. Compost the weight of the judgment.

- Continue to rest on the earth for a while, sharing with the tree an acknowledgment of a life journey that responds to challenge, adapts to it, and survives in beauty and in the bounty of nature.

A number of life-forms on Mount Hamilton, including human beings whose lives are entwined with the mountain, have helped us explore hidden places within ourselves. On the same mountain, we reached as high as the stars, bridged the centuries to share with others the coming of dawn on the summer solstice. The power of the mountain helps us learn to balance between heaven and earth, helps us recognize our place in the universe.

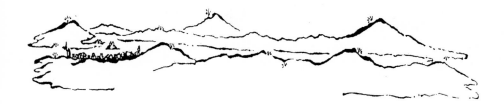

## Chapter Six

# MOUNT UMUNHUM:
# Bridging Ocean and Bay

Each weekday morning and again in the evening, more than twenty thousand people commute between Santa Cruz and Santa Clara,[1] forming a dense line of creeping vehicles. The slowest rush hour today, however, doesn't hold a candle to the slow and arduous pace of the same trip some 160 years ago. This was when Eliza Farnham braved the first buggy trip over the rough trail a few miles north of Mount Umunhum, making her way from the Santa Clara Valley to the summit of the Santa Cruz Mountains.[2] Eliza, a colorful and courageous widow, was known not only for her propensity to take on physical challenges but also for the larger challenge of championing the role of women in the culture.

Today we take for granted our ability to drive over the summit with relative ease. Yet even for many years after Eliza's achievement, wagons could only manage the trip by partially unloading, taking a smaller portion of the total baggage to the summit, and returning for the remainder of the load. The journey often took three days and required the dismantling of the wagons at one point and their reassembly later. In those years, the trail that made such a journey possible was a godsend, circumventing a loop that went as far north as San Francisco in order to get from Santa Cruz to Santa Clara.

## Trails Through the Mountains

When Father Fermin Lasuen was sent to Santa Cruz from the mission at Santa Clara in 1791 to choose the location for the Santa Cruz Mission, he was unaware of the shortest route. As he prepared to return to Santa Clara through San Francisco, the way he had come, the Ohlone people informed him of a more direct, yet rougher, route.[3]

Having occupied the area for more than ten thousand years before the European arrival, the Ohlones were sharing knowledge that was part of their heritage from generations of presence on the land. At the time they described the route to Lasuen and guided him through its convoluted hills and canyons, a wide variety of game roamed the steep valleys. The trails the Ohlones pointed out had begun as a series of animal trails the Indians followed as they hunted grizzly bear, deer, mountain lions, wolves, and jackals.[4] Centuries-long use of the trails had made the pathways more pronounced, but the route was still extremely rugged and difficult.

Lasuen recognized that the trails could become an invaluable pass between the communities that were to evolve around the Santa Clara and Santa Cruz Missions. Lasuen encouraged his guides to widen the trails, and the simple paths eventually became the main transportation route over the Santa Cruz Mountains. The territory would ultimately become known as the Los Gatos Gap. Pack trains used it for transporting goods, cattle, and people, and it continued to be used this way throughout the mission period, which ended around 1835.[5] Generations of roads, including Highway 5 and even a short-lived railroad, eventually became Highway 17, today's primary route between the bayshore communities and the coastal towns near Santa Cruz. Largely unnoticed, the old Ohlone trails still zigzag across Highway 17.

## At the Crossroads of Time: Traversing the Boundary

On a late summer morning, the stillness of the dusty Jones Trail seems to straddle two time lines. We are walking in the St. Joseph's Hill Open Space Preserve along one of the alignments between a segment of the old trail and Highway 17.[6] Our footsteps fall where people have pursued game, moved entire camps in seasonal pursuit of harvests, worked, and visited places sacred to them.

Nature encapsulates us in a bubble of time; the thread of continuity between past and present is held by the heat, the air, the earth, bird sounds. The beginning of the Jones Trail, near the Alma Bridge Road over Lexington Reservoir, is marked with a large sign warning of the presence of mountain lions, with directions about how to handle an encounter. While animal populations are quite diminished since the days of the Ohlone animal trails, the ruggedness of the hills is not. The Jones Trail, more benign than many in the area, represents an immensely valuable characteristic of the Los Gatos Gap—the presence of animal trails pointing out the easiest way through the terrain. This short trail is only about eight miles from the summit of the elusive Mount Umunhum. In spite of its proximity, the mountain goes unseen by the tens of thousands of commuters who pass nearby daily, because the terrain obscures it. And yet Mount Umunhum was prominent enough that the Ohlones considered it to be one of the four sacred peaks around the body of water we call San Francisco Bay.

As the Jones Trail ascends past the crest of the first hill, a cluster of eucalyptus gives way to native plant habitat. We look from the path that parallels Highway 17 into the canyon below, seeing cars crawling along bumper to bumper toward Santa Cruz, and try hard to imagine bushwhacking through the plants to create a path down the hill. Twisted trunks of manzanita reach out and, along with the other plants of the chaparral, create an unassailable ground cover next to the trail. Bay laurel, toyon, manzanita, and chamise are woven into a dense blanket that covers the hills. Animal trails affirm the importance of similar trails to native peoples and to settlers who later navigated this rugged terrain.

The trail enters the deep shade of a peaceful laurel grove. The air is so still that each breath seems to wait to be invited, called forth. On the steep hillsides pale brown leaves carpet the ground beneath the trees. At a bend in the trail, water from countless rainy seasons has cut a narrow channel deep into the hillside, carrying soil away from the base of an enormous bay tree. The roots reach deeply to all sides, seeking an anchor, reminding us that the ground beneath our feet is laced with tree roots making their own pattern of community.

Layers of fallen bay leaves surround us with their rich menthol aroma. The dense woods enfold us in light filtered through the enormous tree canopies rising gracefully from curving trunks that form arches under which we walk.

The slopes of the hills above and below the trail repeat the pattern; the trees are bending, flexing dancers flowing down the hills. So steep is the slope that when we sit at the edge of the path, our legs dangle over the edge. The sensation allows us to feel how difficult it must have been to make one's way through these steep and uncharted canyons, how challenging it must have been to safely lead an animal carrying precious possessions along the precarious trails. With the horizon hidden by the steepness of the land and by the density of the tree growth, you might make many a choice that would turn out to be false progress. Each step would demand your total attention through ankle-deep leaves that mask the presence of roots and stones. The relief of even a slight deer trail would be welcome, and the advice of the native people must have been invaluable.

The sound of whooshing traffic is an irritation for some of us, and we attempt to block it out. For others, however, the sound of the modern world is simply an overlay on another time captured by the stillness of the woods. A group of Rip van Winkles in reverse, we are trying to incorporate the present moment into the past.

Marguerite proposes a breath meditation that will bring the two time lines into a more harmonious relationship. As we inhale, we take in the sounds around us, not resisting the sound of brakes or gunned motors, giving them no more or less value than the occasional chattering of a squirrel. As we exhale, we imagine ourselves being propelled by the power of those sounds along a time line into the past. Fluidly moving through the images that come to mind, we envision the animals that moved by the thousands through the woods, and those who hunted them. We envision the native people who came from Nevada along this trail on their annual trek to the coast to work obsidian stones into arrowheads. We call to mind the missionaries, the natives who helped them, and others who escaped from them and hid throughout the canyons. We visualize a panorama of Caucasian settlers who planted orchards and vineyards. And in the centuries-long progression of people who traveled through the Los Gatos Gap, we envision our own unfolding life journeys.

The stillness of the leaf-carpeted earth and the shelter of the bay trees suspend us magically in space and time. In this place of so many people's journeys, we allow ourselves to flow along the lines of our own life journeys. Our breathing pattern focuses us on the present moment and propels our imaginations backward in time. We are seeking a marker, a moment in our lives when we recognized the seed of the journey each of us is making. We observe how those seed moments sprouted and continue to grow.

## PERSONAL JOURNEYS

Paula: *One day in a sixth-grade math class, the teacher brought up a concept (which I don't even remember now) that had the name of a Greek letter. She discovered that not a person in the class knew the Greek alphabet. She was shocked and talked about how much information there is in knowing Greek origins of language. She put down the math book and immediately began teaching us the Greek alphabet—spending days introducing us to word endings and beginnings. Concepts in math got sidetracked into Greek myths. In that week, I woke up to something quite magical about language and communication. It changed my entire relationship to learning—all because of her passion. I got it that education isn't just rote learning—that it's an active process we need to reach out for and be involved in calling toward ourselves.*

Marguerite: *I was in a marriage that I was trying very hard to make work, but there was nothing I could do that would make my husband happy. That was the way I was trying to fix it—to figure out what would make him happy. We had children, and all of us were suffering from his anger and discontent. One day I was walking down the short hall by our bedrooms, and I had an actual experience like I've seen in comics. An image of a lightbulb came on over my head, and I realized that I would never be able to make him happy—and that I didn't know if I could even make myself happy. I was terrified, but it set me on a totally different path. Even though it took me another year going back to school to prepare to be able to leave, that moment was the turning point in my life.*

## TRY THIS: Journey back and forth across time lines

- Walk very close to the downhill edge of the Jones Trail.

- Choose a spot where you might sit at the edge of this old Ohlone trail, and give your imagination free reign to wander in time.

- Notice what aspects of the terrain drew you to choose this spot—the angle of the hillside, the light and shadow, the growth pattern of the trees, something indefinable.

- Remembering the challenge faced by early travelers, look down the hill into the woods, imagining that whatever you see downhill is the terrain in which you have to develop a trail.

- Comfortably seated, close your eyes and relax. Inhaling, let your senses pull in the information around you—smelling, hearing, feeling, seeing the images and patterns of light, sensing everything around you.

- Exhaling, reach back in time—decades, centuries—toward events that transpired here for human beings, for animals. Feel the ancient spirit of place. Breathe easily and slowly, imagining a scene or scenes unfolding— watching, listening, smelling.

- Inhaling, welcome into your present self the wisdom, the relationship with the earth, of those lives played out here long ago. Ask to comprehend the kinship with the land that we have lost.

- Take your time. When you feel complete, express your gratitude. If that wisdom gives you some new direction, acknowledge it.

- Turn to thoughts of your own life, and once again, exhale purposefully toward the past—this time, the past of your own life.

- Propel yourself backward toward a day of importance to you—yesterday, a year ago, a decade ago—when illumination poured into a moment, a conversation, a vision, a dream that guided the shape of your life.

- Remember that moment when some understanding came to you that allowed you to see, to know, an important direction in some aspect of your life. Allow your senses to amplify your recollection of that event.
- Remember the setting, the people around you, the actions that profoundly affected you, and the way they set your journey in motion.
- Remember what you committed yourself to do or experience on that day and be aware of whether that has been accomplished—whether you are living out that intention now.
- Be aware of what still needs to be resolved to fulfill that journey.
- Residual traces of qualities from those who have preceded you on this trail may be useful to you in fulfilling your own journey. Invite those qualities to come to you, along a bridge across time. Invite them to have a new expression in your life.
- When you're finished, put your hands on the earth. Dig your fingers into the earth; breathing deeply, bring yourself completely back to this time and place, along the Jones Trail on the shoulder of Mount Umunhum.
- Open your eyes and let the scene around you welcome you fully back to the present.

## Approaches to the Summit

Where the Jones Trail meets the Flume Trail, we veer off and follow the Flume Trail. Descending slightly, we're soon walking next to the swiftly moving Los Gatos Creek, which we'd been unable to see from above. We stop at the edge of a huge blackberry patch to graze a bit. Later, with blue lips, we enter Los Gatos, where the trail loops through the edge of town. We pass a lovely brick building with the date of 1893 carved onto the building's façade, then turn uphill past an old stone-and-brick wall to reenter the woods, finally leading us to Lexington Reservoir.

In the days of the Ohlone, community bases and proprietary rights tended to be organized around the presence and flow of water. Fresh water, key to the welfare of the people and animals, flows from two major sources on opposite sides of Mount Umunhum's summit. The headwaters of the Guadalupe River begin near the summit. Emerging from what is now Lexington Reservoir, it runs through the town as Los Gatos Creek, eventually emptying into the lower tip of San Francisco Bay.[7] On the other side of the mountain, the San Lorenzo River tumbles down toward Monterey Bay.

The Sierra Azul Open Space bordering Los Gatos is an ever-growing jigsaw puzzle of land. It uneasily straddles the Santa Cruz Mountains summit area of Mount Umunhum and its slightly taller sister, Loma Prieta.[8] The summit is a distinctive presence. Its silhouette can be seen from many miles away in the Santa Clara Valley, even though high ridges can hide it from close by. Mount Umunhum's impact on weather, its part in the configuration of the Los Gatos Gap and transportation between the bayside and coastside communities, and the Guadalupe River that flows down its side to San Francisco Bay all affect the lives of people on a daily basis.

In spite of its importance, Mount Umunhum has to be explored in a round-about fashion. There are several reasons for this, chief among them that the remarkable summit is contaminated and cannot be approached by the public. From 1957 to 1972, the Almaden Air Force Station occupied the summit area. Radar equipment in a five-story building scanned Monterey Bay, searching for invaders and spy planes.[9] Now, however, the tall rectangular tower stands empty. Easily seen on the horizon even from a distance, it is a silent symbol of errors and abuse of the land perhaps inadvertently committed but left unaddressed by the Air Force.

Mount Umunhum summit from Bald Mountain.
Photo by Debbie Colbert, 2000.

This desecration of a peak once held sacred has involved a trail of toxic debris left by the Air Force when it abandoned Almaden in 1972. Although the Mid-Peninsula Open Space District now owns the summit of the mountain, the Department of Defense is responsible for cleaning up former defense sites. Intense efforts are being made by community, state, and congressional leaders to obtain funding for the cleanup of the site so that it might once again be made accessible to the public. Only then might it fully resume its integral role in the pattern of sacred mountains that surround San Francisco Bay. The mountain was a beacon whose presence helped guide Native Americans for centuries from Nevada along the route to Año Nuevo, where they worked the flint and obsidian on the coast for the three months of winter. Today it acts as a beacon for planes that fly over Monterey Bay to the South Peninsula airports and is an integral part of the greenbelt surrounding San Francisco Bay.

Access to the summit at a certain point along Hicks Road is actively defended against by property owners who—enforcing signs that indicate the limits of public use of the road—sometimes make citizens' arrests of those who stray onto their land. Some ardent survivalists live in the hills, resourceful people who guard their privacy and opinions very convincingly and sometimes ominously. Once, I was startled to see camouflaged men fade into the forest, perhaps engaged in war games. Legs quaking, I made a very careful assessment of where I was in relation to private land.

Precedent for these strong individualists was set by the most colorful early settler in the area, Mountain Charley, who in the 1850s lived in a redwood tree for seven months while he built his log home.[10] Mountain lions devoured the sheep he tried to raise, and a piece of his scalp was torn off by a grizzly bear. He persevered—starting a lumber business, and planting orchards and vineyards. His home became a stagecoach station, where he met travelers with good humor and great true tales of mountain life.

Without access to a route to the summit, we must learn this mountain's identity piecemeal through day trips. Our second foray brings us a little closer to the summit than did the Los Gatos Gap experience on Saint Joseph's Hill. Once again, we cross the Alma Bridge Road at the end of Lexington Reservoir. The beginning of Limekiln Trail is a little more obscure, but at a bend shortly past the Lexington Quarry Road, we find a tiny parking area nearly opposite the unobtrusive gate entrance. A small artesian spring bubbles continuously at the edge of the road, and green plants grow in a pond that's no more than six feet across.

Above the pond on a rocky outcropping, a covey of quail forages, scurrying helter-skelter over the cliff face when a squawking jay warns them of our approach. The jay is taking unnecessary responsibility; the small birds' typical behavior is to scatter in every direction at the slightest provocation to thwart capture by the enemy.[11] Their dull gray coloring camouflages them perfectly against the rock face until they are able to reach the safety of the nearby chaparral.

We hear an occasional rustle of leaves and faint clucks as they hunker down to wait out our departure. They're so endearing that we move forward quickly to put their anxieties to rest. Still, hoping to see more of them, we stand still and give them time to emerge again. While quail are not an uncommon sight in our area, in recent years the size of the coveys has markedly diminished, probably because of household dogs and cats.

We remain very still for a long while, hoping to observe more closely how our state bird moves through its space. We manage to quiet our coughs and random movements. After a time the birds begin to cluck to one another and hop to the ground from their spread-out perches in the chaparral. Regrouping loosely, the covey of about twenty birds forages, picking up seeds from the ground. Murmurs of communication connect them as they move about near us in fluid cohesiveness.

At last we move on. As we approach the gateway to Limekiln Trail, we're already on a gradual climb. We will hike a little more than five miles and climb some eight hundred feet before we're done. There's welcome shade in this section of the trail, but before we're finished, we'll be admiring wide blue sky with virtually no shade to hide the way the clouds move.

## Trembling Earth: An Earthquake Fault

Beneath our feet, the earth is engaged in imperceptible movement. At any moment, that movement might take on the magnitude of an earthquake on the San Andreas Fault, just as it has on innumerable occasions in this region. In the recent past, it has crept as much as one inch a year, keeping the people who live in the mountain communities nearby always somewhat on guard. In 1989, the San Andreas Fault repeated the rupture of nearly twenty-five miles of the fault break that resulted in such devastation in San Francisco in 1906.

When the Pacific Plate slides north along the San Andreas Fault relative to the North American Plate, earthquakes occur along the fault. The plates are also being compressed and pushed over one another. There's a bend in the fault, and the Pacific Plate, like a battling dragon, tries to overcome the restraining bend by pushing itself over the North American Plate. In the 1989 quake, the Santa Cruz Mountains actually grew about fourteen inches in the area of the quake, continuing very rapidly the progression that has formed the mountains over several million years.[12]

The path parallels a stream whose banks are lush and inviting but far too steep to allow us access to the stream. To the right of the path on the uphill side, the dry crispness of the chaparral foliage reminds us that earthquakes aren't the only challenge of living near the summit. The threat of forest fires requires a rather edgy vigilance throughout the dry season. The heat around us is accentuated by the stillness of the air.

During the rainy season, landslides brought on by heavy rains cause similar edginess, and as we round a bend, a slide area looms above us near the top of the hill. Just before it is another impressive sight. A cleft in the earth in front of us divides the path. To continue, we will have to climb into the gully and up the other side. Boulders and smaller stones on the tumbled surface of the ravine mean a scramble for us, but it essentially plunges us just inside the earth that's been opened by a quake.

Earthquake rift along the Limekiln Trail, Mount Umunhum.
Photo by Paul Feder, 2005.

Using our hands to steady ourselves, we clamber inside the shallow rift. Making our way slightly uphill toward the path on the other side, we climb through stones that were once sealed within the earth, once blanketed by grasses, chaparral, and trees. Now, our footing is nothing but a cacophony of stones.

The short expedition becomes a slow, moving meditation; our thoughts follow the quaking that split the earth open. Stones shift beneath our feet; we bend our knees, shifting our center of gravity slightly. Even a few steps are enough to get an awesome sense of the event that opened the earth. "One little shakola," Camila says, "and we're dropped like fleas off a dog. We just don't have the wherewithal internally to feel something so primal as what an earthquake releases. You're virtually helpless. You just have to ride her wave."

We sit among a jumble of exposed rocks that are part of the Franciscan Assemblage. These are rocks pushed up from the ocean basin, rocks from the rising of the continent, shelf settings, volcanic materials—smooth surfaces, layers of sediments, varied textures, shapes, and sizes constantly being changed.[13] Admiring the myriad forms and variations, we pick some of them up, rubbing them over our arms and cheeks to sample their textures.

We move in individual journeys from the present back in time to images of the day when the earth opened. We are in an unending flow of transformation, surrendering to the power of creation, reliving a moment in time when the earth's changes were dramatically exposed. We listen to the rumbling, to the bewildered and sensitive birds, wild animals, and house pets sounding an alarm. Trees crack and fall. The earth moves in waves. In the countless seconds of eternity, this moment is less than the blink of an eye. Returning to the present moment, we look around more attentively to see how the land has settled.

An occasional plant has sprung up on the hard bed. Small willows emerge from between the tumbled stones, an intimate family of slender shoots. I marvel at the power of life to arise out of such apparent devastation, remembering that for the ancestors—Druids, Native Americans, and many others—the willow was a plant of healing. The beauty and innate power of the cascading branches of a willow thicket near a flowing stream are irresistibly attractive.

As I crush a willow leaf between my teeth, saliva rushes to meet the bitter taste. Pointing a narrow leaf like a sword in the palm of my hand, I fantasize about a willow coming to the aid of this wounded earth. Eyes closed, I relax against a large boulder and let the willow speak to me.

"Water," it reminds me—the willow's constant companion. I hear the stream below the earthquake rift bubbling along its journey toward the sea, and I hear again a message water once sent me at San Francisquito Creek, another carrier of Santa Cruz Mountain waters to the ocean.

"These are the gifts that we offer to the Mother of the Waters." This time, I see the willow roots, always reaching toward water, and realize that it is not just the water that nourishes the tree. In the constant give-and-take between all aspects of nature, all plants that grow near water exchange on a cellular level with the water. They not only receive water to grow, they also return to it something of their own chemical structure. And the water moves on toward the sea, touched minutely—and sometimes extravagantly—by everything it touches.

I want to be one of the beings that the humble willow touches and changes. The water has its own means of exchange with the willow, which is open and receptive to the nourishment of the water. I have another.

Pablo Neruda's words pop into my mind, instructing me:

> "Now we will count to twelve,
> and we will all keep still."[14]

As I breathe twelve breaths, my internal rhythm slows; breath descends deeper and deeper, toward my belly. And from my belly, eyes no longer focused, I open to the willow. Just as the willow's roots grow toward water, I extend a pseudopod of attention and desire toward willow essence. Its pale new-life green coaxes my own cells to expand with new life. Willow fills me with the will to thrive. I take it in; every exhalation sends my own roots deeper into the earth. Well-being floods through me. I feel refreshed and revitalized, from head to toe.

This is the gift of the willow, incorporated into me. I store it, certain that I will soon return its power to nature. For now, with the willow already at work changing life in the earthquake rift, I can simply join it, amplifying what it has begun by bearing witness, by appreciating and being fully present to its efforts.

Because of the beauty of the area, many people still choose to live on or near fault lines. Those who do often make preparations for dealing with the immediate repercussions of a quake—a supply of water laid in, a box containing food and other supplies needed to survive for three days without aid.

While the forces of nature may bring people together, those who live near fault lines don't necessarily share views on social, environmental, or political issues. The process of creating agreements is probably as important as the specific concerns that bring them together. The needs for water resources, for fire protection, for emergency response all draw people into finding agreement on solutions. Currently, a periodical called *The Mountain Network News* keeps residents informed about problems, solutions (for example, the use of native plants for fire protection), and events.

Gambling on the chances of an earthquake, those who live in this area make active choices to live on the edge. But there are other kinds of cataclysmic experiences. Thinking about unexpected disruptions turns our talk to the events in our lives that have swept us along in their current, and to the moments when we've been able to extricate ourselves from something that seemed inevitable.

## TRY THIS: Let an earthquake fault become your teacher

- Find the rift on the Limekiln Trail opened by an earthquake.
- Make an offering of tobacco, cornmeal, or something personal and ask permission to sit safely in or next to the rift.
- Relax, listening to the sounds of birds, insects, wind, and rustling leaves.
- Pick up various stones, feeling their texture, noticing their markings.
- Be aware of your body's sensations—the coolness of the stone, the warmth of the sun, the way your body conforms to the stone.
- As you breathe deeply, notice the fragrance of the trees and other plants. Be aware of any other unusual odor.
- With your eyes closed, allow your imagination to go back to the day when the rift was created. Let all your senses come into play as you experience that event.
- Envision the responses of the living beings—plants, animals, birds, insects—to the shifting earth.
- Feel its power and your response to it—surrender, fear, desire to flee, awe…
- When the images of the quake pass, imagine the way the forest area settles—how it adjusts, the stillness or the wind, the feeling of the air.
- Breathe slowly and evenly; be present to the transformations, to the continuation of life, noticing what resumes or shifts.
- Turn your attention to your own life and remember a force that affected and shaped your life strongly. It may have been a turn of political events, a cataclysm of nature, the death of a loved one, the beginning or the ending of a relationship.
- Follow its course—where did it take you? What was your life like before it happened? How did it sweep you along?
- How and when did you differentiate yourself from the movement that carried you in its wake?

- What made it a creative or destructive force in your life?
- What was the personal power or attitude you drew on that allowed you to make the best use of the experience?
- If anything remains to be healed from that time, let that awareness surface now.
- When you are ready, open your eyes. With soft vision, not focusing sharply, pick up a smooth stone, one that's been held in the womb of the earth for millennia.
- Slowly move it over your face, your arms and hands, anywhere on your body that calls to you. As the stone touches each part of your body, ask it to help in that healing. Remind your hands what they will have to do to help. As you touch your eyelids, remind your eyes of what you need to see, to expose yourself to, in order to completely heal. Let yourself be comforted and empowered by contact with the stones from inside the earth.
- When you are finished, thank the stones, the opening in the earth, for their gifts.
- Return their gift by recalling the plants of beauty and health that you've seen on Mount Umunhum and the other mountains circling the bay. Envision them and bring that healing attention to this rift.
- As you begin to move back toward the path, stay silent. Move with the memory of what you experienced. Let your footsteps on this place of transformation ground you in your actions.

## PERSONAL JOURNEYS

Michael: *I remember the '89 quake; my back had gone out, and I was lying on our couch, not able to move quickly to a more protected area. There were windows above me, and when I realized what was happening, I was afraid they would break and fall on me. I covered my face with a pillow and just lay there feeling totally helpless. It's the helplessness I'll never forget—waiting for something to happen, dreading something uncontrollable.*

Paula: *I sat here feeling completely vulnerable, imagining it was happening, and hearing not just the trees falling, which was intense enough, but the sound of the earth crushing itself. It was so loud I felt like my bones were echoing the rocks crashing together.*

# Guadalupe: Following Headwaters to the Bay

As the path resumes on the far side of the gully, blue and green serpentinite stones that have fallen to the path from the slide area uphill glisten like jewels. Around the next curve, the path gradually slopes downward, closer to the level of the streambed. We pick our way to the water's edge, finding separate places to sit along its banks. We decide that each of us will focus on some aspect of life on this stream bank, returning to it over and over, and in the end, sharing our separate pieces.

A tree has fallen across the stream, and stones have backed up behind it. Water spilling over the tree amplifies the sound of the stream. Shaded by laurel, buckeye, and a few oak trees, we sink into quietness, listening to the water play over the stones. Sunlight reaching the surface of the stream transforms the leaves and branches into patterns of light and shadow. Patches of shadow touch the stones and water creatures, shifting ever so slightly as the wind plays its dance tune. Blue jays comment on our presence, and squirrels pick up the complaint that we have invaded their space. We continue to sit quietly. Eventually the animals seem to accept our presence and return to their pursuits. Entranced by the play of light and shadow, I watch the shifting light with unfocused eyes, softening my vision. We patiently melt into the scene, rewarded by the experience of a pace of life that has become very rare for most of us.

No human debris mars the beauty of this stretch of Los Gatos Creek. The path that follows its short journey through Lexington Reservoir is not as frequently traveled as some others on the mountain. I feel opened by the water, in spite of the rumble of trucks along the private quarry road on the far side of the creek.

The water's journey is not always so unfettered. Several of the tributaries that meander down the mountain into the Guadalupe River, finally emptying into San Francisco Bay at Alviso Slough, have been quite devastated by human activity. By the time the river reaches the bay, its very life has been gravely challenged.

We blend the willow's input with that of the headwaters that lead into the creek before us and consider the challenges that face these waters from their emergence near Umunhum's summit on their journey to the bay. We embark on a visionary water journey.

## TRY THIS: Practice reciprocity—cleansing the water

- Sit next to the creek. Close your eyes and listen to the water bubbling over stones, noticing the tranquility of the sound.

- Feel the play of light and shadow on your skin, any slight bit of breeze.

- Smell the plants along the streambed. Be aware of their relationship to the water.

- Bring to mind the image of the willow, making its way through the stony bed of the earthquake rift. Feel its presence within you.

- As you watch its flow through the land contaminated by the Air Force uses and the toxic substances that the water assimilated, hold in your body the healing presence of the willow. Without judgment, bear witness to the water's experience there; stay open, appreciating the water's capacity to transform. Send in its direction the willow's will to thrive. Observe the water in its flow down the mountain.

- Imagine the stream during an earthquake on Mount Umunhum. Envision the heaving earth lifting and dropping, forcing the tributary to shift from its bed, submerging in one area and finding a new path on the surface in another area. Observe the flowing water as it seeks a new balance with the land, participating in the upheaval of life all around it. Throughout the turmoil, bear witness and maintain the willow's intent to heal.

- Watch the new resolutions of earth/water boundaries, the way plants and other life-forms adjust. Send them filaments of the willow's determination to live.

- Blend your intent with the willow's powers of recuperation as it touches the shock suffered by all beings affected by the earth's shifts.

- As you slowly open your eyes, look around, anchoring within your body's wisdom a remembrance of the life-healing cycle of the willow.

## PERSONAL JOURNEYS

Marguerite: *When I think of how much we take water for granted, I realize that our country is in for some big surprises. We don't even realize what we're doing to the water. We can shake our heads at how much people have trashed it, or what we do to it with pesticides, but I hope we can wake up before it's too late to save what we have, and figure out how to share it with all the kinds of lives that need it. I've heard Earth referred to as the Blue Planet—the water planet. But humans won't be part of it much longer if we don't figure out how to be with it more respectfully, in full partnership.*

Paula: *When you're walking, you're just where you are. Sometimes you have a wide view, and sometimes you're in a more closed area. But I really like zooming above it and seeing how everything is related. It expands my understanding and immediately dwarfs me. I feel put into perspective—like one of those water skeeters, only bigger!*

On another side of the mountain, Los Alamitos Creek streams past caves from which Native Americans took cinnabar. The ore was immensely attractive to many tribes, who traded and bought it to make a carmine red paint for ceremonial body decoration. But of far more value to Europeans than cinnabar was the mercury it contained.

When the Native Americans introduced European settlers to their cinnabar treasure, the Europeans focused instead on the mercury, developing the richest of all mines in California. The extraction process poisoned both miners and the waters of the creek. With workers unaware of that danger, the camps were exciting places to live and make good wages. Mine owners provided insufficient precautions for the men or the water, and the consequences descend toward the seventh generation and beyond. The mercury flowing down the creek has for the moment come to rest primarily in the silt of the South Bay. Small amounts of the metal continue to seep into the bay from mines that have long since ceased to operate.

Now attempts are being made to redress the errors of the past, committed largely in ignorance. A long process is under way to reclaim the wetlands in the South Bay, to return them as nearly as possible to their original state. People do not yet understand all that is necessary to accomplish this, and experiments focus on small closely monitored segments. Perhaps willow, tules, or other plants will become some of the partners in this reclamation.

A number of Mount Umunhum's creeks feed into the Guadalupe River in the Santa Clara Valley. In this "Valley of Heart's Delight," the river carried the pulse of the human community. It was a magnet to European settlers that provided food, irrigated wheat fields and then orchards, and provided drinking water and sewage disposal. As time went by, civilization pressed hard on the health of the water. During the Great Depression, a hobo encampment developed on the riverbank. By the 1950s, wastes from industries along the bank were dumped directly into the water. By the 1960s, the river was quite devastated.

When the people of San Jose began to consider the potential of the river to renew the life of the community, they formed an organization—Friends of Guadalupe Park and Gardens. Many volunteers aid the cleanup of the river, the construction of gardens and walkways. Flood control measures are being created to channel the river's quixotic power. Along the riverbank, seven individual gardens mark sister cities' connections with San Jose, and wildlife can once again find suitable habitat.

But on the banks, plastic bags still dangle in the brush marking higher water. An occasional shopping cart lies on its side, water pouring into it and out of it. The river accepts all and responds to whatever actions come to it. At Alviso Slough, the water enters the bay; our mistakes as well as our best efforts pour through. The bay receives them and passes them along with the tide— our gifts to the ocean, Mother of the Waters.

Once, edges of the bay were lined with tule reeds, which helped to purify the water. Now most of them have been cut. But in solstice ceremonies, we honor them, fan the flames of life in those that are left, and encourage decisions to incorporate the plant helpers as partners in repairing the ravages of human actions and decisions.

Later in the year, Meg organizes us to harvest tules at Alviso Slough. We walk on reed platforms created by fallen tules on the banks of the Guadalupe where it feeds into the slough, sometimes sinking ankle deep into the rich river silt. Taking the reeds home, we bundle them together to create a model boat about three feet long. Then at the turning of the tide on winter solstice, we carry the boat to the baylands. Filling it with native flowers and beautiful dried tule blossoms, we add the light of our hopes and wishes for the planet, then send the small craft out to sea, to the Mother of the Waters.

## In the Territory of the Mountain Lion

Our hike on the Limekiln Trail reminds me that it was on just such warm and tranquil days that mountain lions might have been drawn to Laguna Sarjente, a small lake that once existed very near to where Summit Road now crosses Highway 17.[15] Mountain lions were once so common in the area, attracted by the lake, that by 1831 or earlier the summit of the Santa Cruz Mountains was known locally as Cuesta de los Gatos (Ridge of the Cats).[16] The lake ultimately disappeared due to earthquake activity, but the name inspired by the animals it attracted stuck. Thus the town of Los Gatos became one more example of the irony of naming streets, developments, or towns after animals—or native peoples—whose territory has been taken over by settlers or real estate developers.

Dusk is a favorite time for the animals to be active, and I have no doubt that they enjoy the beauty and tranquility of this place just as we do. Solitary and secretive, the great cats are stealthy hunters,[17] and it is entirely possible that one of them is watching us, contemplating us as possible food.

There are between five and six thousand mountain lions surviving in a wide range of habitats throughout California today. Where deer (their favorite prey) are plentiful, we're second choice to them. Rules about what to do in the case of an encounter are posted on many trails. Traveling in groups is virtual assurance of safe passage.

One mountain lion requires between fifty and one hundred fifty square miles of personal territory. As human beings continually encroach on lion habitat and their numbers outstrip the need for habitat, the lions are often driven to extend their range, at times moving into territory settled by humans decades ago.

---

## RULES IN THE EVENT OF A MOUNTAIN LION ENCOUNTER

- Never run. You may be considered prey and stimulate the lion to chase you.
- If you stand and face the animal, you won't be the right shape for prey. Don't crouch or bend over.
- Open your jacket, spread your arms out, and slowly wave them over your head, making your silhouette as large as you can.
- If you're walking with a child, pick him up, so he doesn't panic and run.
- Throw stones or branches, or anything you can reach without bending over or turning your back. Speak in a loud, firm voice. You're trying to convince the mountain lion that you might be trouble to it.
- Slowly back up and don't take your eyes off the mountain lion.
- If you are attacked, fight back. It can make a difference.

---

We're intensely aware that a lion could be stretched out on a limb of any of the trees that create our comfortable shade. The presence of a danger, even if imagined, can make us intensely alive to the present moment. I'm reminded of a Buddhist story about a monk pursued by a tiger. Although this version is not the original version, it came to me as the answer to a prayer when I believed that I was about to die from an act of violence. The story gave me great presence. As I prayed for a way to die without fear, I recalled the complete story in seconds this way:

*A Buddhist monk walking mindfully through a forest became aware of unusually bulky shifting shadows among the branches of the trees. Uneasy, he began to walk a bit faster. Then, out of the corner of his eye, he saw the slinking movements of a tiger, watching him intently. He began to move more quickly, and the tiger kept pace with him. He broke into a run, and in a few moments came out of the woods into a clearing. The tiger followed him, now much closer, and the monk ran as quickly as he could across the clearing. To his chagrin, on the far side of the clearing, he found himself at the edge of a deep chasm, with a swiftly running river hundreds of feet below him. A stout vine dangled over the edge, and with not a moment's hesitation, he lowered himself over the edge with the tiger snarling above him. But he soon realized that his weight was slowly pulling the vine's roots from the ground. Suddenly his glance fell on a strawberry plant growing from the side of the cliff, with a single ripe berry looking plump and delicious. He plucked the berry, put it into his mouth, and said, "How delicious!"*

Suburban residents seldom find themselves in situations where such alertness to danger is real and necessary, but the presence of the mountain lion is the most vivid link to the rugged life people led in California a very short time ago. Knowing that at this moment, we could very well be sharing this calm setting with a lion, we decide to meditate about coexisting with its presence. We find a comfortable position and let ourselves sink into a focused meditation. After a time, we share our experiences, a kaleidoscope of connections.

## PERSONAL JOURNEYS

Carole: *Coming out here knowing we're in territory that a lion may consider his own is a form of sacred trouble—it keeps you in line with who you are, keeps you totally in alignment. You want to be meeting his presence, whether he shows himself or not, with a sense of respect for him, and for yourself.*

Patria: *These lions that have been getting in trouble lately coming into human territory are like our young men, going out to prove themselves, to discover their strengths. It's no different. It comes from the same place, the same needs. They need to find themselves. How can we fault them?*

Debbie: *I think if I were used to the woods, I'd be listening for the other creatures, for what the rest of the forest is doing. I'm on his turf, after all, and if he comes onto mine he might be killed. So why should I be any safer in his territory? I'd like to think that we give each other space until it's a matter of life and death, and then both the lion and I have the right to defend ourselves.*

Peggy: *We come out into the wilderness to experience ourselves. We want to know if we can move through the world with integrity, and to know that, we have to have something to push against. Something has to call up a choice that we make to act with integrity, to honor life, and to make decisions that give us personal dignity. So if we move through the woods with respect for the animals, we'll make right choices if we're challenged. I know I'd be scared to death, but you can't let fear run you, or you'll be killed for sure. You have to rise to the occasion.*

Maya: *There's an ancient Sumerian myth of Inanna, queen of heaven and earth, making a journey into the underworld. She goes through seven gates. At each gate, she protests what's happening to her, but she hears from the gatekeepers, "Quiet, Inanna. The ways of the underworld are perfect. They may not be questioned." It doesn't mean you have to die, but it does mean you're faced with reality and have to show up completely revealed.*

Kayla: *If you go out into nature and make contact with the life force—with trees, for example, and open to their beauty and power, the trees everywhere will know, and form a web of consciousness among those in the forest and those at home. All trees know what you've done and will be available to you. This is about inner connectedness.*

Michael: *There's a Buddhist prayer that says it for me:*

> *"Gate gate paragate*
> *Parasamgate swaha."*

It means

> *"Gone, gone, gone beyond.*
> *Completely gone beyond.*
> *Completely awake, so be it."*

*That's what it's about to walk in the territory of the mountain lion. You better stay awake, and as you do, you're part of something bigger. Your feelers are out in all directions, so you're connecting in a way that's not usual.*

Water gurgling over the stones in the creek washes us with tranquility as we absorb one another's responses. Small insects flit through the air and skate on the water's surface; light and shadow, movement of leaves and branches, warmth of the sun bathe us.

The path, once the road for the Lexington Quarry, climbs to the intersection of Limekiln Trail with the Priest Rock Trail, where we pass from cool shade to open sky. One trail climbs toward Mount El Sombroso, which would take us to the nearest point by trail to Mount Umunhum's summit. The other would return us to our starting point following a more exposed route. We decide to circle back and approach the mountain on another day from Bald Mountain, on the opposite side.

## Bald Mountain: The Far Side of Umunhum

Mount Umunhum Road, which leads to the mountain's summit, is barricaded at a certain point, and only official cars are allowed to pass. From that location, the overshadowing presence of Umunhum's summit, enticing yet unattainable, is reminiscent of the castle in fairy tales: the princess is asleep or held captive, a wall of brambles making her inaccessible to the loving suitor. This close to the summit but unable to move toward it, we all recognize a familiar quality of longing, of desire we can't fulfill.

Near the barricade, however, a trail only a mile and a quarter long provides the closest access to the summit. We leave our cars in the small parking area a few feet from the gated road. Slipping through the opening in the roadside fence, we follow the Bald Mountain Trail.

As we gaze back over our shoulders, the summit appears deceptively close, not much higher than we are. In fact, Mount Umunhum is 3,483 feet in elevation, more than 1,000 feet higher than Bald Mountain at 2,387 feet. I feel an odd sense of aliveness, perhaps due to the elevation, the clarity of the air, or the open space and clear sky.

The Ohlones differentiated between the Sierra Azul (the Blue Mountains) and the Sierra Morena (the Dark Mountains).[18] The northern slopes undulating down toward the Santa Clara Valley are dry and filled with brush, with a few live oak and madrone trees. To the south, deep shadows falling from the high crests create mysterious hollows and green folds. On foggy days, moisture shrouds the redwoods, rendering the mountain as islands in the mist.[19]

The contrast between plant communities on the north-facing and south-facing slopes is striking. Looking from the Bald Mountain Trail, we can see five or six canyons funneling down from Umunhum's summit to the south, like a ribbed fan; other canyons from the Bald Mountain side converge with them in a gorge several hundred feet below. Umunhum's canyons appear to be totally covered with green eiderdown, but as we continue on our path, our perspective shifts, and the patterns of tree growth become more obvious. Shielded from the dehydrating rays of the afternoon sun, the south-facing mountains have more trees. As we climb to a higher elevation, we can see that the greens shift due east of Loma Prieta, turning muddy, a combination of the rust green of fading buckeye blossoms and the needles of gray pine.

## Chaparral: Barriers to Unfulfilled Longing

Lining the trail is chaparral, a community of plants able to survive low rainfall and hot summer temperatures. Chamise, or greasewood, reveals an unusual adaptation to severe conditions; dead wood in the center is surrounded by branches of oily leaves that continue to grow even in times of drought. Deep root systems help the chamise plants conserve water internally. But the unusual growth pattern that creates so much dead wood can fuel conflagrations during dry weather. A thirty-year-old plant may have dead undergrowth that makes up more than 80 percent of the weight of the plant.[20]

Some people speak of chamise as the signature plant of the chaparral. It may grow to twelve feet, sporting beautiful burls and lines that look carved by the hands of a patient woodworker. The needle-sharp leaves, prickly husks, and skin-irritating dried flowers make barriers of the plants simply by their presence. The creamy white flowers of chamise turn a latte brown and last through most of the summer.[21]

The hills appear benign from this viewpoint, but a route overland to reach the summit would be relatively impassable due to the chamise and other chaparal plants. The obstacles remind us even more of the fairy tale brambles separating the seeker from the goal. Poison oak adds its own potent message to stay away, as does the thought of a rattlesnake, not a rare sight here, sunning itself on a rock.

The incredible array of plants and the towering presence of Umunhum's summit form an experience too powerful to rush through. We stop in a small clearing and ask the blended threads of the chaparral to speak to us. The radar tower from the old Air Force installation looms over us impassively. We sit quietly in the warm afternoon, settling more and more into the scene.

The stillness works its magic, slowing us to the tempo of a mountain that seems poised in time. Small clouds move slowly overhead, their shadows drifting over the hills and canyons. There are gifts for all the senses. The fragrance and bright colors of nearby wildflowers—red thistle, yellow sticky monkey, purple lupine—bring buzzing insects. Mahogany-colored branches of manzanita bushes look oiled and polished. Pale green sage and coyote brush add other textures to the chaparral. Wild clematis vines drape over coyote brush, decorating the stems and leaves with white blossoms that look like threads spun into silk spirals. Slender grass stems cast thin shadows in the dust.

Inspired by this little Eden, Carol is moved to pull another fragment of crystal from her pack to pass amongst us. Holding it, we honor the unique perception Mount Umunhum offers us—crossing the boundaries of time, allowing us to look into the heart of an earthquake zone, remembering that we share the territory of mountain lions. We honor the shape of the land and the gap that impacts our lives so profoundly. We honor the summit's toxic legacy in its reminder of the fragility of the natural world and our need to treat it with respect. When the crystal returns to her, Carol buries it where the roots of this beautiful native garden will enfold it.

The prickly chaparral flaunts itself in our presence, perhaps reflecting personal qualities or the circumstances in our lives that get in the way of fulfilling our desires. The sight of the summit and the natural defenses of the chaparral steer our conversation toward airing our feelings of unfulfilled longing—frustration, feeling diminished, helpless, angry, defeated. The plants call us to consider how our own defenses, appropriately or not, might stand in the way of fulfilling our desires, as tough to penetrate as the chaparral.

A meditation takes shape designed to move us past the barriers. Intent, we remind ourselves, can come into play to help us work our way through the underbrush of our personal barriers to unfulfilled longing. While the plant world won't take us physically closer to the summit of Umunhum, it has spoken to us, and we are responding.

Different circumstances evoke diverse threads of understanding, of response, of connection. If we were to come here on another day, different weather patterns, different company, or even direct access to the summit of Umunhum might all affect us differently. Varied threads of the web of life are always present, always available; what we happen to pick up on is a function of many factors, including our own life circumstances on any given day, week, or year. This is the way the weaving is strengthened within ourselves and around us.

To honor that blend of threads, we put some cornmeal on the ground. Some add a few hairs from their own heads. We mark our presence, our gesture of respect to the place, our desire to connect—not too different from the coyote leaving its scat on a path. Pulling our journals from our backpacks, we make a few notes as we talk through our preparation for a writing meditation.

We return our focus several times to the abandoned radar station on the summit, considering several approaches to drawing out from within ourselves the hidden information elicited by the scene. Patria moves our writing forward with some questions to consider. We spend the next twenty minutes writing without stopping.

**TRY THIS: Create a written meditation on longing**

- Think of something you long for—something you want to accomplish, experience, or feel. Perhaps it involves a relationship, a physical or mental skill, a place in the world, an achievement. Write down your goal, and continue to write the images and thoughts that come to you.

- As you engage with your longing, notice obstacles—whether something in yourself or in the environment.

- Ask the chaparral to show you how the obstacle serves you. Consider whether you can do without the benefit of the obstacle, or if you would benefit in some other way without it.

- What would it take to set aside the obstacle? See yourself doing that.

- Now, in your mind's eye, play out the fantasy of the longing completely. If another obstacle arises, deal with it in the same way.

- If your longing involves a relationship with a specific person, imagine or remember the way you want to feel about yourself in that person's presence. Envision the way you handle your body, your emotions, your style of speech—what your sense of freedom empowers you to do.

- Envision the attainment of what you've longed for. What is the picture of your life now? What are you doing and who is with you?

- Envision one act you could initiate in your life, one freedom you could grant yourself that would move your life toward the manifestation of the longing.

- Share the visualization with your companions. Speak in the way you spoke as you envisioned the longing achieved. Move your muscles and take the posture in the way you visualized yourself functioning.

## PERSONAL JOURNEYS

Ann: *For me, longing is tied up with a sense of unfulfilled creativity. I long to feel that however I'm unique has found some form of expression. Fulfillment is hard to figure out. From the time I was a kid, I had a longing I couldn't really describe. I didn't even know what it was about—I just felt a longing. When you're little, people want to know what you're going to be when you grow up. A fireman, a doctor, a nurse—all kinds of futures get sampled in play. For years, I felt like there was one thing that was me, and that I hadn't found it yet. But today, what came up for me was where I am and what I'm doing when I feel like I'm happy and creative. I realize it isn't a question of searching out the one thing I'm "supposed" to do. It happens when I'm with young kids—something gets released, and I feel very free. I teach kindergarten, and something about their spontaneity helps unlock that door for me, too. I can react to them, show them how to do things without making a big deal about it. We get connected, and my self-consciousness gets out of the way. Then I'm in a creative flow that's just absolutely joyful, and exactly the way I want to live my whole life. So right now, you're a circle of kids I'm telling a story to. I'm moving around the way I would if I were with a class telling a story— moving my arms, walking around—and I see that this is a way I can begin to live my life outside of the classroom—just being more animated in expressing whatever I'm trying to say. I don't know what it feels like to you, but I feel more alive than I ever do with grownups.*

After we've all spoken, we celebrate "anything is possible" with a shared feast from our backpacks, leaving crumbs of cookies, offerings to the place, to the small animals, and to the no-see-ums that have been swooping around us as we've been sitting together. Then we turn our backs on longing and head for the top of Bald Mountain.

## Resting Place of the Hummingbird

Umunhum's name comes from a native word meaning "resting place of the hummingbird."[22] Even now, if you're sitting still on an open hillside, you may be visited by a ruby-throated Anna's hummingbird, whose wings vibrate so quickly that the motion hums with intensity. In honor of the hummingbird, we are sporting red shirts in varying hues. Hummingbirds are drawn to the color, and on our hike together, we hope to entice one or more of the birds to pay us a call.

Hummingbird stories are prevalent in Native American mythology. Several themes are common to diverse tribes, such as Hummingbird bringing rain, Hummingbird going between the worlds, and Hummingbird as a manifestation of the sun.

A Mojave legend tells about a time when people lived underground in darkness. A hummingbird, sent to look for light, finds the path that leads people to the sunny open world. A Mayan version describes the hummingbird as the sun in disguise trying to court a beautiful woman, who is the moon.

In a story from Puerto Rico's Taino tribe, two lovers from rival tribes, when their relationship is thwarted, become a hummingbird and a red flower. The

Taino people regard the hummingbird as a sacred pollinator who brings abundant new life.

There are plentiful variations on the theme of how the hummingbirds' work keeps nature in balance. The Apaches tell of a young warrior who, although born deaf, sings magical songs that heal and bring good weather. When he is killed, a devastating winter comes, but it comes to an end when his wife encounters her husband in the form of a hummingbird in the fields of spring flowers. Pueblo shamans use hummingbirds as couriers to the Great Mother, who lives beneath the earth. The Hopi people tell of hummingbirds convincing the gods to bring rain to the people.

To further entice a hummingbird's attention, we draw stories about them from a hat, traveling with them in our imaginations. We find an area where lupine—a flower hummingbirds enjoy—grows, then disperse and sit like overgrown flowers among them. As we wait, we entice the birds with our thoughts, replaying the story lines, letting the stories take us where they will, returning again and again to the images.

Relaxed, my mind wanders between the story I've chosen and the vista before me, holding an invitation to visit. I find myself wondering how a red flower the color of my shirt holds seduction in its body, in its being. I imagine a bud unfolding and then actually stretch my torso and limbs, feeling my heart opening. The image of bees in the center of the flower gathering pollen translates into an itchy cheek, as if a bee's tickling feet were on a pollen hunt across my face. I am a flower, and I'm waiting for my hummingbird.

Although I wait in vain for a long, still time, Marguerite is luckier. The rest of us give up and cluster around to hear her experience.

## PERSONAL JOURNEYS

Marguerite: *I thought about the story line I'd taken and then ended up just relaxing and enjoying the view. I felt more and more like I belonged there, and there wasn't anything in particular that I had to do but just enjoy being alive. All of a sudden I heard a zooming sound, and right in front of me, about 2 feet away, a hummingbird was stopped right in the air! It was just staring at me, or maybe at my shirt. For a minute, I was afraid that he'd dart at my eyes as quickly as he'd come in front of me, and I wished I had glasses on. But all of a sudden he flew straight up, then over to the side a little, still facing me. And then he was gone! There was a little chirping noise; it sounded like he was snapping his fingers and dismissing me!*

*My heart was beating fast—I felt like I'd had a shot of adrenalin. After he left, I realized that the quick movements, the sound of his wings, the unexpectedness of it, all just galvanized me, and I felt totally awake.*

*Then I thought about my story line—I'd picked the story about the humming-bird being a sacred pollinator who brings new life, and I remembered something that happened to me a few years ago.*

*A hummingbird flew into my toolshed, where there's a skylight. He kept trying to get out through the skylight, and when I tried to capture him with a sheet to get him out the door, he seemed so fragile I was afraid I'd hurt him. So I left the door open, but when night came, he still hadn't found his way out. In the morning, I went into the shed and found him on the floor. He was still warm. I ran and got some sugar water and spent the next hour dipping his beak into the water and just holding him in that position for a few seconds, over and over again. After proba-bly half an hour, I saw his throat tremble. I kept it up, and finally, it was like elec-tricity went through his body. He was out of my hand in a flash, hovered in the air for just a moment, and then took off.*

*I wonder if the visit was the hummingbird clan saying thank you for bringing new life to that bird. And I wonder if it would have come to me if I hadn't picked that particular story out of the hat, because it connected me to that old experience, even though I wasn't conscious of it.*

## TRY THIS: Invite a visit from a hummingbird

- Wear a red shirt or jacket when you visit Mount Umunhum, "resting place of the hummingbird."
- Find a sunny spot where plants are growing that hummingbirds are attracted to—lupine, sage, vetch, nettle, columbine, and such.
- Settle in comfortably, patiently waiting.
- Picture a hummingbird in your mind—its size, its color, its unusual flight, the sound of its wings in motion, its constant search for nectar.
- Imagine that you are a flower. Feel the breeze, the sun, the passing clouds that cast shadows over you and then move on.
- Feel yourself becoming part of the scene around you. Relax and breathe.
- Feel and breathe.
- Be as still as a flower, waiting for a hummingbird lover.
- Feel the waiting.
- Feel and be.

# The Weaving from Bald Mountain

We perch on Bald Mountain's promontory, above the lush "Valley of Heart's Delight," where we live. While most of the miles of orchards—cherry, apricot, and others—that early European settlers planted have been replaced by the industries of Silicon Valley, enough of the beauty remains to justify using the name given to it by those early arrivals. The trails we walk on these mountains, the views from the high ridges, still delight our hearts.

Mount Umunhum has sharpened our awareness of partnerships with various aspects of nature, including those with human beings. Weaving Mount Umunhum into the circle of sacred sites we've visited around San Francisco Bay, we call out some of the experiences that anchor us to this mountain. We honor the way the quail maintain their tight community; being in the territory of mountain lions and paying attention to sharing space with those who are different from ourselves; looking into the depths of an earthquake zone; the cooperation of very independent people in the mountain communities coming together for mutual needs and protection; the animal trails that thread through the Los Gatos Gap, and the way their habits in the terrain have fused into such an integral part of our own transportation between bay communities and ocean communities; the mystery of passing back and forth between time lines. We walk again in mind's eye along Los Gatos Creek, dappled light and shadow creating patterns on its surface. We're inspired by the Guadalupe River running to San Francisco Bay, persistently enduring the assaults of human beings over decades, responding to attention and care as we attempt to restore what we've destroyed.

The wide vista before us reveals Umunhum's place in the scheme of the mountains of the Bay Area. On the far side of the south end of the bay, the Mount Hamilton Wilderness marks the eastern horizon.

From the promontory of Bald Mountain, we look toward our homes and neighborhoods in the valley, remembering the sources of nourishment in our human communities—our loved ones, our friends. Exploring the area near Mount Umunhum, we've rounded the foot of the bay. As we begin to close the circle, the sacred space within these mountains holds the possibilities and promises of paradise, becoming a powerful container of inspiration and vision for the future.

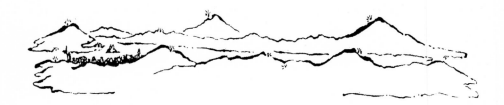

## Chapter Seven

# SAN BRUNO MOUNTAIN:
# Guardian of the Earth's Heritage

The stars have faded in the sky when I pull into the Bank of America parking lot in Brisbane, City of the Stars. Huge electric stars are scattered on buildings throughout the small town, handed out by the Chamber of Commerce to anyone who agrees to maintain one. I like the official whimsy of this act, particularly given the important role San Bruno Mountain plays in its connection to the Bay Area's geological history. The star-studded buildings link me to all the stars and planets of the universe, to the pull of the moon on the ocean tides, to the slow reshaping of the land at the edge of the ocean, to the natural transformation of life as we know it.

### The Franciscan Habitat

The buildings of San Francisco have buried its Franciscan habitat, a totally unique biological and historical treasure that once extended from the city onto the southern limb of San Bruno Mountain. The last remnants of the Franciscan ecosystem on earth endure only on San Bruno. Here lives Pacific manzanita, one of the world's rarest plant species. The San Francisco silverspot butterfly, once widespread on the northern peninsula, is now found only on this mountain. Sixteen plants and animals living on San Bruno are on the rare and endangered list.[1]

As warm Central Valley air rises, cold wet Pacific air is drawn inland through the Golden Gate and the Lake Merced Gap. The encounter of this foggy air with the hills results in what appears to be a treeless landscape on the mountaintops. Some Ice Age plants have survived here, as well as a variety of coastal plants that have evolved into specimens existing nowhere else on the earth. The ravines, too, hold unexpected secrets; fog from the Pacific pours into their sheltered recesses, and luxuriant plant life awaits the person willing to explore beyond San Bruno's seemingly bland appearance.

Jo and I pop into the donut shop at 5:45 a.m. for a wake-up cup of coffee to sip on the drive toward the summit. We pass through an industrial park, then connect with the summit road. Part way up the mountain, Jo suggests a side trip. She wants to take me to a favorite place of hers, unknown to me, for a sunrise view. We park, then follow the faint beginnings of a footpath through fields of brown grasses and bracken fern, sparsely studded with chaparral. As we walk, Jo bends the thick stems of invasive exotics that crowd the path—fragrant fennel, Scotch broom, others—to check their growth. The robust plants lust for more space. If they persist and spread, unhampered by the ecological checks of their own native habitat, the more fragile native plants will soon be taken over.

Hillsides are covered with pearly everlastings, their downy gray-green stems and leaves topped with clusters of silver-white blossoms. The carpet of plants is more expansive than I've ever seen in one place. Lizard's tail adds splashes of bright yellow. The fields of flowers form a backdrop to a garden of miniature native plants that surrounds a rock formation Jo calls Eagle Rock. I'd call it Bearded Rock—various kinds of small gray-green lichens dot its surface and give the rock the look of someone's crew cut or stubbly beard. The diminutive plants are precious specimens in this unique environment of the Franciscan zone and I feel like I've been catapulted into another era or even onto another planet, a Gulliver in Lilliput. A tiny cairn, appropriate in size to the scene before us, sits on the highest rock of the formation, a marker of human attention honoring the wonderland next to us.

## Lichen's Tenacity

Lichens are aptly called pioneer plants;[2] they grow in conditions where other plants still fear to tread—on cold mountain peaks, in jungles and deserts, and beyond the Arctic Circle on the tundra. The marriage of algae and fungus that constitutes lichens begins a life-generating succession of events. The lichens secrete weak acids that gradually dissolve mineral matter out of the rock.

Very slowly, they "eat away" the rock surface, and the rock crumbles into minute particles. A time-lapse movie of the process would take generations of photographers, but eventually the lichens are the creators of a layer of soil that may be sufficient to host other plants.[3]

The determination of the lichen reminds me of a teaching story a shaman once told me as we sat together on a mountain cliff:

> *An eagle had a nest very high on a mountain's granite boulder. Her three fledglings were ready to leave the nest, and it was becoming quite crowded. She said to the first one, "You are a great eagle. Your wings are so well developed that you are now ready to fly very far. Go now, and see how much ground you can cover in a day's flight." The eagle was proud of his mother's praise and left the nest immediately. To the second one, she said, "You are strong and vigorous, and deserve a territory that is spacious and full of prey. It awaits your discovery." He was proud of his mother's words and left to claim his space. To the third, she said, "You are the finest of the fine. You can see for many miles around, and when you have found your aerie, you will be king of all you survey." Quite full of himself, he fluffed his feathers and left for the highest cliff he could find so that he could have an enormous kingdom.*
>
> *He found a spot and sat very high on a cliff, preening his feathers, feeling regal and proud, king of the vast domain that spread before him. He stretched his wings, puffed out his chest, and gloated. Before long, his leg began to itch; looking down, he saw a tiny ant plodding with determination up his leg. Enraged, he shouted, "You! How did you get here, and how dare you! What are you doing here? This is my domain!" The little ant replied, "I crawled up. I like the view!"*

A similar tenacity keeps the lichen clinging to the rock. Through magnifying glasses, we peer closely at the lichens slowly blanketing Eagle Rock. We very gently touch their surfaces, inspecting their grip on the rock. We pull out a bit of sacred tobacco and blow on it, imprinting the tobacco with our feelings of appreciation for the lichens' power to create and sustain new forms of life. Placing the tobacco just under the boulder, we find a place to sit where we can continue to have the lightest contact possible with the lichen, letting one finger move slowly over a small part of the rough surface. Closing our eyes, we surrender to the power of the lichen, asking it to take us to a place in our own lives where tenacity is called for, asking for a message there from the lichen.

**TRY THIS: Let lichen show you how to be tenacious**

- Place a small offering on the earth by a lichen-covered rock; if you feel welcomed to stay awhile, sit down and make yourself comfortable.
- Notice the position of the lichen on the rock, the way light falls on it.
- Lichen breathes, thriving where the air is clean. Notice the air surrounding the lichen's home and any source of pollution that might pose a threat to it.
- Relax your vision and look at the lichen with soft eyes.
- Let the lichen's slow breath guide your own; breathe deeply and slowly, allowing yourself to come into harmony with the lichen.
- Imagine the minute spores of fungus coming together with the algae, remembering the long slow passage of time as the partnership evolves and takes hold of the rock. Envision the infinitesimal slow growth, fed by rock, sun, and moisture, tested by the wind and storms.
- Let your breath slow more and more, breathing in rhythm with the lichen.
- Honoring the perseverance and tenacity of the lichen, drift in your awareness to your own life, to a situation facing you that may involve more challenges to accomplishment than you anticipated.
- In your mind's eye, consider the obstacle that has slowed your progress—someone's actions, a regulation, an attitude you hold or someone else holds about you or your plan.
- Offer the situation to the spirit of the lichen, asking for guidance, for an incremental way to move toward your goal.
- Relax and open yourself to whatever there is to be experienced. An image may come to you, a song, a sensation, or some other phenomenon.
- Thank the lichen, and when you return to ordinary reality, write down or tell someone every single part of what you experienced. Pay attention especially to the incongruous parts of the image or experience that came to you.

Lichen on Bearded Rock, San Bruno Mountain. Photo by Paul Feder. 2005.

The sky grows lighter as we quicken our pace toward the vista point over-looking the park formerly known as Candlestick. The plants here are shock-ingly different from those in the delicate native garden we've just left. Wildly invasive gorse consumes the hillsides, overrunning everything in its path. Gorse plants are very vigorous, with long, sharp needles. It's hard to imagine how any animals, let alone people, could make their way through the brush. A lone coyote bush, the only native left visible in this stand, is being smothered under the weight of the expanding gorse.

From our vantage point, we look down on foothills and canyons toward the northeast as they taper down and curve, cupping the low basin of filled land next to the bay. This basin is where San Francisco sent its garbage from 1920 until 1960. The garbage-filled basin was topped off with soil chopped from the top of the hill next to it, creating a huge flatland. The ridge of hill that once connected McLaren Park and Candlestick Park is now a ghost, removed to fill the bay so that train tracks could be built between the Peninsula and San Francisco.

Highway 101 is built on that fill, but for many years major development of the mountain was held in abeyance by several conditions. No one was inter-ested in living near the land at the foot of the mountain due to the dreadful smell from the combined odors of the dump and several tanneries. Furthermore, winds blow almost constantly on the mountain, and fog is very common. More hospitable land for building homes could be found elsewhere. However, the dump and tanneries were eventually closed, the odors diminished, and desirable land elsewhere grew scarce. Sections of the filled basin are now strewn with industrial developments. Clusters of unexplained illnesses plague homeowners in the area. The battle to preserve San Bruno Mountain in its natural state began and continues to this day.

## Bringing Balance: Weather

We choose to welcome the dawn from a place where Candlestick Hill marks the northern frame of the low basin and the shoreline. Out of sight, behind the hill, is the beloved ballpark formerly known as Candlestick, now called 3Com Park. Just as we arrive, the sun begins to rise above the horizon, slightly to the right of Mount Diablo in the distance. At the same moment, a small arm of fog comes in from the ocean over the summit behind us. The fog streams toward the east, rushing to meet the sun. As it does so, the fog is rewarded by the touch of sunlight, filling its drops of moisture with pink radiance. Pinkness streams over our shoulders as the sun rises over the fog bank that drapes the hills of the Diablo range. Before us, two sage plants sparkle with drops of morning mist. The same fog brings imperceptible moisture to our own bodies, and I look down to see if our arms sparkle in the way the sage does.

As the fog bank on the Diablo range reaches up toward the sun, the gold is tamed into silver. Sunlight creates a silvery path on the bay's water and on the rooftops of buildings in the basin below us. On the hill's slope just beneath us, sunlight streaks the slender leaves of a patch of wild iris, plastered to the earth by the wind. Behind us the moon, just past its full phase, is beginning to wane. Streams of silver from the sun reach westward toward his lingering sister before she leaves for the day. A cycle is playing out around us, wrapping us in relationship and rhythm. We're embraced by the sun and the moon. In just a moment, the spell is broken, the moon disappears, and the sun takes on its full daytime character.

### TRY THIS: Do a moving meditation to bring balance to your life

- Near the full moon at the time of the "hour of power"—dawn or dusk— find a place on San Bruno Mountain or a hill that allows you to see the horizon to the east and west.

- Stand facing the east and turn in a slow circle. Pace your turning with your breathing, as you affirm, "Here I am…I am here." Let your awareness, your slow circling, take in and affirm your presence in this very place, this very moment.

- Circle slowly once again. Let your arms move in response to the place you're standing—perhaps in greeting or in tracing the line of the horizon.

- Circle again, allowing your body and your legs to move as if dancing with the stars and planets as they dance with each other and the earth—yourself a star being, circling, circling.

- Give yourself to the movement. Close your eyes or look around you with soft eyes, an unfocused seeing. Keep your breathing slow and even as you bend your knees to feel well planted as you dance.

- Invite thoughts of some situation in which you have felt off balance or of a relationship that feels out of balance.

- As you move, let your arms and hands offer that imbalance to the sun as it moves across the sky, to the moon as it begins to rise or to set. Ask the sun and the moon to receive the issue, incorporating it into the balance of the universe. You do not need to envision a specific resolution—only invite the restoration of balance.

- Let go of any attachment to the situation as it has been. Dance in harmony with the balanced movements of the universe.

- When you are ready, open your eyes or regain your focused vision. Be aware of your capacity to restore balance in your life.

The fog glides low over the summit from the west, then slithers down into Buckeye Canyon and Owl Canyon, and veils the ledges of the quarry where the hillside is being eaten away. Everything is touched and softened by the fog. In its journey from the ocean into the canyons, the fog shape-shifts—first a dragon, then a stalking lion, then a luxurious woman stretching her limbs—as it's lifted by the wind, guided by the conformation of the land, and melted by the sun.

We sit a long time watching the show, hot tea from our thermoses warming our hands. Constantly changing fog patterns are visits from an unseen source, giving a drink to one plant and passing over its neighbor.

A phrase from Biology 101 pops into my mind: "regeneration of lost parts," the ability of frogs and lizards to regrow a missing limb. This morning the mountain itself is gifting us with a peek at its regeneration. The delicacy of the process that sustains the endangered species on the mountain is especially visible in this habitat, which has existed in its current form for centuries. Once again we are in a miniature native garden—Diablo rock rose, San Francisco owl's clover, San Francisco campion, white-rayed pentachaeta, native bunchgrasses, and others. Its precarious perch here is obvious, where civilization presses in with an industrial complex, a housing development, and the stream of cars racing down Highway 101. Through its link with the past, an essential quality of the mountain is presenting itself—both in the lineage of human habitation and in its preservation of plant habitat.

In the late 1960s, when the odors of tannery and dump had subsided, developers started taking an interest in the beauty of San Bruno Mountain. Almost simultaneously, David Schooley discovered the mountain and, after exploring it, dedicated himself to its preservation. David and a few others formed the San Bruno Mountain Committee, which began efforts to defend San Bruno. They brought attention to the threat to this natural treasure, one of the world's biodiversity "hotspots" and home to endangered species that rely on the mountain habitats in which they evolved. A fragile ally living on the mountain came in the form of the mission blue butterfly. When it was placed on the endangered species list, its presence here helped San Bruno Mountain Watch (successor to the SBM Committee) bring about the creation of San Bruno State and County Parks during the 1970s.

As time passed, builders chafed to find a way to build on this prime land. Finally, an amendment to the Endangered Species Act was developed, a compromise whose effectiveness has never been scientifically and impartially studied.[4] The Habitat Conservation Plan developed for San Bruno proposed measures to provide alternative habitat for two endangered butterflies—the mission blue and the San Bruno elfin—and to allow landowners to build on the butterflies' prime habitat. Twenty years later, gorse gobbles up what was to have been the new habitat. Houses now occupy the former butterfly habitat. The streets bear the names of the various butterflies, and the unproven conservation plan is in use all over the United States, spreading like the invasive nonnative plants that continue to flourish on San Bruno.

## Butterfly Transformation

We return another day and meet at a parking lot part way up the mountain. We are bent on a walk to another favorite spot on the mountain. We move through acres of lizard's tail, with its golden blossoms and forked leaves. It's a "Sound of Music" scene. Yellow blossoms of mustard on long stems wave in the breeze, and vast fields of wild radish add a pristine note with their delicate white blossoms. These two invasive plants add their beauty even as they crowd the natives. A healthy patch of native mugwort, now only a few inches high, will soon grow to perhaps eighteen inches.

Just a few years ago, we loved walking along the path here, where curtains of manroot vines laced through the eucalyptus trees. However, beauty and good health for a site don't always go hand in hand. A well-intentioned but poorly executed effort to control the expansion of the non-native eucalyptus grove went sadly awry. Insufficient funds and physical help resulted in a lack of protection from invasion by other plants once the eucalyptus was removed. This would prove disastrous; an array of gorse and other non-natives took advantage of the new conditions and threatened to overwhelm the attempt to make space for the native plants.

In spite of this setback, a garden of native plants has been put in, and volunteers now work to help bring back the mountain's original flora and fauna. The work of these volunteers has far-reaching implications; when native plants are lost, the populations of animals and insects they support dwindle and eventually disappear. Although the task of reviving the habitat seems overwhelming, those who work here do so with camaraderie and the satisfaction of recognizing that they are working to sustain what they love. Some come alone, to work in quiet relationship with the mountain.

It's a warm morning. As we wait for friends to gather, we spread out in the native plant garden, weed a bit, and then sit quietly, watching the activities of butterflies, bees, and other flying insects. Life slows for us as we watch various kinds of butterflies around us. We feel no impatience in waiting for our friends. Butterflies possess nearly full-circle vision, protecting them from birds and human beings alike. So rather than try to catch them, we simply admire their dance.

The Papago Indians tell a story about Elder Brother being inspired to create something by the sound of children happily playing. He put the colors from flowers and leaves, pollen and cornmeal, pine needles and sunlight into his magic bag. When he invited the children to open the bag, the first butterflies flew out, delighting the children.[5]

No animal or insect represents transformation more than the butterfly. Miraculously passing from egg to larvae to pupa to mature butterfly, its form completely changes through each stage.[6] As I watch this beautiful culmination of the process in action, I remember a dream that came to me during a visit to Cuzco.

*I had gone to the Andes with a friend to watch the last full eclipse of the sun in the twentieth century in this hemisphere. I had arranged to visit the shaman Americo Yabar. We met in Cuzco, and he proposed that we travel together a few days, going up to his home in the mountains. I was overwhelmed by his invitation. As I went to bed, I asked myself, "What am I doing here? I didn't anticipate this, and I wonder if I really want to do it."*

*That night, a dream gripped me so powerfully that I awoke crying and walked around the room in great distress. In the dream, I was in my California home. An old woman came to the door and said, "Your husband was my granddaughter's pediatrician. It was unsuccessful, and she is dying anyway. I've taken your husband prisoner, and when you come with me, I'll release him."*

*She and I went to her home, and as we entered, I understood that my husband was no longer a prisoner. But she locked the door behind us, and I found myself among a group of people milling about. She left the room, going down a corridor. There were seven of us left to our own devices, equally bewildered by why we were there.*

*Finally, I decided to find her. I went down the short corridor and found her in a bedroom, where a child lay comatose in bed. The woman sat by her side, totally focused on the child. She paid no attention to me but was fully present with the child, and I immediately understood why I was in her home. I had come to be a witness to the transformation of the child's existence. And I had come to Peru to learn to witness the transformation of life as we know it on the planet.*

Now on San Bruno, in the presence of this butterfly, queen of transformation, "transformation of life as we know it" takes on new possibility. When the rest of our friends arrive, we take a moment to sit among the flowers at the edge of the garden, watching the fluttering wings of butterflies. I lead a meditation on butterfly transformation as we hold ourselves open to their wisdom. Each person calls to mind some personal transformation she would like to make—of a habit or relationship she finds herself in, a position, a personal goal—and then I begin.

## TRY THIS: Let the butterfly's life cycle guide you through a transformation

- Watch the butterflies nearby, dancing in the air—silent and yet vividly sending information to one another.

- Notice the way their wings move—the unexpected darting and returning. With the image of their dance in your mind, close your eyes.

- Allow the butterflies in their light fluttering to carry you with them on their journey. Imagine the pheromones, the scents they send, invitations to one another.

- Visualize the butterflies touching, mating, and moving away from one another.

- In your imagination, watch the female butterfly as she seeks out a gray-green lupine pod and lays her eggs on its rough, lined surface.

- Picture the texture of the lupine pod, where the butterfly eggs are independent from their mother, receiving their nourishment from the life of the lupine. Already they have begun their journey of transformation. They feed on the lupine, then rest, feed, and rest.

- Imagine the tiny caterpillars crawling to the base of the plant, curling up, and resting in a long sleep. Feel the peaceful rest sustaining them, as a chrysalis forms and blankets each small being.

- Resting, they let nature take its course, changing them effortlessly into a totally different form, surrendering to the change.

- Picture the butterfly working its way out of the chrysalis, slowly fanning the air with damp wings, drying them in the air, readying itself to fly. At last it lifts into the air for the first time, then up into the treetops, far above the earth where it began its life and went through its transformations.

- Let your mind turn toward your own evolving life.

- What powerful desire for transformation draws you? What is it that you wish to change in yourself in order to feel more fulfilled?

- Allow yourself to name that desire, to see yourself in a new form, having evolved into the transformed person you wish to be.

- Remember the nourishment in your childhood—cuddling, being fed, being sung or read to, hearing bedtime stories.

- If you yearned for that caring and felt deprived of it, remember the feelings of yearning.

- Remember the people of your community as you grew up, the support or nourishment you received from teachers, friends, parents of friends, aunts and uncles, grandparents—each with a different perspective, a different way of connecting. Remember what they gave you.

- If you knew there was something you were reaching for that hadn't yet crystallized, remember those feelings of longing.

- Remember a time when you, too, may have drifted in your becoming, when it was not yet time to move toward your transformation. How were you marking time?

- Are you still drifting in that state? If so, what has to happen before you are ready to emerge?

- Conscious transformation: What will it be? How will you emerge? What will it look like when you fly?

- Open your eyes and enjoy the butterflies.

## PERSONAL JOURNEYS

Marguerite: *When I watched the life cycle of the butterfly, I felt a huge sense of wonder at the effortlessness and inevitability of the urge to go from one step to the next in its cycle. The butterfly-to-be just surrendered to an inner urge, doing what comes naturally. When I looked at my own process, I realized how much garbage I carry around self-doubt, around embarrassment about my body and not wanting to look foolish. There's none of that in a butterfly's trip, so I decided to use that falling-into-the-process attitude as I thought about my goal, which is to walk the Coast Trail from Mexico to Canada. I can sabotage the plan very easily—where will I find the time, who would want to do this with me, fear about being alone out in the world and something happening, not having the discipline to actually get in shape to do this. But I decided to set aside all these things that keep me from actually creating a plan to prepare for this adventure, and just envision what I had done in the past that made me want to do it, and the little experiences that have given me a sample of the pleasure of distance walking. I remembered the adventurous people who visited our household when I was a kid (never mind that they were all men), and the sense of being alive that they gave off. I remembered being in a race as a kid and feeling like I might truly be flying—looking down to see if my feet were touching the ground. I pictured all the hikes we've taken in circling San Francisco Bay, and how many other wonderful places I could go while I'm getting in condition. That made it seem like the butterfly's falling-into-the-process mode. You just do the next thing without worrying about the end.*

As we continue up the path, the butterflies flit soundlessly away. Invisible to us, an olive-sided flycatcher insists over and over again "Quick, three beers! Quick, three beers!"[7] while a Hutton's vireo cheers him on from the treetops. We move through the native garden and skirt the remaining eucalyptus trees draped luxuriantly with the ivylike leaves of manroot, wild cucumber vines. Its grace veils an unusual power: as we pass along the vines, we are moving past a large, unseen village of roots. These huge roots are sometimes shaped like a man's body, or a skull, and through them flows an intense poison, which has been used both to stun fish and, paradoxically, for medicine.[8]

We climb the path effortlessly and steadily. It curves several times, until we find ourselves on a flat plateau large enough for our small group to sit together. We draw and write. Beyond the eucalyptus woods, directly in front of us, loom the buildings of San Francisco. Past them, and a bit to the left, Mount Tamalpais dabbles its foot in the Pacific. On the right is San Francisco Bay. From this vantage point, the union of the two bodies of water is hidden, but its existence holds a key to our paradise. The Golden Gate is the conduit between our lives in the Bay Area and the lives of all those to whom the Pacific Ocean flows.

## Giving the Mountain a Voice

Once again Patria is our guide in a writing practice, and she poses the topic. "I am the mountain," she proclaims. We write for twenty minutes, not stopping. The flat terrain allows us an expansive view. Even though the plateau itself is actually out in the open, it is sheltered from the wind by the wooded ridges nearby, so we are comfortable. Sparsely scattered quartz crystals wink in the sunlight.

The protection of the plateau inspires us; in the open air, freedom of expression and the mountain itself flow through us. We all become creative, celebrating the mountain. We picture the occasional small crystals on the ground as receiving our expressions and sending them to the heart of the mountain. They carry our gratitude for the beauty that transforms our states of being into peacefulness, the trust of open hearts, and a sense of belonging. Opening our senses and our hearts, we're gifted by San Bruno Mountain. As we thank her, our creativity is expanded through her inspiration.

Meg writes: *I am the mountain....I am warm inside, deep, bone-connected to the other mountains. Hidden springs course through my bones, flowing into the water that covers me and surrounds me. The bay lies across my body, filling my curves and crevices. My breasts and elbows make small islands; my nose and knees rise high up above the water. My bones connect me with all the other mountains; we are one...*[9]

Sandy expresses the gifts of the mountain as she describes her writing experience: *The mountain talked to me as I wrote.... I came today feeling weighed down with responsibility for things I really can't change. All my efforts have been focusing on worry, and how can I work to change things....I'm used up. The mountain was laughing at me for walking along being so focused on my pain that I wasn't receiving all the healing energy around me. Getting filled this way will give me the juice I need to get out in the world again, but first things first. I think I have something to learn about healing myself before I'm ready to heal anything else.*

Later, Patria shares a poem inspired by her writing that day. The first verse:

A Full Brief Light

I am the mountain.
I endure, sustain
Through massacre and conquest,
under cement, steel, and glass
my heart beats steady, even.

I am the mountain.
I know death is not forever.
Each summer I adorn myself.
Sun yellow poppies, sticky monkey,
and rivers of pearly everlasting

cascade down my great thighs
to the center of my pleasure
where iris, wild cucumber,
azaleas just pink ripple down
my rich brown curves

to the heart of my crevices
where elfin butterflies
quiver, my music hastens
on blue wing
from bright blossom to fading flower.

I am the mountain.
In my lengthening, moths live
and die many times
before my next breath.
Red flickers see for me—

fine hawks
make a circle round
the sick
seize the tender flesh
feast fast like daylight vision.

Thus, my creatures come
to me solitary as the bee
one by one before
all their descendants
take flight.

## TRY THIS: Do a writing practice to give the mountain a voice

- On San Bruno Mountain, spend as much time as necessary walking to release distractions, particularly any heaviness or worry you may be carrying. Give it to the mountain as you walk along, intending that it pass through your footsteps, composting the mountain with your feelings.

- When you've set aside distractions in this way, find a place that calls to you, a place where you feel a strong connection to the mountain.

- Lie down, making as much direct contact with the mountain as you can, feeling its support of your body, the different textures that touch your skin directly. Notice how the surface feels through your clothing.

- Put your fingers onto the earth and nestle your fingertips into the soil on the surface of the earth.

- Imagine that you and the mountain are not separate, that you are one being. Feel what there is to feel—sun or wind on your body. Listen to the sounds flowing over you—birds, wind, or traffic. Notice the fragrances that waft over you.

- Let your slow breathing become an extension of the breathing mountain. Breathe with the mountain, allowing your breath to sink deeply into the mountain and then to carry the mountain's presence beyond your body, into the air around you. Become the mountain.

- Feel the union and allow your breath, coupled with the mountain's, to sustain this bond until you can speak for the mountain.

- When you are ready, open your eyes and write, "I am the mountain." Give the mountain a voice and let it speak through you.

- If you become momentarily blank, write again the phrase, "I am the mountain," and just let your hand and pen continue to write without thought, without editing, without judgment. Even if it seems irrelevant, just continue to write for fifteen minutes. For this space of time, your hand is the mountain's hand, the vehicle for its opportunity to be heard. Even if what you are writing is some reflection of a personal experience of your own, keep writing.

- If you've come with friends, read to one another and discover the mountain's dialogue in community.

We continue walking the circuitous trail to the summit, where we pick up the Ridge Trail. It's been some time since we've been here. The small village of satellite dishes and forest green communication towers has grown, tuned as ever toward the sky. On our latest visit, a small red fox, hoping for food and tame enough to cautiously approach cars, was rewarded by visitors for its courage and charm. However, like the bears in national parks, these animals don't understand human rules and quixotic behavior; they are risks and are themselves at risk. Today, the fox is nowhere in sight, and I wonder what's become of it.

## A Hermit's Focus

Once, when I visited Thelma and Besh, a homeless couple who lived in Owl Canyon, Thelma described an experience with a red fox. She had been alone for an extended period—Besh was gone for a month, and Thelma slept in a sleeping bag next to the mud-oak wall of the structure in which they lived. The fox, who had taken up with them from a distance, began to spend time outside the same wall, just next to where Thelma slept. Every time she'd cough or roll over, the fox responded with curiosity. After a few days of this behavior, the fox began to jump up when she coughed and then to come to the entrance, peering in. Thelma finally became unnerved by the fox's actions when it actually came into the open-ended little room. Reluctantly, she chased it away.

Besh and Thelma lived many years on the mountain, essentially in wilderness surrounded by civilization—modern-day hermits who served the mountain as unpaid, unofficial caretakers, doing the day-in, day-out steady work of habitat restoration. The canyons in which they lived are now completely clear of French broom and fennel, and almost free of pampas grass, Italian thistle, and hemlock. Their work opened up habitat for endangered butterfly species, whose presence has increased in these canyons. They repaired trails, cut back poison oak, removed litter. Thousands of schoolchildren from all over the Bay Area came to visit and learn from them about ecological action.[10]

The mountain's patron saint, San Bruno, would have been very able to relate to their presence here; although he was a highly regarded priest and theologian in the Catholic Church at the turn of the twelfth century, he loved most of all to commune with God in the wilderness. Another Bruno, also a priest and theologian, lived just after the time of Copernicus. He so passionately viewed nature as divine that he was burned as a heretic.[11] Perhaps his link to the mountain was through Besh and Thelma, who were also banished for political reasons, and their living space on San Bruno Mountain destroyed by the county.

## Shell Mound: The Presence of the Past

At the foot of San Bruno Mountain, just next to San Francisco Bay, is a sheltered lagoon that once served as a prime fishing spot for the Ohlone people who lived less than a mile away. Just a little north of here, near Candlestick Park, the bay water is much choppier. However, the protected lagoon made it relatively easy for people to fish. At that time, the creek that still runs through the shell mound meandered through a marshy area—now covered by Highway 101—all the way to the lagoon. The tule reeds for their fishing boats were probably gathered very close by.

The shell mound, six feet deep in places, was in use for about five thousand years and extended all the way down to the bay. The village was clustered around a spring that flowed year-round near the southern edge of the shell mound and was the gathering spot for many shared community activities. Because the shells in the soil make it hard for plant life to persist, not many trees grow directly on the mound. But next to the stream a willow stand marked the presence of water; buckeyes, bay laurels, and oaks grew nearby. Sedge, used for making baskets, still grows along the creek, and patches of watercress skim the water's surface.

Some one thousand years ago, a large earthquake shifted the land above the main village, and the whole ridge collapsed into the canyon. Originally, the creek ran straight down the hillside, but the quake gave it a bend, and it now flows down a slightly altered streambed. When the ridge dropped, it left a flat plateau that provided a second shell mound area. From that upper shell mound, one has a clear view all the way down the Peninsula. It was probably the last camping area of the Indian people before the full takeover by the Spaniards. The approach to the shell mound by way of the bay's shore would have been too difficult for the explorers to access easily, so the Spaniards who stumbled on the community probably came by way of El Camino Real, the route several miles to the west that connected the California missions.

Through all of the changes in the land over the last few hundred years, the upper mound has retained the most native habitat. Next to Bayshore Road, a eucalyptus grove grew, then was cut down. Cattle were kept on the land. More recently, it was dug and prodded and shaped into roadbed. Then a small miracle took place.

For decades, developers have wanted to build houses and commercial buildings at the base of San Bruno Mountain. The plans have been protested in courts and on the streets. About three years ago, a new developer took possession of the property. Activists with San Bruno Mountain Watch invited him to go for a hike on the land the Ohlones occupied, where rare and endangered habitat presence was evident in and around the village site. Jack Myers accepted the invitation and was touched by the importance of the site. An agreement was reached among all concerned parties. The shell mound in its twenty-five acre valley was made available for purchase. While it may become part of the state park if sufficient funds can be generated for its upkeep, recent funding cuts now threaten the success of the agreement.

The significance of shell mounds is becoming more fully understood. While they were once considered simply the garbage pits of Indian villages, it is now clear that they mean much more than that. Some were occupied in a transitory way as people moved from place to place gathering food. Others were the sites not only of villages but also of ceremonial activities and burials of the Ohlone people. The artifacts in the mounds provide information that expands knowledge about community life and practices. For example, the condition of a mortar and pestle found at this site was consistent with a practice in which the mortar was purposely broken when the woman who had used it died. Despite their value for expanding knowledge, many people feel that the mounds should not be subjected to scientific examination but respected and left intact.

At this particular mound, the remains of at least fifteen people have been found. Probably hundreds of other burials exist here as well. It's hard to say exactly how many people occupied this site, but it's likely that the entire southeastern side of the mountain contains remnants of Ohlone settlements.[12] The Ohlones burned their dead, and although human remains have been found in six of the seven drills on the site, they are mostly charred bones. At least one intact skeleton was found and reburied. In nearby Brisbane, a man, woman, and child were discovered together, which probably means they fell victims to a disease introduced by Europeans.

During the time when the fate of this shell mound was being debated, some of us gathered with David Schooley on the site. We walked slowly over the land, fragments of shells and dark earth linking us with many forms of life that once existed here. We sat together, where friends and relatives in an ancient community once talked and worked with one another. We made a ceremonial offering, a *despacho*, to the mountain and then lay on the earth with our eyes closed. Geoff's didgeridoo sounded a low and evocative call. In mind's eye, we sank into the mound, our attention focused on the presence of the past, and we walked in another time.

## PERSONAL JOURNEYS

Marguerite: *I was lying on the ground, very close to the didgeridoo. When he began to play, I started to feel like my body was being very faintly vibrated, like each cell of my body was responding, in very tiny movements. Then I felt like the ground under me, the shell mound, was vibrating, and I was sinking back in time. There were no roads, no buildings. There was movement in the background, as if there were people, but I felt invisible, like a ghost.*

*It was quiet—I just had a feeling of slow activity in the community. And even though I felt invisible, I also felt like I was present—that I was someplace in the past that wasn't any different from being in the present. When the didgeridoo stopped, I didn't open my eyes right away, because I felt like the people had come back with me, and I didn't want that sense to go away. Even though I didn't see anyone that I didn't expect to see, it still feels that way. Something is here that has always been here that I wasn't even aware of before.*

Jo: *It was after the Peruvian ceremony you did in the beginning....When Geoff played the didgeridoo, I felt a sense of presence. I interpreted it as spirits rising from the mound to join us in that music. I had been on that shell mound several times before and never had an experience like it. I wrote this poem:*

> *Listen, Listen*
> *Big crowd, many people*
> *Man, Boat on water*
> *This, no change, forever.*

## TRY THIS: Feel the presence of the past

- When you are at a shell mound, or in a place where others have lived before, find a comfortable place where you can melt into time.

- Ask permission of those who were here before to move through time to visit this place in another era.
- Let your body relax and begin to breathe slowly.
- Feel the temperature of the air and of the ground—a breeze or warm sun—any tactile experience of your body. You are sharing timeless sensations that others have felt in this very place.
- As you breathe deeply, notice the fragrances borne on the air around you. As they do now, ancestors of the sedges, the herbs, the buckeyes— plants that may no longer be here now—perfumed the air in generations past.
- How long might their minute traces have lingered? Let your senses of smell, of sound, of presence, open to the earth's gifts that may linger here.
- Feel the rhythmic breathing of your environment, a breathing made up of no individual person, plant, or animal but a rhythm that encompasses all life that is present.
- Breathe with the rhythm of this place and feel your own breath contributing to that rhythm. You are not separate from the place nor separate from the flow of time here.
- When you feel yourself breathing as part of the whole, let your senses relax and experience whatever there is to be experienced. Even with your eyes closed, see what there is to see, hear what there is to hear.
- When you are ready to return to a separate sense of yourself and to the present time and place, take three deep breaths, touching the earth with your fingers.

## Buckeye: Gathering Power

There's a particular pleasure in discovering something newly revealed in a familiar place. Perhaps you are present at different times of the day, or during different seasons or weather patterns. Animals and birds might move differently. The scents of plants change with varying exposure to moisture. When you tap into the variations of the mountain's life, new perceptions and new relationships emerge.

On another visit to the mountain, my extended family comes with me. We make our way up through the industrial park on the west side of the mountain. Our destination, Buckeye Canyon, is the site of another of San Bruno's shell mounds. Once an inlet of the bay occupied the area, which is now thoroughly filled with offices and warehouses. Enormous trucks lumber down the access road from a quarry; the path toward Buckeye Canyon begins just before the quarry's tall cyclone fence marks the boundary of the quarry.

Near the beginning of the trail, fennel leaves on six-foot stalks waft their tantalizing licorice odor into the air. I gather some for tea later, breaking the stem close to the ground so that the growth of this intensely invasive plant is inhibited. It's a small gesture, however; for this and the other invasive plants that endanger the more fragile native plants, the only way to eliminate their presence is to dig them out.

Years ago my son gave me a flute made from the thickest fennel stem I've ever seen. Gaily painted, it has come with me many times and lends its voice to the wind, an acceptable way for this invader to be harmlessly present on the mountain. Blackberries in a patch at the side of the trail are not yet ripe, but the crop is so bountiful that we'll return another time when the berries are ready.

From that point on to the shell mound, only native plants are present. The approach to the shell mound is relatively flat, and the trail winds through toyon, coyote brush, and poison oak. A bit to the left of the trail, a stand of willow hints of the creek that once flowed into the marshy inlet at the foot of the hill. I wonder what happens these days to its seasonal flow, its natural path now blocked by buildings and streets. Scatterings of mint appear—people food— and an occasional lupine—butterfly food. The pale green coastal sage is soft to the touch. Rattlesnake grass will rattle in the late summer, when the little pods have dried.

The path gradually merges with the stream bank and dips abruptly into it. Here the dry creek bed flares wide, and at its center, a fire circle appears to have been recently used. An ancient buckeye grows on the far bank, branches and broad leaves overhanging the creek bed, creating a cool retreat from hot sunshine. Sitting beneath it, the people from the shell mound community would have ground up acorns harvested from nearby live oaks and put them into baskets in the creek's running water for a week to leech the tannin, creating an edible acorn meal.

Buckeyes produce nuts—beautiful golden brown globes that hang on the trees wrapped in protective coats long after the leaves have dropped in late summer. Because the tree concentrates its water in the roots, putting its efforts into nurturing the nuts rather than the leaves, the branches lose their leaves very early. When the first rains come, the nuts fall to the ground, and the trees seem denuded overnight.

Under the buckeye, a special feeling of protection, of nurturance, permeates the area. Relaxing, we let the tree become our teacher.

**TRY THIS: Following a buckeye teacher, gather your power**

- When buckeyes lose their leaves late in summer, sit beneath one of the bare-branched trees.

- Close your eyes, relax, and lean against the spreading trunk.

- Take some of the dry leaves from the ground and crumble them between your fingers. The tree has let them go to concentrate its water supply for the important task of creating and nourishing what is to come, bringing the nut to fruition.

- Envision the mahogany-colored buckeye nut hanging from the tree, protected by the husk that begins to part even while it's still on the tree. The hidden promise of the nut is peeking out, showing itself.

- Envision the shiny golden nut still clinging to the bare branches, still nourished by the life coursing through the tree.

- In your mind's eye, watch the buckeye nut falling from the tree, falling onto fertile ground.

- As you continue to pick up the dry leaves, crumbling them in your fingers and dropping them, let an image or word appear that epitomizes what, in your heart of hearts, you most passionately desire to create.

- Let the crackling sound of the dry leaves bring to mind the static and clutter of your own life—the obligations and connections that fill too many hours, take too much attention, distract your focus from whatever matters most to you.

- Continue to crackle the dry leaves in your fingers, as you consider the distractions one by one. How do they feed you? What keeps you bound to them? Is it guilt or habit, lethargy or social expectation, fear of changing your life?

- As you listen to the sound of the dry leaves returning to compost the earth, imagine crushing whatever drains your attention, whatever habitual patterns of behavior or responding to demands are no longer appropriate for you. Imagine them crumbling like the leaves in your fingers.

- Remembering the buckeye tree nourishing the nut as it clings to the tree, see yourself nurturing your own unfolding creation.

- How can you protect it, help it to grow? See yourself feeding it—giving it space in your life, practicing, learning, risking trials.

- Imagine your creation being launched, coming to fruition. Feel and see the fruits of your efforts.

- Take a deep breath and open your eyes. Search out a fallen buckeye nut and hold the nut in the palm of your hand. Feel its smooth and perfect shape, its coolness; admire its color and fragrance.

Holding onto the buckeye tree anchored on the far side of the stream helps us climb the short steep bank. We take care to avoid the tree's poison oak guardian. Passing under the buckeye canopy, we look for buckeye nuts to take home, plant, and grow for a while. They will witness the unfolding of the journey we've begun here with the buckeye teacher, and when the desire we're working toward is well on its way, we'll return the plants to San Bruno Mountain. As we return here again and again, the new trees' sprouting will help us check on the progress of the growth of our personal creations seeded here today.

Near the top of the bank, we find ourselves in an open grassy field, where rich dark earth studded with bits of white shells is the unmistakable mark of a shell mound. Five thousand years of continuous habitation has gifted the earth with buried secrets of generations, left undisturbed here. The shell mound is marked on the surface only by the shell fragments and by a slender totem pole piercing the earth. In 1990, Earth First!, San Bruno Mountain Watch, and several other organizations commemorated the site by erecting the pole. Even though it is not traditional to the Ohlone people who lived here, the pole is a tribute of honor to the generations who were then stewards of the land and a commitment to be the responsible stewards of this generation.

We sit near a hummingbird sage plant and eat, sharing plant folklore that comes to mind—of the hummingbird who stole fire for the people and brought it back to be stored in the buckeye tree for everyone to use; of the yarrow stalks used to cast the I Ching; of hazelnut, used for divining rods to discover water, valuable minerals, or buried treasure. Ancient uses are carried through folk tradition, through cultural myths and songs of all countries and traditions, and even through investigations in scientific laboratories. My favorite way to experience the plants is at their source, growing from the earth.

Later, we return to the streambed and begin to wind our way up toward the summit. We're surrounded by the green leaves of a variety of plants and are so sheltered from the sun overhead that for a long time, only the lime green light of sun filtered through the trees shines down on us. Tree roots sometimes extend into the damp bed, and the hike grows more strenuous. We climb over boulders and step up onto ledges created by the roots. Wildflowers take us by surprise; our path has been strewn by an unseen welcoming committee. We take advantage of the beauty, stopping often to catch our breath and marvel at bright color in filtered shade.

As the path through the streambed ascends, we sometimes sidestep, digging our boots into the steepness for a better purchase. The group becomes spread out, some more able than others to deal with the steepness and challenge of the terrain. Obstacles present themselves—slippery muddy spots, stones slick with emerald green mosses that look like they're hiding entrances into leprechaun's homes, hanging branches of poison oak. We help one another over the tricky spots, solicitous and encouraging. Sometimes the next step isn't a step at all but clinging with hands and knees to take advantage of whatever purchase is available. The trail rises and falls.

We pick up a trail to the left of the streambed and enter a series of very old groves. Oak trees drip with mossy-looking old man's beard. Pale yellow catkins decorate hazelnut bushes. No one would have recognized the ancient Islay cherry grove as cherry, but the proof was passed down the line—small handfuls of nearly black cherries, sweet and juicy, with large pits that we spit back into the moist forest earth. A few still "cherry red" are not quite ripe; sampling them makes my mouth pucker. Weeks ago the last garden cherries were harvested, but here enough fruit clings to the trees to make a small feast.

Suddenly, blue sky appears through the canopy, azure fragments of a jigsaw puzzle whose main picture was green foliage and mossy stones. The woods release us completely; moving through fields of wildflowers, we finally gain the rolling Ridge Trail. The astonishing shift from a forested world to open hills and sky makes it hard to believe it is the same mountain. A short distance below, a completely different microclimate exists.

## Burn Area: Unknotting the Regeneration Mystery

Transformation and regeneration is taking another form on San Bruno Mountain. A controlled burn early in the summer of 2003 became a spreading wildfire and cleared 72 acres of well-entrenched exotics, plants that were almost impossible to eradicate any other way.[12] We decide to visit the area. We want to see what it might have looked like after a traditional Native American burn and to see the effect of the fire on the plant community. Although the fire has taken everything in its path, it helps the exotics as well as the natives regenerate. The window of opportunity provided by the burn is small, and only timely replanting by volunteers will allow native plants to get an advantage.

A year-round spring trickles through the burned ravine. Lining the path leading to the running water, blackened skeletons of tangled plant stems form patterns that resemble Celtic knots, the elaborate designs of old Ireland that represented the intricacies of creation and man's circuitous path through life.[13] To our consternation, we notice that pale-green eucalyptus leaves are beginning to emerge at the roots of trees burned to ground level by the fire. Very near, however, are other plants, infinitely more precious. Islay cherries vie for a place in the landscape; native to Franciscan habitat, these plants have grown for centuries on the mountain. Although far more fragile than the eucalyptus, the leaves of the cherry plants have grown as high as those of the exotics. With the eucalyptus and gorse temporarily held in check, the centuries-old cherries have breathing space and a new chance to survive. Jo sits on Nine Fern Rock and plays her Celtic harp to them. Its sweet notes swirl around the plants and dip into the ravines. A healing peace envelops all of us—Jo, her harp, the cherries, the ravine, the nearby stream, and me.

The threat posed by the presence of exotics on San Bruno has become increasingly obvious to visitors. Time and the failed efforts of the Habitat Conservation Plan have revealed the difficulty of controlling them. Even with the fire's helping hand, the task seems nearly impossible. We decide to work with the fire, looking to its impact on the land for guidance on how to continue the work. We'll use the blackened stems and branches of trees that made it through the fire for inspiration. The twisted plant stems will be our Celtic knots, our doorways for dialogue with the fire.

Picking up charred pieces of wood lying about, we pull out our journals, open them to clean white pages, and settle ourselves among the tree trunks for a new kind of conversation. We observe the plants rather than the paper and charcoal. Each of us holds in our minds some form of a question: How do we continue the regeneration begun by the fire? Guided by the interwoven branches, we allow our hands to move, and images begin to emerge on paper. We hold the question in our minds and hearts, and follow the path our hands offer us.

## PERSONAL JOURNEYS

Ginny: *Holding the charcoal made me feel connected to the fire itself. I followed the swooping pattern of the burned branches, and it began to feel like the fire had scrubbed things. It was as if the fire did its work, then sat back, asking me what I would do—like being given a blank slate to create on. I was drawn to plant, and I think I must find out how to take part in the efforts being organized to do that. I also had an image of wood carvers working on the blackened stumps to create a hillside of Watchers—so that as the plants grow back, there would be guardians, ancestors of the plants that had died, who would be overseeing the next genera-*

*tion. I like to imagine coming back and seeing faces peeking out through the next growth! That probably isn't very practical, but I really like the idea. I could imagine music here, playing to the plants.*

## TRY THIS: Let your hand guide you through a burned knot doorway

- Go to a burn area and locate a bush or small tree whose tangled skeleton draws your attention.

- Find some charcoal on the ground nearby.

- Sit and observe the bush whose tangled skeleton draws your attention.

- With the charcoal in your hand, look at the bush.

- Formulate clearly the information you're seeking. You may choose to focus on the regeneration of this place. Or you may resonate in a very personal way about deep loss in your own life and reconstructing your own future.

- Keep your eyes on the bush and let its image guide the movement of your hand. Keep the charcoal in constant contact with the paper, like the continuous cord used to make a Celtic knot.

- Let the charcoal continue to move over the page without looking at it.

- Ask the bush to show you how to move through the doorway of regeneration that the fire has provided. Ask how you can be of greatest benefit to the native habitat.

- As you draw, let any words, images, or songs come to you. Notice ideas, thoughts—whatever comes to your mind or your inner senses.

- Keep the charcoal moving; it is your guide through the doorway of the knotted stems and branches.

- Let the image or words develop fully. Try to follow a theme, asking for clarification or elaboration. "Thank you. And what else?" or "Thank you. And can you show me more?" Participate in a dialogue with whatever senses are stimulated.

- When you feel complete, thank the plant and the fire. Stretch a bit to return completely to ordinary reality.

- Leave a small offering at the base of the bush—a pinch of tobacco or cornmeal, a hair from your head, or some water from your water bottle.

- Look at your drawing; it may look like a child's scrawl over the page— but it has been your doorway to information and action.

- Write down a description of what you saw, or the words that came to you. Include the process, the path you followed—even if the elements seem irrelevant or inconsequential. Often, the small details hold information that has meaning only to you.

- Follow through with the actions that came to you. When we ask for information and it comes to us, the more often we act on what we've received, the more likely it is that future attempts will also be successful.

## Mountain's Ridge: A Walking Meditation

On the windblown ridgetops, the undulations of the mountain's bare ridges extend to the northwest. Only the low and bowing plants that have made their bargains with the fierceness of the wind have a home here, but just off the summit, the canyons teem with buckeye and oak. I fantasize having hands large enough to mold my palms around the mounded hills, as though they were warm clay or the soft contours of a human body.

Like the view from the plateau of our earlier visit, the vista from the hilltops also includes the Pacific on one side and San Francisco Bay on the other. While the plateau felt protected by the woods on nearby hills, here the land is almost continuously scrubbed by the wind. The sky is constantly changing—enormous billows of white clouds piling higher and higher, dark streaming clouds moving swiftly. Cloud shadows move across the landscape, reverse spotlights closing out details and then moving away to reveal them once again. Like mysterious animals, they stalk the hills and valleys. We smooth sunscreen on our faces, put on backpacks filled with water, cheese, and fruit, then maneuver through the fence onto the path of the Ridge Trail.

None of the other mountaintops around San Francisco Bay offers a trail that extends so far in a single direction. As we move forward, the convergence of ocean and bay is visible in our imaginations, although we'll never quite arrive at that point on this day. We would have to cross the streets of San Francisco that now bury the rest of the Franciscan zone before we would finally reach the Golden Gate at Baker Beach.

On the Ridge Trail, the rough stones of the uneven path help us focus our attention on walking, and we watch for the first appearance of one of the sparkling fragments of quartz crystal that may favor us near the end of the trail. This trail is the backbone of the mountain, an obvious boundary between coastal and bayside climates. It moderates the fierce ocean winds in the winter, bearing the brunt of a force that can arrive at eighty miles an hour. It shapes the intense summer fogs, guiding their direction over the slopes; today, its presence simply ushers wisps of fog over the ridge.

Once again, our walk becomes a meditation. Moving very slowly, we pay continuous attention to the contrast between the two sides of the ridge. Right side: a rare manzanita, hugging the hummocks and blanketing the rocky sides of the path. Left side: coyote brush and native grasses. Right side: the city of Colma; on the left, Mount Diablo. Right side: the ground being prepared for more houses; left side: the canyons with their hidden groves of buckeye and oak. Right side: the existing housing developments; left side: the industrial park. Right side: the Pacific Ocean; left side: San Francisco Bay. We become foglike conduits of the wind, carrying the calmness and tranquility of the ocean side toward the bay side of the mountain. Inhaling, we breathe in the wisps of fog; exhaling, we direct the cleansing wind through our bodies from the ocean side to the bayside. Feeling the swirl of the fog around our upright bodies, we become upright extensions of the mountain. "I am the mountain," we murmur to ourselves as we move slowly forward.

**TRY THIS: Send fresh air from the ocean to the bay**

- Walk along the Ridge Trail; feel the winds blow in from the ocean.
- As you walk, pay attention to each footfall on the rocky path.
- Match your breathing to the pattern of your steps. Inhale when you step to the right, on the ocean side, and exhale as you step to the left, on the bay side.
- With each breath, extend your attention to the plants on either side of the path, pulling in the winds that pour over the plants on the right side and pouring them out toward the plants on the left side.
- After a while, extend your awareness to the slope of the hills, receiving and sending the winds from these greater distances.
- Reach with your breathing to the plants on the hills to your right. Inhale the spirit of those plants and exhale them to the plants on the left, linking the plant worlds on the ocean side and the bay side.
- When you are comfortably sending the essence of the plants and sloping hills on the right toward those on the left, extend your awareness and your breath to the land and the plants beyond.
- Inhale the air from the ocean side and exhale toward the bay.
- Feel yourself amplifying the air coming in from the ocean, helping to refresh the air over the region of the bay.

Red-tailed hawks soar through the valleys below us and a bullfinch swoops over our shoulders. Coyote brush and low manzanita edge the path; Dellalou points out how the manzanita snuggles against the stone for protection against intense winds. Bright yellow blossoms of lizard's tongue vie for attention with the deeper orange hues of monkeyflower among them. Two stalks of foxglove side by side, one deep pink and the other cloud white, invite a ruby-throated hummingbird to touch down. In a moment, a second bird comes to the same flower, and the two immediately fly away together.

## Cleansing Winds

Meg carries a tule cape on this journey. Months earlier, she and Patria visited Kirby Cove. There, they were inspired in a shamanic journey by Ohlone grandmothers to create the cape, something neither of them had done before. They sought out Norm Kidder at Don Edwards San Francisco Bay Wildlife Refuge, who builds boats and other objects from tules. Following his advice, they collected tall tules from the banks of the bay, prepared them, and finally created the cape that would be used in many community gatherings and rituals.

Now Meg spreads the cape on the ground. Avoiding the newly sprouting yarrow and California poppies, we sit next to it. Fresh leaves of hummingbird sage grow nearby. Because this type of sage is found at many shell mounds, its presence here at the top of the mountain causes us to recollect previous visits to the mountain. Sitting quietly, we anchor ourselves here by envisioning the plants, the paths, the insects, birds, and animals that form our associations with the mountain.

Previously, on Mount Tamalpais and on Mount Diablo, we'd used fire ceremonies to help us transform unwanted thoughts and residues of pain. Elsewhere, running streams shifted the way we see ourselves and the world around us. We'd used shamanic meditation practices to compost our individual toxins into the earth. Earth, water, and fire have transformed us. Now the wind over San Bruno shows us that it, too, has the potential to sweep away unwanted residue, and we give ourselves over to its elemental power for a thorough personal cleansing.

One at a time, we lie on the reed cape, our faces turned toward the drifting clouds. Debbie takes the first turn. Carol reaches into her backpack and retrieves the group *mesa* we'd made together at Ring Mountain, the assemblage of power objects to which each person contributed. She places it on Debbie's heart to connect each of us to Debbie. Hera brings out a small vial of water taken from the ocean during the outgoing tide at Kirby Cove. As she passes it among us, each of us sprinkles a few drops onto Debbie. We form a circle around her and begin very gently to stroke her, brushing from her filaments of energy any shadows of pain or sorrow she is carrying.

Debbie begins to tremble but gives herself to the powerful event that is happening. Later, she says, "I felt like I was in my grave and looking up. The wind was blowing, and a cloud claimed my body for a moment. But I was also feeling that everyone who was in the circle surrounding me was protecting me, helping to cleanse me. It was unbelievable."

When each of us has had a turn, we hug each other, overwhelmed, laughing and excited. Finally, we share our experiences over sandwiches, water, and chocolate.

"I felt transported," says Sarah. "I felt lifted up and just surrendered. I felt completely safe, even though we're out here totally exposed." Others echo her sentiments in various ways. Marguerite comments, "I always feel like the mountains we visit feed me. But today, I really understood that threads of my self also impregnate the mountain. I leave a trace of myself—through my attitude, my appreciation, my awareness, my motivation to care for open space."

Our pleasure in this unique experience draws us very naturally to the final installation of the crystal. As the sparkling stone passes among us, we remember the dawn that bound the passing of time with the rising sun and the setting moon; the fragile and unique environment of the plants of the Franciscan zone; the stench of landfill that protected the mountain from thoughtless early development; the fog that allowed us to bring balance to our lives with a moving meditation; the endangered butterflies who guided us through personal transformation; the inspiration of the land itself to give the mountain a voice; the humble dedication of Besh and Thelma tending the space they occupied on the planet; the shell mounds' reminder of the lingering presence of other lives on the mountain; the buckeye's unique capacity to concentrate its life force; a burn area teaching us about renewing life; the Ridge Trail allowing us to become extensions of the mountain; and our spirits cleansed by the wind.

When the crystal returns to Carol, she moves a large stone to one side. Remembering aloud the act of separation at Kirby Cove that shattered the cluster of crystals, she encourages us to envision the crystal connected around the bay, like the planets of the solar system, orbiting around the sun. She places the crystal into the hollow she created by moving the stone. We replace the stone and move away, leaving the crystal to San Bruno Mountain, gatekeeper of our circle.

## Gratitude to the Mountains: Spinning the Web, Making An Offering

We gather our belongings and move farther along the Ridge Trail. We dawdle, searching for a spot to create the final offering in our circle of mountains around the bay; because it's so special, we're determined to locate the spot that will draw together most powerfully the seven sites we've visited.

We could have stayed where we spread the tule cape and placed the crystal, but without even speaking of that as a possibility, we all seem to want to give that powerful event its own space. It belonged particularly to San Bruno. We want something that will give equal importance to Kirby Cove and all the mountains. We choose one spot and then move on, choose again and walk farther. Walking farther along the ridge gives us a chance to center ourselves and to prepare for the wider scope of our intent.

At last, we agree on a place that pleases us all, then settle down, facing San Francisco Bay. The wind has blown away the clouds, and most of the mountains in our circle are visible from this vantage point. Assembling a *despacho* will celebrate that powerful circle. I spread a beautiful Peruvian weaving on the ground, then place a smaller weaving on its surface to hold our offering as we create it. I secure a Chinese prayer paper embossed with a gold medallion with small stones to keep it from blowing away. Sprinkles of brown sugar, sage, and incense form the bed for the offering; we remember how at each mountain visit we found sweet experiences of beauty and friendship. We recall ways we found at each site to cleanse our spirits of whatever heaviness had come with us. We pray that the sage in the offering brings a similar purification to the mountains' beleaguered lives. As the incense is placed on the gold prayer paper, we call up memories of wind-borne mists and pollens, of rubbing our fingers on leaves of cedars, pines, wild mints, and other leafy plants, and visit the image of each mountain being cloaked in unseen fragrances.

From the familiar bag of fragrant bay leaves, each person chooses three perfect leaves of a similar size, a reminder to focus actions, feelings, and mental images on the site she is honoring. Each location around the bay, including the opening of our way at Kirby Cove, will be represented by someone's contribution. This time, as each person places the grouping of leaves on the offering, she shares what the yearlong process has meant to her. One by one, we call the mountains in this way and honor them.

With a husky voice, Hera begins the process with Kirby Cove. Blowing on the leaves she's chosen, she places them on the offering. "I'll never forget our first trip—to Kirby Cove—walking down that hill to the beach. Oh, it was breathtaking. You were showing us the world we'd never get to see if it weren't for your vision of a circle of sacred places around the bay. I got to know the land in a way I'd never known it, even though I've lived here for years.

"It gave us a feeling of being a real community, a high experience that made *me* feel special. Having a hand in planning it made *us* a fantastic community experience. I met people of all different ages who, because of their love for the land, the trees, and the rocks, were very attractive to me."

Patria follows her, honoring Ring Mountain. Placing three leaves on the offering, she acknowledges the importance of the circle to her.

"It was so much a matter of expanding my awareness. It wasn't the number of them—there are more places I still want to get to—but more experiencing them in a way that connects the meditations with the mountains. It gave me a lot of creative inspiration. It was tremendous for me—increased the depths of experience of being in nature. The circular aspect of it was important, too. I meditate every day—it changed my life and provided tremendous grounding for me. The book of poetry and painting that Barbara and I put together based on our visits to the mountains was a rich collaboration for both of us."

Maya adds, "Circling the bay was a brilliant idea—and so much fun! To really attend to the sacredness of the mountains and the land where we live was tremendously fulfilling. Even though I've lived in the Bay Area for almost 35 years, there were a number of places we visited that I had never seen before. I remember my first reaction to Ring Mountain, seeing the spring streams running down the mountainside, the wildflowers, and the amazing huge rock formations—I was stunned by the power and beauty of this place so close to the freeway and yet so ancient and wild. I'll never forget it."

Blowing on her three leaves as she places them on the offering, Carol honors Mount Tamalpais. "I was born in the Bay Area," she says. "I've lived here all my life. Through this circle, I've seen places I've never visited—never even heard of. Circling San Francisco Bay, I became integrated into the physical world around me. In all my years, I never had such an intimate relationship with any place. Each mountain has its own personality, and I felt like I had come home. But I'm also committing to give something back to the land. I know that it will continue to affect what we do, how we relate to the earth, that we are integrated into this place."

Debbie honors Mount Diablo, her voice choked with emotion, as she places her leaves on the gold paper. "One of the biggest things that sticks in my mind is, of course, Mount Diablo…all the work we did around the issues with my mother and the brutality of my life, and the healing that occurred. Not only for me, but for other people, too. Conventional therapy didn't work for me. *This* is what helped me get better. Jails are full of people with my kind of background. I didn't want to go that route.

"Then there are the ancestors of that mountain, who continue to strike me today, especially at times when driving to Lake Tahoe and seeing Mount Diablo in the distance….And then there is the music….I almost always heard a song in my head when we were doing our journeys on the mountains, usually a popular rock/folk song. Remember when we went to Mount Diablo and I brought with me a tape I had made of different songs that were relevant to me at that time? You and Hera were helping me with something about my mother, and I played my tape and journeyed alone on my spot overlooking a ridge. I still have that tape and play it from time to time. I have wonderful memories of so much love and healing. Those will stay with me forever."

As she honors Mount Hamilton, Marguerite speaks about the web: "I think about my relationship to the environment in a different way. When we weave the web from the mountain we're on to all the others we've visited, it makes me a dweller in a larger community than even the Bay Area. There's a bigger context I'm connected to. I do feel like a weaver—a protector of life around me, fed by the environment to protect not only me but the environment itself. Mount Hamilton wove my life into that of the universe. It's been a wonderful experience of human community and physical community, and I'll never forget it. Being in nature feeds me in a way that's absolutely necessary for me to stay balanced."

Honoring San Bruno Mountain, Barbara says, "It was a high point in my life. It opened up the whole world to me. I've done paintings about it and refer to it in my art classes. And even though I only go out here when we're together, I have it. I have it all inside. I think about it and talk about it. And when I do, I get it right back again. It gave me a new way of looking at nature and being in a place I love."

Meg, who comes here often for San Bruno's special gifts, adds, "Circling the bay introduced me to mountains I did not know and taught me the value of developing and maintaining a relationship with mountains. Now I connect daily with, and draw energy from, five of those that surround the bay. My whole experience of life is richer and more profound because of the connections."

"Kayla muses, "Mt. Umunhum woke me up to notice things around me in nature that are always present, but that I tend to overlook. I'm more appreciative of the everyday world around me."

When we finish sharing, we sit quietly. Clearly, these mountains and everything on them are our sources, our nourishment for the efforts we will continue to make to protect the earth. This is where we can come to regroup, to find solace, guidance, and pleasure, to remember what we're continuing to protect. Without the insight, the protection, the peace they offer us, we'd run on empty in no time at all. Our efforts would become disconnected from heart and spirit, and all would be lost.

When each location has been called and honored, we enhance the *despacho* with decorations of flowers, chocolate, corn, and rice, of sparkling mica and tiny symbols of the elements—contributions that call up the sustenance, beauty, and pleasure that the circle itself has given us. Onto the completed offering, we blow a mist of red wine from a tiny vial passed among us. I fold the corners of the paper securely over the offering, and Meg ties it with a thin gold thread.

Standing in a circle, each person in turn holds the offering bundled in a small weaving and strokes the person next to her from head to toe with it. It is a final sharing between ourselves and the offering, a symbolic act of personal involvement in the creation of the offering and of the circle, and of distributing the blessings from each location to every participant.

## TRY THIS: Through an offering, spin a web to encircle the bay

- Somewhere along the Ridge Trail that rises and falls over San Bruno's crest, find a comfortable spot to sit overlooking the bay and the circle of mountains that surround it.

- Notice the mountain silhouettes that can be seen from here; remember those that can't be easily seen, and their location around the body of water below us. Remember Kirby Cove, the ocean's entrance into the bay. Extend your awareness in all directions.

- Follow the horizon's outline with your finger, as if you were tracing a path along the horizon itself, the path you followed in your circling.

- As your hands engage in this activity, imagine a filament, a thread of your own energy, moving from your center, through your finger, connecting you to the area that you are observing.

- Place next to you anything you have gathered to contribute to an offering, each carefully chosen to be part of your expression of appreciation for the gifts you've received at the mountains—foods you enjoy, something beautiful, flowers, a poem, seeds or twigs you've found in the woods.

- Spread a beautiful cloth on the ground, a context for the offering to honor the mountains and your relationship to each site.

- Place a smaller cloth on the "table," and on it, place the paper, simple or fancy, that will hold the offering itself.

- Place California sage on that foundation to purify the offering.

- Add something sweet, as you would offer a guest in your home, to communicate the pleasure you take in the mountains' company.
- Sprinkle incense, inviting connection with the spirits of place in the mountains.
- From a bag of bay leaves brought for the offering, find three perfect leaves of a similar size to represent the alignment of your heart, your actions, and your intent toward each mountain you've chosen.
- Take turns placing bundles of leaves on the offering until each site has been honored.
- As you place the bundle of three leaves on the bed of the offering, recall your relationship to the mountain it represents—reliving your physical experiences there, the way the mountain moved or inspired you, and your vision for the well-being of the mountain.
- Decorate the offering with symbols of the natural elements (earth, air, fire, and water), symbols of male and female—whatever beautiful, cheerful, or tasty additions are available from the hidden stores of backpack and pockets.
- Fold the corners of the paper securely and tie the offering with a thread of gold.
- Take turns stroking one another with the bundled offering, a final sharing between each person and the offering, a symbol of personal involvement in its creation and of the blessings from the mountains to every participant
- Burn the offering, if it is safe to do that, or bury it under a rock.

We live in paradise, a weaving of places and life-forms, of weather and human actions, of vision and intent. We partake in all aspects of our paradise, from the smog to the wind over the mountains, from the oranges and vegetables we raise to our jobs and the trails we walk and bike. We are not separate from it—and we create it. We are Spirit and participate in shaping our world by our attention, involvement, and energy. We feed ourselves with everything in our surroundings and feed what surrounds us with our choices and behavior. Here in the mountains, we can surrender to the pleasure of being fully alive in the moment and know that what we receive creates the power to sustain that which gives us life.

# Epilogue

# On the Summits: Weaving the Web

A few months after completing the first circling of the bay, we arrange an unusual meeting. Each person from our original group revisits a separate site that holds special meaning for her. She brings friends or family who have not previously participated in our excursions.

From each site to every other one, we "broadcast" the experience, weaving current images and sensations with recollections of the original visits. Through our imaginations, our hearts, and our intent, we become weavers.

From Kirby Cove, where the circle began, Patria's new circle listens to the waves lapping the shore; gathering threads sent from the other mountains, they breathe them out in rhythm with the tide. Focusing on the outgoing tide, they send our life choices out toward the shores of other Pacific countries. Bathed in light fog, this cove group sends that wispy veil on the wings of a red-tailed hawk to receptive weavers on other summits. Those seated on the promontory of Bald Mountain send the ocean fog that rolls over Mount Umunhum's summit into the weaving. Another group of friends sends the fog fingers from San Bruno's canyons to join the emerging warp of the weaving.

Conscious of the elusive opening to San Francisco Bay at Kirby Cove, Patria's circle sends to the other mountains the discovery of portals. On Mount Tamalpais, Dellalou and her group send a resonating thread from the portal that leads from a sunny meadow into the dappled woods along the Matt Davis Trail. Crisscrossing the threads affirms variations in the ways that openings present themselves.

The blue schist on Ring Mountain carries Maya's group into the tumultuous geological story of the Bay Area. They send its thread outward into the weaving, where it might meet a thread from Kirby Cove's ancient radiolarian cliffs. Maya and her friends offer up beginner's mind—touch a responding thread from those who descend mindfully four hundred feet into Kirby Cove and from those who breathe the Pacific air toward the bay as they walk San Bruno's ridge.

The friends sit before a carving thousands of years old. Diving into the past centuries toward a day when a petroglyph was etched and pecked so deeply that it might one day reach helpers in other worlds and realities, the group calls out to ancestors, to their own descendants, to the weavers on the other mountains, creating a multidimensional weaving across time and space. And on Mount Umunhum, those who cross into the past on the Los Gatos Gap send another time bridge into the pattern.

Those with Dellalou on Mount Tamalpais sit on the serpentine formation, travel its umbilical cord into Mother Earth—pull in Her nourishment, then send it toward the other mountains. They voyage back to the ancestors of humanity itself—and later draw that wisdom forward into the weaving. Dellalou remembers her early morning wakening by the wind, with its invitation to witness an enormous lavender moonset.

Debbie and her friends climb to the summit of Mount Diablo, where we first enacted the weaving among the mountains' sacred sites. The view immediately draws them—as weavers—into the weaving itself.

Debbie remembers tiny embers outlasting a fire ceremony, ready to begin their work of consumption anew. On San Bruno, skeletons of bushes charred by wildfire send their resonating response. The people on Mount Diablo paint mental images of cloud-filled valleys at sunrise and send them out to the peaks where others receive Diablo's threads.

Other vivid images spill out to this group—drops of moisture falling into a tiny pond created by an ancient oak's spreading roots; the vulture's search for carrion and his lessons for searching out their own inner carrion; sky-blue baby blue-eyes that fill them with enough peace to share with a mountain quarry, enveloping the torn hillside in conscious and compassionate awareness. As they weave the strands, the invisible connection among the mountains is strengthened.

At the foot of Mount Hamilton, Jenny and her friends sit at the foot of one of the ancient oaks in the Avenue of the Sun. She describes the reluctant sunrise on a solstice morning. The people weave in strands of the sun's light of day enflaming the meadows and tree-dotted hills of Joseph Grant Park. On all the other mountains in the circle, the sun's rising on each mountain is a unique gift, binding earth and sky together. From San Bruno comes the memory of fog veil that turns the rising sun to silver.

On Mount Hamilton, the weavers cross the boundaries of time and space, traveling to the stars and returning with filaments for the weaving. Perhaps at the same moment, the people bearing witness at Mount Umunhum walk again in their mind's eye across time lines at Los Gatos Creek, dappled light and shadow creating patterns on its surface, bringing subtle shading to the weaving.

From Mount Hamilton, the fragrance of buckeye blossoms perfumes the weaving. Recalling the festive bread on the summer solstice brings the sweet taste of raisins to the people's tongues, adds a flavorful dimension to the strands. On San Bruno Mountain, near a midden in Buckeye Canyon, a buck-eye drops its foliage to divert its growth into the shiny brown nuts suspended on the bare branches, and the power of concentrating, being essential, comes into the weaving.

Rounding the foot of the bay, the position of Carol's group begins to close the circle. They sit on the promontory of Bald Mountain, the gaunt tower on Mount Umunhum's peak at their backs. Across the foot of the bay, the dome of Mount Hamilton's glistening white observatory sends them reassurance that the human desecration symbolized by the tower behind them can change. Farther down the mountain, the Guadalupe River echoes that faith, as people envision the water's response to restoration efforts.

The Mount Umunhum witnesses entwine the earthquake rift into the fabric, the shape-shifting a reminder of the earth's own agenda of change. Mount Hamilton's "melted-ice-cream topography" echoes its way into the weaving.

Mount Umunhum sends forth threads of animal power—the hummingbird's darting quest for nourishment, drawn to partner with wild blossoms; the quail moving in tight community; the mountain lion's reminder of sharing space with those different from ourselves.

The people at Mount Umunhum remember animal behaviors guiding humans to traverse the mountains efficiently, and thrust the importance of animal guides into the weaving. On Mount Diablo, witnesses note the vulture's example of dealing with carrion, and from Mount Hamilton comes the wild pig wisdom of the worthy adversary.

Along the Ridge Trail of San Bruno, Barbara's group turns from ocean view to bay view, choosing finally to observe the bay and the circle of the mountains visible to them. From this vantage point, San Francisco Bay seems an enormous womb, and around its edges their communities are implanted—to be nourished and to return their own energy to the mountains and to the waters that host our very existence.

Barbara recalls the mountain's guardian role—protecting the last native plants of the Franciscan ecosystem, moderating weather patterns from the ocean. As she speaks of it, the people bring guardian quality to the weaving. Calling attention to the natural guardians, they honor the entire greenbelt surrounding and guarding the bay. They remember Besh and Thelma, humble people caretaking the mountain—envision them and many others contributing simple acts of restoration and preservation. They envision themselves and all who live around the bay as guardians, sharing the task of preserving life.

A quartz crystal found on the path reminds them of crystal's capacity to broadcast, to reflect. With attention and intent, they ask the crystal to broadcast the message of its own wisdom. Looking across the bay, they honor

Mtount Diablo's widespread influence, Mount Hamilton's bringing information from the universe. From mountain to mountain, the weaving takes shape.

*          *          *          *

We live in paradise. As we walk its sacred space, we open ourselves to deeper relationships with all the beings who share it. In the audible silence of nature, we risk exposing our deepest fears, hopes, and feelings to the trees, to the wind, to the waters. In the canyons and on the peaks, we hear what we must do in order to live harmoniously with the other beings of the natural world. We discover new capacities and approaches from the natural world itself. Here in the mountains, we surrender to the pleasure of being fully alive in the moment and know that what we receive creates the power to sustain that which gives us life. The sacred space within these mountains becomes a powerful container of inspiration and vision for the future.

# Appendix A: Useful Contacts

California Open Space Project: www.californiaopenspace.com

California Native Plant Society: www.cnps.org

Committee for Green Foothills: www.greenfoothills.org/

Growing Native: http://www.growingnative.com/

Kirby Cove Day Use Area:
http://www.nps.gov/goga/spug/picnic/p_kcdu.htm

Save Mount Diablo: http://www.savemountdiablo.org/

Mount Diablo State Park:
http://www.parks.ca.gov/default.asp?page_id=517

Mount Hamilton and Lick Observatory:
http://www.irving.org/xplore/lick/contents.html

Mount Tamalpais State Park:
http://www.parks.ca.gov/default.asp?page_id=471

Mount Umnhum and the Sierra Azul Open Space Preserve:
http://www.openspace.org/preserves/pr_sierra_azul.asp

Ring Mountain:
http://www.marinopenspace.org/os_park_24.asp

San Bruno Mountain Watch:
http://www.mountainwatch.org/

# ENDNOTES

## INTRODUCTION

1. Dolan Eargle, *The Earth Is Our Mother: A Guide to the Indians of California, Their Locales, and Historic Sites* (San Francisco: Trees Co. Press, 1986), 12.
2. "A Timeline of San Francisco History."
Available from: http://www.zpub.com/sf/history/sfh2html
3. Among the shamans were Don Americo Yabar, Don Juan Nunez del Prado, and Alberto Villoldo. Juan and Americo held respectively the "left side" (heart) and the "right side" (mind) teachings of their shamanic lineage. Alberto Villoldo has been an important link in bringing together the traditions and strengths of North America and South America in the "flight of the eagle and condor."
4. Paul Devereux, *Shamanism and the Mystery Lines* (St. Paul: Llewellyn Publications, 1993), 48.
5. Paul Devereux, *Earthmind: A Modern Adventure in Ancient Wisdom* (New York: Harper & Row, 1989), 110.
6. James Swan, *The Power of Place: Sacred Ground in Natural and Human Environments* (Wheaton, IL: Theosophical Publishing House, 1991), 15.
7. Ginni DuPraw-Anderson, "Working with the Stone People," *Proceedings of the Twelfth International Conference on the Study of Shamanism*, ed. Ruth Inge-Heinze (San Rafael: Ruth Inge-Heinze, 1995), 105-115.
8. California Geological Survey, "Serpentine: California State Rock" (CGS Note 14). Available from: http://www.consrv.ca.gov/cgs/information/publications/cgs_notes/note_14/
9. Thomas Berry, *The Great Work: Our Way into the Future* (San Francisco: Sierra Club, 1999), 4.

## CHAPTER ONE

1. This personal communication occurred during a visit in which Richard and I walked along the rim of Kirby Cove and then into the cove itself. Richard Feather Anderson is the founder of the American School of Geomancy. Among his teachings are ecology and earth-based spirituality.
For more information: http://www.richardfeatheranderson.com
2. Paul Huson, *Mastering Herbalism* (New York: Stein and Day, 1983), 77; Mrs. M. Grieve, *A Modern Herbal, Vol. II* (New York: Dover Publications, 1971), 700-708.

3. Harold Gilliam and Ann Gilliam, *Marin Headlands: Portals of Time* (San Francisco: GGNRA, 1993), 8.

4. "Travels of the Marin Headlands."
Available from: http://www.nps.gov/prsf/geology/mhland.htm

5. Gilliam and Gilliam, *Marin Headlands*, 38.

6. GGNRA information sheet on Kirby Cove, 3.

7. Gilliam and Gilliam, *Marin Headlands*, 40.

8. Ibid., 33.

9. Harold Gilliam, *Tides in the Sky* (New York: Doubleday, 1957), 271-272.

10. David Alt and Donald Hyndman, *Roadside Geology of Northern and Central California* (Missoula, MT: Mountain Press Publishing Company, 2000), 1.

11. GGNRA information sheet on Kirby Cove, 5.

12. Druids were the magician priests of the Celtic people, an educated and elite class who served as judges, educators, doctors, historians, astronomers, and astrologers. The source of their wisdom was nature—the sea, the sun, the wind, the earth, plants, and animals. They gathered the people in the woods to teach them, often through story, poetry, and music. For more information: http://www.crystalinks.com/druids.html

13. GGNRA information sheet on Kirby Cove, 1.

14. Ibid., 6.

15. Gilliam and Gilliam, *Marin Headlands*, 11.

16. GGNRA information sheet on Kirby Cove, 1.

17. For more information on Potato Patch Shoal: http://content.surfline.com/sw/content/travel/surfmaps/us/sanfrancisco_monterey/potato_patch.jsp

18. Fred Alan Wolf, *The Eagle's Quest: A Physicist's Search for Truth in the Heart of the Shamanic World* (New York: Summit Books, 1991), 163.

19. Sandra Ingerman, *Medicine for the Earth: How to Transform Personal and Environmental Toxins* (New York: Three Rivers Press, 2000), 2.

20. Ibid., 2.

21. In the Orkney Islands, selkies were seals that were believed to have the capacity to transform into beautiful human beings. They delighted in the change, dancing on the beach and sometimes having human lovers. If their skins were lost or stolen, they were unable to return to their seal forms. They bore human children but often began to pine for their homes in the sea. When they found their skins, they returned to the ocean and often took their children with them. For more information: Sigurd Towrie, "The Origin of the Selkie Folk," http://www.orkneyjar.com/folklore/selkiefolk/selorig.htm

# CHAPTER TWO

1. Larry Serpa, "Ring Mountain Self-Guided Nature Trail, Winter Edition" (The Nature Conservancy, date unknown), 2.

2. "IVM Technical Bulletin: Smooth Cordgrass (Spartina)." Available from: http://www.efn.org/~ipmpa/Noxspart.html

3. Thomas Lescohier, *The Coast Miwok People* (Novato: handwritten, 1977), 22.

4. Randall Milliken, *A Time of Little Choice* (Menlo Park: Ballena Press, 1995), 180.

5. "Ring Mountain Preserve" (The Nature Conservancy, date unknown).

6. Robert Torrez, "New Mexico's Spanish and Mexican Land Grants." Available from: http://www.nmgs.org/artlandgrnts.htm

7. "Turbidity Currents." Available from: http://www.soc.soton.ac.uk/CHD/classroom@sea/general_science/turbidites.html

8. "Ring Mountain Preserve."

9. Edward Ball, *Early Uses of California Plants* (Berkeley: University of California Press, 1962), 30.

10. Ibid., 72.

11. Jeannine Gendar, *Grass Games and Moon Races: California Indian Games and Toys* (Berkeley: Heyday Books, 1995), 83.

12. Ibid., 22.

13. Lescohier, *Coast Miwok People*, 30.

14. Matthew Seiple, *Ring Mountain Petroglyph Rock* Volume IV, Number 2, Winter 1994 (Berkeley: Sacred Sites International Foundation, 1994).

15. "San Quentin." Available from: http://www.Rotten.com/library/crime/prison/san-quentin/

16. Shunryu Suzuki, Zen Mind, Beginner's Mind (NY: Westerhill, 1998), 14.

17. Lyrics from Naomi Littlebear Morena and Holly Near, "Old and Strong/The Mountain Song," on *Epiphany* by Circe's Tryx (Kairong, Australia: The Realm of White Magic, 1999). For more information: http://www.whitemagic.com,au/magickmusic/epiphany.htm

18. Blue Schist on Ring Mountain Available from: http://www.marin.cc.ca.us/~jim/ring/block.html, 2/28/2006

19. Song by Diana Hildebrand-Hull

20. M. Leigh Marymor, *Proposal to Manage and Protect the Ring Mountain Petroglyphs, CA-MRN-442* (San Francisco: Bay Area Rock Art Research Association, 1998), 5.

21. Ibid., 5.

## CHAPTER THREE

1. A phrase used in the Andes, and shared with me by the shaman Americo Yabar in 1996, that refers to the light and atmosphere of twilight and dawn.
2. Lincoln Fairley, *Mt. Tamalpais: A History* (San Francisco: Scottwall Associates, 1987), 7.
3. Ibid., 115.
4. Dan Totheroh, *The Mountain Play* (Mill Valley Library, 1970).
5. Fairley, *Mt. Tamalpais*, 1.
6. Ibid., 2.
7. Ibid., 2.
8. Joseph Bruchac (ed.), *Silver Fox and Coyote Create Earth—Native American Animal Stories* (Golden, CO: Fulcrum, 1992), 3.
9. DuPraw-Anderson, "Working with the Stone People," 283.
10. Reda Davis, *California Women: A Guide to Their Politics, 1885–1911* (San Francisco: California Scene, 1968), 134.
11. Fairley, *Mt. Tamalpais*, 46.
12. Ibid., 1.
13. Devereux, *Earthmind*, 111.
14. Wolf, *Eagle's Quest*, 163.
15. Devereux, *Earthmind*, 111.
16. Grieve, *A Modern Herbal, Vol. II*, 464

## CHAPTER FOUR

1. Elsie Richie, "Marvels of Being a Turkey Vulture," *Mt. Diablo Review* (Summer/Fall 1993), 3.
2. John Weminski, "Creating a Mountain" (text of the geology display at Mt. Diablo Summit Building, undated).
3. Rick Yarborough, "Coal and Sand Mining in the Mt. Diablo Foothills" (Antioch, CA: Black Diamond Mines Regional Preserve, undated), 1.
4. Brian Branston, *Gods of the North* (Guilford, Surrey: Biddles Ltd., 1980), 77, 79; Kevin Crossley-Holland, *The Norse Myths* (NY: Pantheon Books, 1980), xxiii.
5. Bev Ortiz, "Mt. Diablo as Myth and Reality," *The American Indian Quarterly, Journal of American Indian Studies, Special Issue: The California Indians* 13, no. 4 (Fall 1989), 457–460.
6. Christine Colasurdo, "Out of an Ancient Sea: Notes on the East Bay Landscape," *Bay Nature* 1, no. 2 (April-June 2001), 18.
7. Ortiz, "Mt. Diablo as Myth and Reality," 459.
8. Jose Ignacio Rivera, "Fire, Grazing, and Native Californian Resource Management," *Mt. Diablo Review* (Summer/Fall 1993), 4.

9. Glenn Keater, "Fire as Shaper of Vegetation," *Mt. Diablo Review* (Winter/Spring 1993–94), 4.

10. Lois Duncan, *The Magic of Spider Woman* (New York: Scholastic Books, 1996).

11. Stephen Naylor, "Indra," *Encyclopedia Mythica Online*. Available from: http://www.pantheon.org/articles/i/indra.html

12. Crossley-Holland, *Norse Myths*, 188.

13. Alan Ereira, *From the Heart of the World* (New York: Mystic Fire Video, 1991).

## CHAPTER FIVE

1. Jim Arnosky, *Watching Water Birds* (Washington, DC: National Geographic Society, 1997), 23.

2. Frank Staub, *Herons* (Minneapolis: Lerner Publications, 1997), 18.

3. Colasurdo, "Out of an Ancient Sea," 18.

4. Ibid., 18.

5. David Rains Wallace, "Old Hills, New Economies: A Natural History of the Mount Hamilton Ridgelands," *Bay Nature* 1, no. 2 (April-June 2001), 13.

6. Barry Breckling, "Sada." Available from: http://www.coepark.org/sada.html

7. Jim Carter, "Joseph D. Grant House." Available from: http://www.ghosttrackers.com/joseph_d.htm, 2/17/04

8. Eric Carlson, "Notes from the Underbelly: The Ranchscapades," *Metro, Silicon Valley's Weekly Newspaper*, June 14–20, 2001, 3. http://www.metroactive.com/papers/metro/06.14.01/underbelly-0124.html

9. Joseph Grant Park brochure, http://www.parkhere.org/scc/assets/docs/644504Grant%20Brochure.pdf

10. Tony Misch and Remington Stone, "The Building of Lick Observatory." Available from: http://mthamilton.ucolick.org/public/history/bldg_the_obs.html

11. Betty Fullard-Leo, "Star Struck by Wayfinding." Available from: http://www.coffeetimes.com/may98.htm

12. Jean Guard Monroe and Ray A. Williamson, *They Dance in the Sky: Native American Star Myths* (Boston: Houghton Mifflin, 1987), 2.

13. Veronica S. Schweitzer, "The Pleiades Rise." Available from: http://www.coffeetimes.com/pleiades.htm

14. Oregon Women's Land Community, "A River of Birds," recorded on *A Circle Is Cast*, Libana, 1986.

15. Reginald Barrett, "Feral Swine: The California Experience." Available from: http://texnat.tamu.edu/symposia/feral/feral-15.htm

16. Joe Eaton, "Mastodons in Our Midst: The East Bay's Miocene Menagerie," *Bay Nature* 1, no. 3 (July-September, 2001), 10.

17. Laura Martin, *Wildlife Folklore* (Old Saybrook, CT: The Globe Pequot Press, 1994), 22.

18. Buffie Johnson, *Lady of the Beasts* (New York: Harper & Row, 1988), 262.

19. Varaha Avatar, "The Boar Incarnation of Vishnu." Available from: http://www.indiayogi.com/content/indgods/varaha.asp

20. Margo Adler, *Drawing Down the Moon* (Boston: Beacon Press, 1979), 55.

21. Starhawk, *The Spiral Dance: A Rebirth of the Ancient Religion of the Goddess* (New York: Harper & Row, 1979), 178.

22. For more information on the Fall TarantulaFest and Barbecue: http://www.coepark.org/tfest.html

23. Jennifer Dewey, *Spiders Near and Far* (New York: Dutton, 1993), 31-33.

24. Alexander Crosby, *Tarantulas: The Biggest Spiders* (New York: Walker & Co., 1981), 9.

25. "Gray pine (digger pine)." Available from: http://www.geocities.com/Yosemite/Trails/5335/Plants/graypine.html

26. Andrew Storer, Thomas Gordon, Paul Dallara, and David Wood, "Pitch canker kills pines, spreads to new species and regions," *California Agriculture* 48, no. 6, 9-13. Available from: http://frap.cdf.ca.gov/pitch_canker/prevention_management/cal_ag.html

## CHAPTER SIX

1. Chuck Purvis, "Commuting to Silicon Valley." Available from: http://www.mtc.ca.gov/maps_and_data/datamart/census/county2county/commute_siliconvalley.htm

2. George Bruntz, *History of Los Gatos: Gem of the Foothills* (Fremont, CA: Valley Publishers, 1971), 33.

3. "The History of Los Gatos: How Los Gatos Got Its Name." Available from: http://www.los-gatos.org/main/history.html

4. Billie J. Jensen and Reece C. Jensen, *A Trip Through Time and the Santa Cruz Mountains* (Gardnerville, NV: Ghastly Gallimaufry, 1994), 3.

5. "How Los Gatos Got Its Name."

6. Mid-Peninsula Regional Open Space District brochure for Saint Joseph's Hill.

7. Jensen and Jensen, *A Trip Through Time*, 1.

8. Mid-Peninsula Regional Open Space District brochure for Sierra Azul.

9. Neil Wiley, "The Good, the Bad, and the Ugly," *The Mountain Network News*. Available from: http://www.mnn.net/goodbaduglyhtm.htm

10. Robert Aldrich, "Los Gatos History: Pride and spirit prevail in our mountain folk." Available from: http://www.losgatos.com/history/aldrich1.html

11. Ted Andrews, *Animal-Speak: The Spiritual and Magical Powers of Creatures Great and Small* (St. Paul: Llewellyn Publications, 1995), 187.

12. Jeffrey Marshall, Dan Orange, and Alfred Hochstaedter, "Earthquakes." Available from: http://www.es.ucsc.edu/~es10/fieldtripEarthQ/EarthQWelcome.html

13. Phil Stoffer and Paula Messina, "Field-Trip Guide to the Geology of the Lexington Reservoir and Loma Prieta Areas in the Santa Cruz Mountains, Santa Clara and Santa Cruz Counties, California," U.S. Geological Survey Open-File Report 02-221. Available from: http://geopubs.wr.usgs.gov/open-file/of02-221
14. Pablo Neruda, *Estravagaria: Poems* (New York: Farrar, Straus, & Giroux, 1994), 23.
15. "How Los Gatos Got Its Name."
16. Ibid.
17. Andrews, *Animal-Speak*, 259.
18. "How Los Gatos Got Its Name."
19. Jensen and Jensen, *A Trip Through Time*, 1.
20. County of Los Angeles Fire Department, "Official Report: Old Topanga Incident." Available from: http://www.lafire.com/famous_fires/931102_OldTopangaFire/110293_official_report_old_topanga_inci.htm
21. Plant Index, "Adenostoma fasciculatum." Available from: http://www.mcssb.org/sbpanda/chemise.html
22. Larry and Terrie Gates, Hummingbird World Web site. Available from: http://www.portalproductions.com/h/native_american.htm

## CHAPTER SEVEN

1. "Facts You Should Know About San Bruno Mountain," *San Bruno Mountain Watch*. Available from: http://www.mountainwatch.org/mountain/
2. Floyd Shuttleworth, *Non-Flowering Plants* (New York: Golden Press, 1967), 93.
3. William Grimm and M. Jean Craig, *The Wondrous World of Seedless Plants* (New York: Bobbs-Merrill, 1973), 68.
4. Rasa Gustaitis, "The First-Ever HCP: Did This Habitat Trade-off Work?" *California Coast & Ocean* 17, no. 1 (Spring 2001). Available from: http://www.scc.ca.gov/coast&ocean/spring2001/pages/thre.htm
5. Laura Martin, *Wildlife Folklore* (Old Saybrook, CT: The Globe Pequot Press, 1994), 108.
6. Larry J. Orsack, "The Endangered Mission Blue Butterfly of California," *San Bruno Mountain Watch*. Available from: http://www.mountainwatch.org/mountain/fauna/missionbluebutterfly.htm
7. John Farrand, *National Audubon Society Field Guide to North American Birds* (New York: Alfred A. Knopf, 1995), 601.
8. Helen K. Sharsmith, *Spring Wildflowers of the San Francisco Bay Region* (Berkeley, CA: University of California Press, 1965), 158–159.
9. Meg Beeler, "Meditating on the Wild Mountain: Entering Sacred Space," *PanGaia* 18 (Winter 1998–99), 33–35.

10. David Schooley, "Demolished Home, Destroyed Stewardship," *Street Spirit* (San Francisco, Vol. 9, No.3, March 2003 A publication of the American Friends Service Committee), 11.

11. Jo Coffey, "The Saints Bruno," *San Bruno Mountain Watch*. Available from: sanbruno@mountainwatch.org

12. Sara Gaiser, "Fire Killed Bad Plants," *Burlingame Daily News*, October 5, 2003, 3.

13. "Celtic knots," Wikipedia, the free encyclopedia. Available from: http://en.wikipedia.org/wiki/Celtic_knots

978-0-595-39191-2
0-595-39191-5